Ember.js in Action

Ember.js in Action

JOACHIM HAAGEN SKEIE

MANNING

SHELTER ISLAND

For online information and ordering of this and other Manning books, please visit
www.manning.com. The publisher offers discounts on this book when ordered in quantity.
For more information, please contact

>   Special Sales Department
>   Manning Publications Co.
>   20 Baldwin Road
>   PO Box 261
>   Shelter Island, NY 11964
>   Email: orders@manning.com

Manning Publications Co. 20 Baldwin Road PO Box 261 Shelter Island, NY 11964	Development editor: Susanna Kline Copyeditor: Lianna Wlasiuk Proofreader: Melody Dolab Typesetter: Marija Tudor Cover designer: Marija Tudor

ISBN: 9781617291456
Printed in the United States of America
1 2 3 4 5 6 7 8 9 10 – MAL – 19 18 17 16 15 14

brief contents

contents

preface

Since 2006, I've worked with the development of web applications in one form or another. I started out writing a web application for Norway's largest retailer, which was based on JavaServer Pages (JSP) and later migrated toward JavaServer Faces (JSF). At the time, these technologies were great, and they served their intended purpose. Back then (before Ajax became widely used), the request-response cycle of HTTP demanded that most of the logic be put on the server side and that the server deliver complete markup, scripts, and style sheets to the browser on every request.

Even though these server-side approaches to writing web applications did their job, issues arose whenever state was a concern. Because the server is required to do the bookkeeping for all the logged-in users, managing state quickly becomes a difficult and memory-hungry task. How do you deal with users opening multiple tabs in your application and switching between them? How do you persist your session data when you want to scale the service across multiple (virtual) machines? How can you easily scale out horizontally in a consistent fashion if you have user-state stored on the server side?

As I started working on the open source project Montric (named EurekaJ at the time), I quickly decided that if I wanted to scale the application horizontally without requiring a separate session cache, I'd need to invest in learning one of the JavaScript frameworks that had started to gain momentum and popularity.

I assessed multiple frameworks and built prototypes in both Cappuccino (www.cappuccino-project.org) and SproutCore (http://sproutcore.com). Although Cappuccino had more complete tooling and promised a detailed and good-looking user interface for my application, I chose SproutCore because it enabled me to use my existing skills, while promising an easier integration with third-party libraries. Sprout-Core also offered powerful views, which act as components that can be combined into a fully functional web application. Coming from a component-based, server-side framework world, these features made me feel at home with SproutCore. But despite this initial delight, I discovered that integrating SproutCore with third-party libraries wasn't as easy as I had anticipated.

When the SproutCore team was acquired and the momentum of the framework slowed down, the SproutCore community began to shift. Work on SproutCore v2.0 was well underway, but the gap between the original SproutCore and what was to become SproutCore v2.0 was widening. As a result, Ember.js was born as a fork of SproutCore.

Ember.js promised a framework that was thoroughly rooted in the technologies that drive our web experience, enabling you—as a developer—to use the skill set that you already have to develop JavaScript applications. Ember.js doesn't abstract or hide the details of your JavaScript, HTML, or CSS code, but instead it embraces these technologies to lift them up into the twenty-first century.

Needless to say, I followed along with Ember.js and decided to rewrite EurekaJ's front end with Ember.js. In the process I renamed the project Montric (http://montric.no). I've been on the Ember.js roller coaster ever since. Being part of the pre-v1.0.0 Ember.js community had its highs and its lows. With constantly changing APIs, and concepts being rethought and revisited on what felt like a weekly basis, the lows have mostly been ironed out, leaving only the highs. Deciding to write a comprehensive book about Ember.js in its pre v1.0.0 days undoubtedly exaggerated the lows in my mind.

As I'm writing this, Ember.js v1.2.0 is out, the API is stable, and the project is healthy and growing. Ember.js has become an awesome framework that lets you push the envelope on the applications you build for the web.

acknowledgments

This book is the most comprehensive and cohesive writing I've done to date, and it has been an experience with a steep learning curve. Crafting and writing this book has been an extremely humbling, difficult, and educational experience.

I wish to thank the Manning team for being willing to publish a book about Ember.js and for pushing to get the book realized as the story/journey that you're about to embark on. I would especially like to thank development editor Susanna Kline for putting up with my many missed deadlines and endless Skype questions, and for always giving great feedback on needed improvements. I also would like to thank the team of copyeditors—Lianna Wlasiuk along with Rosalie Donlon, Sharon Wilkey, and Teresa Wilson—who caught and fixed an embarrassing number of spelling and grammar mistakes throughout the text. Thanks also to proofreader Melody Dolab, compositor Marija Tudor, and project managers Mary Piergies and Kevin Sullivan.

The reviewers also made sure that the book remained on point and relevant during the various stages of its development, and I'd like to extend my gratitude for their work along the way. Thanks to Benoît Benedetti, Chetan Shenoy, Dineth Mendis, Jean-Christopher Remy, Leo Cassarani, Marius Butuc, Michael Angelo, Oren Zeev-Ben-Mordehai, Philippe Charrière, Richard Harriman, and Rob MacEachern. Finally, thanks to technical proofreader Deepak Vohra for his careful review of the manuscript shortly before it went into production.

I wish to extend a special and huge thank you to my beautiful wife, Lene, and my two amazing children, Nicolas and Aurora. Lene's support and understanding have been incredibly important during the writing of the book, especially as it consumed a lot of my spare time during evenings and on weekends. Knowing that your family is safe, secure, and happy is of utmost importance when deciding to prioritize your spare time elsewhere.

about this book

Ember.js is the most ambitious web application framework for JavaScript. With the release of the final v1.0.0 version, after just under two years of development, the APIs have stabilized and the project has steadily moved on, quickly reaching versions 1.1.0 and 1.2.0.

Writing large, ambitious web applications is hard work. Ember.js exists because its creators wanted to build a framework that simplified and standardized the way we write applications for the web. This book aims to present the features and highlights of the framework while keeping the text driven by real-world examples.

Roadmap

The book is divided into three parts:

- *Part 1*—Ember.js fundamentals
- *Part 2*—Building ambitious web apps for the real world
- *Part 3*—Advanced Ember.js topics

Part 1 uses simple, self-contained examples to introduce you to Ember.js, its core features, and what Ember.js expects from your application:

- Chapter 1 introduces you to Ember.js and explains where the project comes from, as well as where it fits into the world of web applications. You'll learn the fundamental concepts and terminology used in Ember.js.
- Chapter 2 builds on chapter 1 by explaining the core features of Ember.js. In this chapter, you'll learn about bindings, computed properties, observers, and the Ember.js object model.

- Chapter 3 is dedicated to Ember Router, the glue that holds your entire application together.
- Chapter 4 presents Handlebars.js, the template library of choice for Ember.js applications. You'll learn the features Handlebars.js brings to the table for Ember.js applications as well as the Ember.js-specific add-ons that Ember.js adds to Handlebars.js.

Part 2 introduces the case study, Montric, which is used for the majority of the remaining chapters. This part delves into the harder parts of web application development: how to interact with the server side efficiently, both with and without Ember Data; writing custom components; and testing your Ember.js applications:

- Chapter 5 dives into how to use the third-party Ember Data library to communicate with the server side. Based on Ember Data beta 2, this chapter details what Ember Data expects from your server-side API and your Ember.js application before showing how to customize Ember Data to fit your existing server-side API.
- Chapter 6 shows how to interact with the server side without relying on a framework to help you. This chapter also shows how to build a complete CRUD data layer from scratch.
- Chapter 7 is all about custom components, a feature added late to Ember.js. Using Ember.js components, you can build atomic, self-contained components that can be reused either on their own or as building blocks of more complex components.
- Chapter 8 is dedicated to showing how to test your Ember.js application. You'll use QUnit and PhantomJS to build up a viable testing solution.

Part 3 moves into the more obscure parts of Ember.js and discusses other services and tools to facilitate application development and increase your understanding of Ember.js:

- Chapter 9 walks you through building in authentication and authorization by using a third-party authentication system. This chapter specifically implements Mozilla Persona, which is an open source solution.
- Chapter 10 eases you into the Ember run loop, called Backburner.js. This background motor drives your Ember.js application and ensures that your application views are always kept up-to-date while keeping performance high.
- Chapter 11 teaches you how to structure your Ember.js application as your source code grows and how to build, assemble, and package your application in preparation for deployment.

Who should read this book

This book is written to help you become familiar and productive with Ember.js. Depending on your background, developing JavaScript applications with a framework such as Ember.js may involve a steep learning curve. This book helps you learn the concepts of Ember.js quickly and familiarizes you with the Ember.js terminology and application structure. This book is approachable to newcomers to Ember.js, as well as to developers with previous Ember.js experience.

As a prerequisite, this book expects you to be familiar with JavaScript as a language, as well as to have some familiarity with jQuery.

Code conventions and downloads

The following typographical conventions are used throughout this book:

- *Italic* type is used to introduce new terms.
- `Courier` typeface is used to denote code samples, as well as elements and attributes, method names, classes, interfaces, and other identifiers.
- Code annotations accompany many of the code listings and highlight important concepts.
- Some of the lines of code are long and break due to the limitations of the printed page. Because of this, line-continuation markers (➡) may be included in code listings when necessary.

This book includes many code snippets and a large amount of source code. The source code for part 1 is available via the book's GitHub pages or as a downloadable zip file from the publishers's website at www.manning.com/Ember.jsinAction. Parts 2 and 3 are based on the Montric source code, and as such, the code is available on GitHub.

Because the examples are living projects, the source code will invariably have changed since this text was written. To account for this, use the following direct links to view the source code as it was during the writing of this book:

- Chapters 1 and 2—https://github.com/joachimhs/Ember.js-in-Action-Source/tree/master/chapter1/notes
- Chapter 3—https://github.com/joachimhs/Ember.js-in-Action-Source/tree/master/chapter3/blog
- Chapters 5, 7, 8, 9, and 11—https://github.com/joachimhs/Montric/tree/Ember.js-in-Action-Branch
- Chapter 6—https://github.com/joachimhs/EmberFestWebsite/tree/Ember.js-in-Action-branch

I've tried to document as much about Ember.js as possible, while keeping the examples real and down-to-earth. Using the Montric source code led to the occasional difficulty in isolating good examples, but I think this gives the book more depth. In addition, the number of updates and changes to the book's examples give you an idea of how much Ember.js has grown since its initial release.

Author Online

The purchase of *Ember.js in Action* includes free access to a private web forum run by Manning Publications, where you can make comments about the book, ask technical questions, and receive help from the author and from other users. To access the forum and subscribe to it, point your web browser to www.manning.com/Ember.jsin-Action. This page provides information on how to access the forum after you're registered, what kind of help is available, and the rules of conduct on the forum.

Manning's commitment to our readers is to provide a venue where a meaningful dialogue between individual readers and between readers and the author can take place. It isn't a commitment to any specific amount of participation on the part of the author, whose contribution to the forum remains voluntary (and unpaid). We suggest you try asking the author some challenging questions, lest his interest stray!

The Author Online forum and the archives of previous discussions will be accessible from the publisher's website as long as the book is in print.

About the author

Joachim Haagen Skeie is self-employed though his company Haagen Software AS. He spends his time working as a freelance consultant and an instructor of Ember.js and RaspberryPi courses, while working on launching the products Montric (an open source application-performance monitor) and Conticious (an open source CMS API used to host Ember.js-based RIAs). Both Montric and Conticious are based on Ember.js on the front end, with Java on the back end.

Joachim has worked on the development of web applications, big and small, since 2006, primarily focusing on Java and Ember.js. He lives in Oslo, Norway, with his wife and children.

about the cover illustration

The figure on the cover of *Ember.js in Action* is captioned "A theater director in Paris." The illustration is taken from a nineteenth-century edition of Sylvain Maréchal's four-volume compendium of regional dress customs published in France. Each illustration is finely drawn and colored by hand. The rich variety of Maréchal's collection reminds us vividly of how culturally apart the world's towns and regions were just 200 years ago. Isolated from each other, people spoke different dialects and languages. In the streets or in the countryside, it was easy to identify where they lived and what their trade or station in life was just by their dress.

Dress codes have changed since then and the diversity by region, so rich at the time, has faded away. It is now hard to tell apart the inhabitants of different continents, let alone different towns or regions. Perhaps we have traded cultural diversity for a more varied personal life—certainly for a more varied and fast-paced technological life.

At a time when it is hard to tell one computer book from another, Manning celebrates the inventiveness and initiative of the computer business with book covers based on the rich diversity of regional life two centuries ago, brought back to life by Maréchal's pictures.

Part 1

Ember.js fundamentals

Ember.js is a JavaScript MVC framework that helps you organize and structure the source code for large web applications. In comparison to other popular JavaScript application frameworks, it delivers a more complete MVC pattern, while also including features to help you build applications for the web of tomorrow. It's also one of the more opinionated frameworks available, relying heavily on convention over configuration to help you structure your application.

Because of its large number of features coupled with the conventions that it expects from your application, Ember.js has a steep learning curve. Part 1 of this book, comprised of the first four chapters, eases you into the mindset of Ember.js application development, while ensuring that you build something useful right from the get-go.

The first two chapters focus on the core features that Ember.js brings to the table. Chapter 3 focuses on Ember Router, and chapter 4 focuses on the template library of choice for Ember.js developers: Handlebars.js.

Powering your next ambitious web application

1

This chapter covers

- A brief history of the single-page web application (SPA)
- An introduction to Ember.js
- What Ember.js can provide you as a web developer
- Your first Ember.js application

This chapter introduces the Ember.js application framework and touches on many of the features and the technologies in the Ember.js ecosystem. Most of these topics are covered in more detail in later chapters. This chapter gives a quick overview of what an Ember.js application might look like and what strengths you get from basing your application on Ember.js.

The chapter also includes an overview of the building blocks of an Ember.js application and touches on the different aspects of the Ember.js framework. If you initially find any code presented here confusing or hard to understand, don't worry! All aspects of the source code development are explored in detail, every step of the way, in the book.

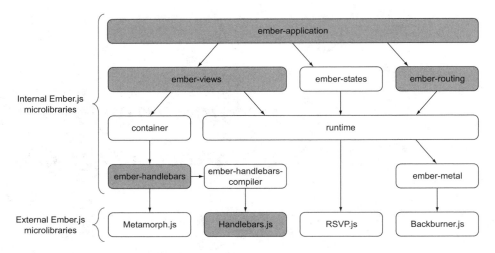

Figure 1.1 The internal structure of Ember.js

Ember.js comes with a steep learning curve if you're used to writing server-side generated web applications. The code examples presented in this chapter and the Notes application example go through the different concepts of structuring an Ember.js application.

The structure of Ember.js is based on a set of microlibraries. Each chapter of this book starts with a diagram that shows these microlibraries and highlights the ones that the current chapter discusses. We'll touch on many of the microlibraries in Ember.js in this chapter, as shown in figure 1.1.

If you are building a single-page web application that pushes the envelope of what's possible on the web, Ember.js is the framework for you!

1.1 Who is Ember.js for?

Websites that serve content based on the traditional HTTP request-response lifecycle, such as the websites for the *New York Times* or Apple Inc., render most of the HTML, CSS, and JavaScript on the server. As shown in figure 1.2 (at left), for each request, the server generates a new, complete copy of the website's markup.

At the other end of the spectrum are rich internet applications (RIAs), such as Google Maps, Trello, and, to a certain degree, GitHub. These websites aim to define new application types and rival native installed applications, and they render most of their content at the client side. As shown in figure 1.2 (at right), in response to the first request, the server sends a complete application (HTML, CSS, and JavaScript) only once. Subsequent requests return only the data required to display the next page in the application.

Strengths and weaknesses are at both ends of the spectrum. The pages toward the left of the spectrum are easier to cache on the server, but they tend to rely on the request-response cycle and full-page refreshes in response to user actions.

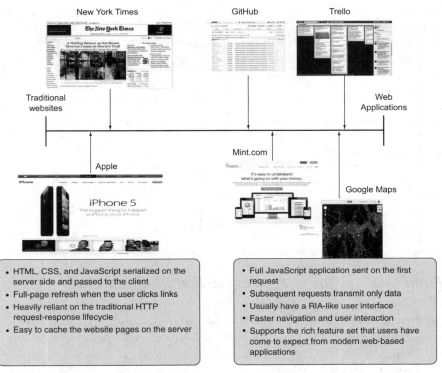

Figure 1.2 The Ember.js framework works with a variety of web applications.

The applications toward the right of the spectrum typically have richer user interfaces, deliver a better user experience, and resemble and behave like familiar native applications, but they're more complex and require more from the browser software in terms of computing power, features, and stability.

Single-page applications (SPAs) have become more common because RIAs—and SPAs in particular—feel more like native, installable applications, and they have a more responsive user interface with few or no complete page refreshes. Within this domain, Ember.js aims to be a framework that provides the best solutions for web application developers and pushes the envelope of what's possible to develop for the web. As such, Ember.js fits well with applications that require long-lived user sessions, have rich user interfaces, and are based on standard web technologies.

If you build applications toward the right of the spectrum, Ember.js is for you. Ember.js also makes you stop and think about how you want to structure your application. It provides powerful tools for building rich web-based applications that stretch the limits of what's possible, while providing a rich set of features that enable you to build truly ambitious web applications.

Before you get started with developing an Ember.js application, let's discuss why we have frameworks like Ember.js in the first place, as well as the problems that Ember.js promises to solve.

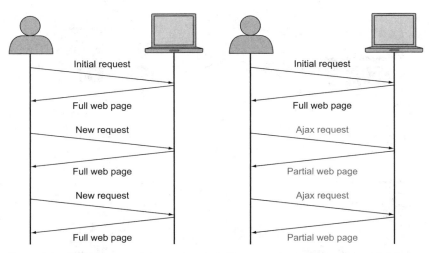

Figure 1.3   The structure of the early web (left) versus the promise of Ajax (right)

1.2 *From static pages to Ajax to full-featured web apps*

From the introduction of the World Wide Web (WWW or W3) in the mid-1990s, up until Ajax arrived in the mid-2000s, most websites were static in nature. The server responded to any HTTP page requests with a single HTTP response, which contained the complete HTML, CSS, and JavaScript required to display a complete page, as depicted in figure 1.3 (at left).

Although many websites still rely on the full-page refresh approach shown at the left in figure 1.3, more and more developers are building dynamic content into their websites. Today, users expect websites to act and feel like applications with no page refreshes occurring.

1.2.1 *The rise of asynchronous web applications*

With the introduction of the asynchronous call came the ability to send specific parts of the website for each response. Dedicated JavaScript code received this response on the client side and replaced the contents of HTML elements throughout the website, as shown in figure 1.3 (at right). As nice as this seems, this approach came with a gigantic caveat.

It's trivial to implement a service on the server side that, given an element type, renders the new contents of that element and returns it back to the browser in an atomic manner. If that was what rich web application users wanted, it would've solved the problem. The issue is that users rarely want to only update a single element at any one time.

For example, when you browse an online store, you search for items to add to your shopping cart. When you add an item to the cart, you reasonably expect the item quantity and the shopping cart summary to update simultaneously. This lets you know the total number of items as well as the total price of the items in your shopping cart.

Because it's difficult to define a set of general rules that define which elements the server will include in each of the Ajax responses, most server-side frameworks revert to sending the complete web page back to the client. The client, on the other hand, knows which elements to replace and swaps out the correct HTML elements.

As you can guess, this approach is inefficient, and it significantly increases the number of HTTP requests that the client sends to the server. This is where the power of Ember.js comes into play. As a developer, you probably understand the issues with the model presented in figure 1.3, in which the server side returns the updated markup for single elements on the page. To update multiple elements, you need to take one of the following approaches:

- Require the browser to fire off additional Ajax requests, one for each element that updates on the website.
- Be aware of—on both the client and server sides—which elements must update for every action a user performs in your application

The first option multiplies the number of HTTP calls to your server; the second option requires you to maintain client state on both the client and the server. As a result, you significantly increase the number of HTTP requests that the client issues against the server, but you don't decrease the amount of work that the server needs to do for each of these requests. Don't get me wrong, this model supports partial-page updates by replacing elements based on the element identifiers and cherry-picking these elements from the complete markup returned from the server. If you're thinking this is a waste of both server- and client-side resources, you're absolutely right. Figure 1.4 shows this structure.

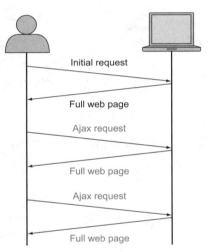

Figure 1.4 The structure of a server-side framework

Ideally, what you want to do is to serve the application only once. After the full application is loaded, you want to submit requests for data only from the client. This brings us to the model that Ember.js employs.

1.2.2 Moving toward the Ember.js model

These days, websites rely less on passing markup between the server and the client, and more on passing data. It's in this realm that Ember.js comes into play, as shown in figure 1.5.

In figure 1.5, the user receives the full website once, upon the initial request. This leads to two things: increased initial load time but significantly improved performance for each subsequent user action.

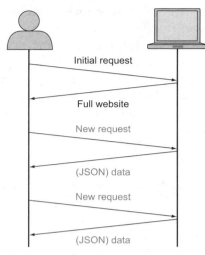

Figure 1.5 A modern web application model

In fact, the model presented in figure 1.5 is similar to the traditional client/server model dating back to the 1970s, but with two important distinctions: the initial request serves as a highly viable and customizable distribution channel for the client application while also ensuring that all clients adhere to a common set of web standards (HTML, CSS, JavaScript, and others).

Along with the client/server model, the business logic involving user interaction, the GUI, as well as performance logic has shifted off the server and onto the client. This shift might pose a security issue for specialized deployments, but generally, as long as the server controls who has access to the data being requested, the security concerns can be delegated to the server where they belong. With the responsibilities of the client and the server clearly separated, the client and the server can get back to doing what they do best—serving the user interface and the data, respectively.

Now that you understand which types of web applications Ember.js is created to build, let's delve into the details of Ember.js.

1.3   Overview of Ember.js

Ember.js started its life as the second version of the SproutCore framework. But while working on version 2.0 of SproutCore, it became clear to the SproutCore team members that the underlying structure of the framework needed a radical change if they were to meet their goal of building an easy-to-use framework that applied to a wide range of target web applications but was still small.

What Is SproutCore?

If you're not familiar with SproutCore, it's a framework developed with a highly component-oriented programming model. SproutCore borrowed most of its concepts from Apple's Cocoa, and Apple has written some of its web applications (MobileMe and iCloud) on top of SproutCore. Apple also contributed a large chunk of code back to the SproutCore project. In November 2011, Facebook acquired the team responsible for maintaining SproutCore.

In the end, part of the core team decided to make these changes in a new framework separate from SproutCore's origins.

Ember.js does borrow much of its underlying structure and design from SproutCore. But where SproutCore tries to be an end-to-end solution for building desktop-like applications by hiding most of the implementation details from its users, Ember.js does what it can to make it clear to users that HTML and CSS are at the core of its development stack.

Ember.js's strengths lie in its ability to enable you to structure your JavaScript source code in a consistent and reliable pattern while keeping the HTML and CSS easily visible. In addition, not having to rely on specific build tools to develop, build, and assemble your application gives you more options and control when it comes to how you structure your development. And when the time comes to assemble and package your application, many reliable tools are available. In chapter 11, you'll learn about a few of the available packaging options.

You must be eager to get started with Ember.js by now, but before you move on to create your first Ember.js application, let's explore what Ember.js is and what parts make up an Ember.js application.

1.3.1 What is Ember.js?

According to the Ember.js website,[1] Ember.js is a framework that enables you to build "ambitious" web applications. That term "ambitious" can mean different things to different people, but as a general rule, Ember.js aims to help you push the envelope of what you're able to develop for the web, while ensuring that your application source code remains structured and sane.

Ember.js achieves this goal by structuring your application into logical abstraction layers and forcing the development model to be as object-oriented as possible. At its core, Ember.js has built-in support for the following features:

- *Bindings*—Enables the changes to one variable to propagate into another variable and vice versa
- *Computed properties*—Enables you to mark functions as properties that automatically update along with the properties they rely on
- *Automatically updated templates*—Ensures that your GUI stays up to date whenever changes occur in the underlying data

Combine these features with a strong and well-planned Model-View-Controller (MVC) architecture and you've got a framework that delivers on its promise.

1.3.2 The parts that make up an Ember.js application

If you've spent most of your time developing web applications with server-side generated markup and JavaScript, Ember.js—and, indeed, most of the new JavaScript frameworks—has a completely different structure from what you're used to.

Ember.js includes a complete MVC implementation, which enriches both the controller and the view layers. We'll discuss more about the MVC implementation as we progress through the chapters.

---

[1] http://emberjs.com/

- *Controller layer*—Built with a combination of routes and controllers
- *View layer*—Built with a combination of templates and views

NOTE   Ember Data, which you'll learn about in chapter 5, enriches the model layer of Ember.js.

When you build an Ember.js application, you separate the concerns of the application in a consistent and structured manner. You also spend a decent amount of time thinking about where to best place your application logic. Even though this approach does take careful consideration before you delve into the code, your end product is better structured, and, as a result, is easier to maintain.

Most likely, you'll opt to follow the guidelines and standard conventions of Ember.js, but in some cases you may need to spend some time off the beaten track to implement the more intricate features of your application.

As you can see in figure 1.6, Ember.js introduces extra concepts at each of the layers in the standard MVC model. These concepts are explored in detail in the first five chapters of this book.

With that figure in mind, let's take a closer look at each of the MVC components.

MODELS AND EMBER DATA

At the bottom of the stack, Ember.js uses Ember Data to simplify the application and provide it with the rich data-model features that you need to build truly rich web-based applications. Ember Data represents one possible implementation that you can employ to communicate with the server. Other libraries exist for this functionality, and you can also write or bring your own client-to-server communication layer. Ember Data is discussed in detail in chapter 5, and rolling your own data layer is covered in chapter 6.

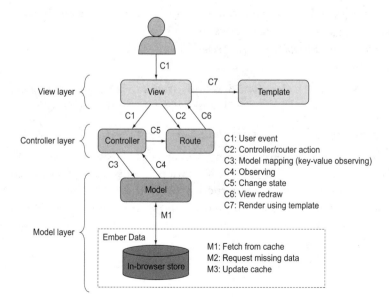

Figure 1.6   The parts that make up Ember.js and how they fit in with the MVC pattern

The model layer holds the data for the application, which is typically specified through a semi-strict schema. The model layer is responsible for any server-side communication as well as model-specific tasks such as data formatting. The view binds the GUI components against properties on the model objects via a controller.

Ember Data lives in the model layer, and you use it to define your model objects and client-to-server API, as well as the transport protocol between the Ember.js application and the server (jQuery, XHR, WebSockets, and others).

CONTROLLERS AND EMBER ROUTER

Above the model layer is the controller layer. The controller acts mainly as a link between the models and the views. Ember.js ships with a couple of custom controllers, most notably the `Ember.ObjectController` and the `Ember.ArrayController`. Generally, you use the `ObjectController` if your controller represents a single object (like a selected `note`); you use the `ArrayController` if your controller represents an array of items (like a list of all `notes` available for the current user).

On top of this, Ember.js uses Ember Router to split your application into clearly defined logical states. Each route can have a number of subroutes, and you can use the router to navigate between the states in your application.

The Ember Router is also the mechanism that Ember.js uses to update your application's URL and listen for URL changes. When using Ember Router, you model all your application's states in a hierarchical structure that resembles a state chart. Ember Router is discussed in detail in chapter 3.

VIEWS AND HANDLEBARS.JS

The view layer is responsible for drawing its elements on the screen. The views generally hold no permanent state of their own, with few exceptions. By default, each view in Ember.js has one controller as its context. It uses this controller to fetch its data, and, by default, uses this controller as the target for any user actions that occur on the view.

Also by default, Ember.js uses Handlebars.js as its templating engine. Therefore, most Ember.js applications define their user interfaces via Handlebars.js templates. Each view uses one template to render its view. Handlebars.js and templates are discussed in chapter 4.

> ### Handlebars.js
>
> Handlebars.js is based on Mustache, which is a logic-less template library that exists for a number of programming languages, including JavaScript. Handlebars.js adds logic expressions (if, if-else, each, and so on) on top of Mustache. This, along with the ability to bind your templates to properties on your views and controllers, lets you build templates that are well-structured, specific, and hand-tailored to your Ember.js application.

Ember.js ships with default views for basic HTML5 elements, and it's generally a good practice to use these views when you're in need of simple elements. You can easily create your own custom views that either extend or combine the standard Ember.js views to build complex elements in your web application.

Now that you understand the parts that make up an Ember.js application, it's time to start writing your first app.

1.4   *Your first Ember.js application: Notes*

The source code for the Notes application weighs in at about 200 lines of code and 130 lines of CSS, including the templates and JavaScript source code. You should be able to develop and run this application on any Windows-, Mac-, or Linux-based platform using only a text editor.

> **TIP**   I generally use WebStorm from JetBrains to write JavaScript-based applications, but this is not a requirement.

To get an idea of what to expect from an Ember.js application, you'll dive in and write a simple web application that manages notes. The application has the following features:

- *Add a new note*—The application has an area that allows users to add notes to the system.
- *Select, view, and edit a note from the system*—Available notes appear in a list at the left. Users select one note at a time to view and edit its content in an area at the right.
- *Delete an existing note*—Users can delete the selected note from the system.

A rough design of what you're building is shown in figure 1.7.

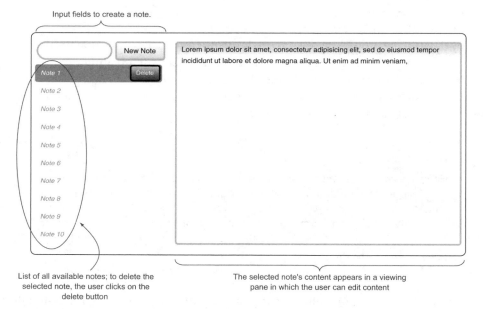

Figure 1.7   The design and layout of the Notes application

To get started, download the following libraries. The versions of each library may vary, depending on the current version of Ember.js:

- Ember.js version 1.0.0
- Handlebars.js version 1.0.0
- jQuery version 1.1x
- Twitter Bootstrap CSS
- Twitter Bootstrap Modal
- Ember Data version 1.x Beta
- Ember Data Local Storage Adapter

Your options: start from scratch or get the code from GitHub

To start from scratch:

1 Create a directory on your hard drive to store all the application files.

2 Create the directory structure as shown:

To get the code from GitHub:

If you'd rather get the source code all packed up and ready to go, download or clone the Git source repository from GitHub: https://github.com/joachimhs/Ember.js-in-Action-Source/tree/master/chapter1. The GitHub repo is the finished result at the end of chapter 2.

After you're set up, open the index.html file.

1.4.1 Getting started with the Notes application

Wire the application files together inside your index.html file, as shown in the following listing.

Listing 1.1   Creating links in the index.html file

```
<!DOCTYPE html>                          Standard doctype declaration        Standard elements to
                                                                             start an HTML document
<html lang="en">
<head>
    <meta http-equiv="Content-Type" content="text/html; charset=utf-8">
    <meta name="viewport" content="width=device-width,
        initial-scale=1.0, maximum-scale=1.0">

    <title>Ember.js Chapter 1 - Notes</title>
    <link rel="stylesheet" href="css/bootstrap.css"                 Links to Twitter
        type="text/css" charset="utf-8">                            Bootstrap CSS file
    <link rel="stylesheet" href="css/master.css"
        type="text/css" charset="utf-8">                            Links to custom
                                                                     CSS file
    <script src="js/scripts/jquery-1.10.2.min.js"
        type="text/javascript" charset="utf-8">
    </script>
    <script src="js/scripts/bootstrap-modal.js"
        type="text/javascript" charset="utf-8">
    </script>
    <script src="js/scripts/handlebars-1.0.0.js"
        type="text/javascript" charset="utf-8">
    </script>
    <script src="js/scripts/ember-1.0.0.js"
        type="text/javascript" charset="utf-8">
    </script>
    <script src="js/scripts/ember-data-beta-1.js"
        type="text/javascript" charset="utf-8">
    </script>
    <script src="js/scripts/ember-data-localstorage.js"
        type="text/javascript" charset="utf-8">
    </script>
    <script src="js/app/app.js" type="text/javascript"
        charset="utf-8">
    </script>                                      Adds application
                                                   source code
</head>
<body>

</body>
</html>
```

The code in this listing is enough to get you started developing the Notes application.

Where to place your templates

For simplicity, you'll place all your application templates inside the index.html file. This simplifies your setup, and it's a convenient method to start on a new Ember.js application. Once your application grows, you typically extract your templates into separate files and bring them in via build tools. Build tools will be discussed in chapter 11.

In most production-ready Ember.js applications, the code in listing 1.1 is all the code that will ever be inside the index.html file. This might be different from the web development that you're used to; it was for me before I was introduced to Ember.js. Unless you specify anything else, by default the Ember.js application places its contents inside the `body` tag of your HTML document.

Nothing special is happening in the code. The document starts by defining the `doctype` before starting the `HTML` element with the standard `HEAD` element. Inside the `HEAD` element, set the page's title, along with links to both the Twitter Bootstrap CSS as well as to a separate CSS file where you'll put the custom CSS required by your Notes application. The `script` elements of the `HEAD` tag define links to the scripts that your application is dependent on; the last `script` tag links to the source code for the Notes application, which you'll develop throughout the rest of this chapter.

1.4.2 *Creating a namespace and a router*

In this section you'll build the first part of the Notes application with the basic web application layout in place.

> **NOTE** The source code for this section is available as app1.js in either your code source directory or online at GitHub: https://github.com/joachimhs/ Ember.js-in-Action-Source/blob/master/chapter1/notes/js/app/app1.js.

The first thing any Ember.js application needs is a namespace that the application lives inside. For your Notes application, you'll use the namespace `Notes`.

After your namespace is created, you need to create a router that knows how your application is structured. Using the router isn't a requirement, but as you'll see in this book, it greatly simplifies and manages the structure of your entire application. You can think of the router as the glue that holds the application in place and connects different parts of it together.

The code required to get the Notes application up and running to serve a blank website is minimal:

```
var Notes = Ember.Application.create({    ◁─── Creates a namespace
});                                              for the application
```

This code creates your `Notes` namespace on the first line via `Ember.Application` `.create()`. Any code that you write related to this application is contained in this `Notes` namespace. This keeps the code separate from any other code that you might bring in via third-party libraries or even inline inside your JavaScript file. But serving a completely blank website is rather boring. Let's see how to get some content onto the screen.

Currently Ember.js has created four objects with default behavior, all off which are related to the Notes application:

- An application route
- An application controller
- An application view
- An application template

You don't need to know what these four objects do at this point in time. What's important to know is that you can override these default objects to include customized behavior.

To write some text onto the page, you'll override the default `application` template with custom markup. Add a `script` tag inside your `head` tag of index.html. The type of this script tag needs to be `"text/x-handlebars"` and must include the name (`id`) of your template, as shown in the following example.

Listing 1.2 Overriding the `application` template

```
<script type="text/x-handlebars" id="application">
        Hello Notes Application!
</script>
```

Creates a Handlebars.js template named application.

Contents of template will be written to the screen.

Remember to close your script tag!

Load your index.html file into your browser and you should see the text "Hello Notes Application!" as shown in figure 1.8.

Hello Notes Application!

Figure 1.8 Rendering the `application` template

Running your application

Although you can run the Notes application by dragging the index.html file into the browser, I recommend hosting the application in a proper web server. You can use the web server that you're most comfortable with. If you want to start up a small lightweight web server to host the current directory you're in, you can use either the asdf Ruby gem, or a simple Python script.

If you have Ruby installed

1 Install the asdf gem by typing `gem install asdf` into your terminal (Mac or Linux) or command prompt (Windows).

2 Once the gem is installed, host the current directory by executing `asdf –port 8080` in your terminal or command prompt.

3 Once the gem starts, navigate to http://localhost:8088/index.html to load your Notes application.

If you have Python installed

1 Execute `python -m SimpleHTTPServer 8088` in your terminal or command prompt.

2 Once Python starts, navigate to http://localhost:8088/index.html to load your Notes application.

Now that you've got some text on the screen, you can move on to defining the setup for the rest of the Notes application. To do this, you'll need to think about which states (routes) your application can be in.

But first delete the `application` template you added in listing 1.2. For the rest of the chapter, you won't need to override the default `application` template, so go ahead and delete it.

1.4.3 Defining application routes

Looking back at figure 1.7, you can see that the Notes application can be in one of two logical states; the list of notes at the left of the application window represents one state, and the selected note's content at the right represents the second state. In addition, the selected note's state is dependent on the selection made in the list at the left. Based on this, you can split the application up into two routes. Name the initial route `notes`. Once a user selects a route, the application transitions to the second route, which you'll name `notes.note`.

The Ember Router and how routes work are thoroughly explained in chapter 3. For now, add the following route definition to your app.js file as shown in the next listing.

Listing 1.3 Defining the application's router

```
Notes.Router.map(function () {                          ⟵  Defines application router
    this.resource('notes', {path: "/"}, function() {
        this.route('note', {path: "/note/:note_id"});   ⟵  Defines subroute,
    });                                                     notes.note, responding
});                                                         to URL "/note/:note_id"
```

Defines top-level route, notes, responding to URL "/"

This code creates a map of your application's routes inside the `Notes.Router` class. Your router has two routes. One is named `notes` and belongs to the URL "/"; the other is named `note` and is a subroute of the `notes` route. A route that can have subroutes is referred to as a *resource* in Ember.js, whereas a leaf route is referred to as a *route*.

Both resources and routes derive their fully qualified names as combinations of their parent route names and their own names. For example, the `note` route in the listing is referred to as the `notes.note` route. This convention extends to controllers, views, and templates, too. Based on the router you defined, Ember.js creates the following default object implementations:

- `Notes.NotesRoute`
- `Notes.NotesController`
- `Notes.NotesView`
- `notes` template
- `Notes.NotesNoteRoute`
- `Notes.NotesNoteController`
- `Notes.NotesNoteView`
- `notes/note` template

In addition, each of your application's routes binds itself to a relative URL path for two-way access, meaning that it responds as expected to URL changes, while at the same time updating the URL when you transition between states programatically. The concepts of routes might seem confusing at first, but rest assured they're thoroughly explained in chapter 3.

> **NOTE** Even though Ember.js creates default implementations of each of the files listed above, you only need to override the files you want to modify. As a result, your Notes application won't have an implementation for all the classes listed.

Now that you've defined which routes your application has, you also need to tell your Notes application what data is available to each route. The following listing shows the definition of both the notes and the notes.note routes.

Listing 1.4   Defining the application's routes

```
Notes.NotesRoute = Ember.Route.extend({          ⟵─── ⟵  Defines notes route
    model: function() {
        return this.store.find('note');              Defines data
    }                                                available
});                                                  to this route

Notes.NotesNoteRoute = Ember.Route.extend({
    model: function(note) {                      ⟵
      return this.store.find('note', note.note_id);
    }
})
```

Defines notes.note route ─▷

This code introduces a couple of new concepts. The most obvious is that each of your routes extends from Ember.Route. Next, you use the model() function to tell each of your routes what data is valid within them. We won't discuss what the code inside the model() functions does in detail here.

Using Ember Data, you tell your notes route to populate a NotesController with all the notes registered in your system. Similarly, you tell the notes.note route to populate a NotesNoteController with only the selected note. In addition, you use the Local Storage Adapter for Ember Data, which means that the notes you create are stored locally in the browser and made available to the application across site refreshes. The concept of Ember Data might seem confusing to you at this point. Don't worry, though; we'll go through Ember Data in detail in chapter 5.

Now, you'll add some real content to your application.

1.4.4   Creating and listing notes

Inside the notes route, you'll include an input text field and a button so that users can add new notes to the application. Beneath these items, you'll provide a list of all the notes that are registered in your application.

Because you already defined your routes, all you need to get started is to add a new template called notes. The following code shows the text field and the button added to index.html.

Listing 1.5 Adding a template, input field, and button

```
<script type="text/x-handlebars" id="notes">
    <div id="notes" class="azureBlueBackground
        azureBlueBorderThin">
        {{input}}
        <button class="btn btn-default btn-xs">
            New Note
        </button>
    </div>
</script>
```

Defines template named notes

Wraps template contents inside div with id notes

Adds text field to template

Adds button labeled New Note

You wrap the contents of your `notes` template in a `div` element with the `id` of `notes` to ensure that the correct CSS styling is applied to the list of notes. Inside this `div` element, you add the text field and the button. For now, they don't have any functionality because you haven't told Ember.js what to do with the text entered in the text field or what to do when the user clicks the button.

To get text onto your application, you created a custom implementation of the `application` template in listing 1.2. Because you no longer want to include this text in your Notes application, go ahead and delete the `application` template you created. Relying on Ember.js's standard application template works just fine for the Notes application.

> **NOTE** Whenever Ember.js requests a template that you haven't defined yourself, it uses a default implementation, which contains only a single `{{outlet}}` expression.

The end goal is to allow the user to enter the name of a new note in the text field and then click the button to create the note and save it to the browser's local storage.

To achieve this, you need to bind the content of your text field to a variable on the `NotesController` and add an action that triggers on the `NotesController` when the button is clicked. Ember.js automatically created a default `NotesController` for you, but to implement your action, you need to override it. The following listing shows the additions made to the app.js file.

Listing 1.6 Creating the `NotesController`

```
Notes.NotesController = Ember.ArrayController.extend({
    newNoteName: null,

    actions: {
        createNewNote: function() {
            var content = this.get('content');
            var newNoteName = this.get('newNoteName');
            var unique = newNoteName != null && newNoteName.length > 1;

            content.forEach(function(note) {
                if (newNoteName === note.get('name')) {
                    unique = false; return;
                }
            });
```

Extends Ember.ArrayController

Binds newNoteName property to text field

Defines the actions on controller

Defines createNewNote action

Ensures that note name is unique

If name is unique, creates note using Ember Data createRecord, persists note to browser's local storage, and resets contents of text field

```
if (unique) {
    var newNote = this.store.createRecord('note');
    newNote.set('id', newNoteName);
    newNote.set('name', newNoteName);
    newNote.save();

    this.set('newNoteName', null);
} else {
    alert('Note must have a unique name of at
        least 2 characters!');
}
    }
  }
});
```

If note name isn't unique, alerts user

A lot is happening in the code in this example. First, you created a controller named `Notes.NotesController`. Because this controller contains a list of notes, it extends `Ember.ArrayController`.

Next, you define a `newNoteName` property on the controller. You'll bind this to your input text field. You could omit this declaration here, because Ember.js would create it automatically for you the first time the user typed into the text field, but I like to be explicit with the properties that my templates are using. This is a personal preference, though, and your opinions might differ.

The contents of the `createNewNote` action are straightforward:

- Verify that the name of the new note contains at least two characters.
- Ensure that no other notes exist in the system with the same name.
- Once the new note name has been verified, create a new note and persist it into the browser local storage.

To add notes via the application's user interface, you need to update the `notes` template. But first you need to initialize Ember Data. The next listing shows the code added to app.js.

Listing 1.7   Initializing Ember Data

```
Notes.Store = DS.Store.extend({
    adapter: DS.LSAdapter
});

Notes.Note = DS.Model.extend({
    name: DS.attr('string'),
    value: DS.attr('string')
});
```

Specifies to use Local Storage Adapter

Creates Notes.Store class extending Ember Data's DS.Store

Creates definition for Note model object

Specifies name property of type string

Specifies value property of type string

Now that your application is set up to use the browser's local storage through Ember Data, you can bind your text field value and button action to the `Notes.NotesController`. The following listing shows the updated `notes` template in index.html.

Listing 1.8 Adding a binding

```
<script type="text/x-handlebars" id="notes">
    <div id="notes" class="azureBlueBackground azureBlueBorderThin">
        {{input valueBinding="newNoteName"}}
        <button class="btn btn-default btn-xs" {{action
        "createNewNote"}}>New Note</button>
    </div>
</script>
```

Adds action to trigger createNewNote action on NotesController

Binds value of text field input to newNoteName property

Now that you can add new notes to the application, you also want the ability to list all notes in the Notes application. To implement this functionality, edit the notes template with the code shown in the next listing.

Listing 1.9 Creating the list of notes

```
<script type="text/x-handlebars" id="notes">
    <div id="notes" class="azureBlueBackground azureBlueBorderThin">
        {{input valueBinding="newNoteName"}}
        <button class="btn btn-default btn-xs"
            {{action "createNewNote"}}>
            New Note
        </button>

        <div class="list-group" style="margin-top: 10px;">
            {{#each controller}}
                <div class="list-group-item">
                    {{name}}
                </div>
            {{/each}}
        </div>
    </div>
</script>
```

Adds Twitter Bootstrap list group to hold notes list

Iterates over each note registered in NotesController

Prints out name of each note

The additions to the code are straightforward, if a little unfamiliar at this point. You use the {{#each}} Handlebars.js expression to iterate over each of the notes inside the Notes.NotesController. For each of the notes, you print out the name. You use Twitter Bootstrap to style your user interface. Figure 1.9 shows the results of loading the updated index.html.

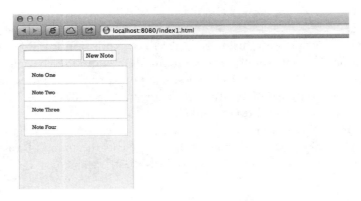

Figure 1.9 The updated Notes application after loading index.html

At this point, you might think that you went through quite an ordeal to get a list of notes onto the screen, but as you'll soon discover, all that hard work will pay dividends.

Next, you'll implement part two of the application: selecting a note in the list to transition to the `notes.note` route and viewing the contents of each note.

1.4.5 *Selecting and viewing a note*

What's a notes application without the ability to write text into the individual notes? By the end of this section, you'll have implemented this part of the application.

> **NOTE** The complete source code for this section is available as app2.js in either your source code directory or online via GitHub: https://github.com/ joachimhs/Ember.js-in-Action-Source/blob/master/chapter1/notes/js/app/ app2.js. You'll find the complete source code for this section in the index2.html and app2.js files. This example uses Ember.js 1.0.0, and thus the {{#linkTo}} helper. In newer versions of Ember.js, this helper has been renamed to {{#link-to}}. If you are using a newer version than 1.0.0, Ember.js will tell you that the {{#linkTo}} helper has been depricated.

Listing 1.10 Linking each note to the `notes.note` route

```
<script type="text/x-handlebars" id="notes">
    <div id="notes" class="azureBlueBackground azureBlueBorderThin">
        {{input valueBinding="newNoteName"}}
        <button class="btn btn-default btn-xs"
            {{action "createNewNote"}}>
            New Note
        </button>

        <div class="list-group" style="margin-top: 10px;">
            {{#each controller}}
                <div class="list-group-item">
                    {{#linkTo "notes.note" this}}          Wraps name of note
                        {{name}}                           in linkTo expression
                    {{/linkTo}}
                </div>
            {{/each}}
        </div>
    </div>
</script>
```

Wrapping the {{name}} expression inside a {{linkTo}} expression is the most common way to transition the user from one route to another as the user navigates your Ember.js application. The {{linkTo}} expression takes one or two attributes: the first is the name of the route to transition to; the second attribute specifies the context that the {{linkTo}} expression injects into the linked-to route.

In the case of your Notes application, you want to transition the user from the NotesRoute to the NotesNoteRoute whenever the user clicks the name of a note. In addition, you want to pass in the selected note to the NotesNoteRoute.

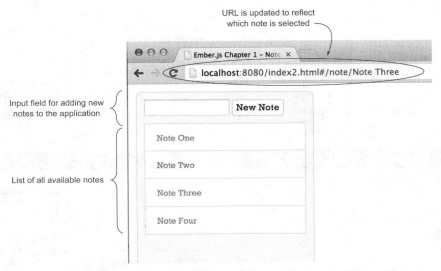

Figure 1.10   The notes in the list are HTML hyperlinks, and the browser URL updates when a note is selected.

Refresh your application and select a note by clicking it. Each note name in the list is now an HTML hyperlink. When you click a note, notice that the application URL updates to reflect which note you're currently viewing (see figure 1.10).

Now that you can view and select your notes, you also want to be able to display the contents of the selected note at the right of the list.

To display the selected note, you'll create a `notes/note` template. But before you do, you need to tell the `notes` template where it should render its subroutes by adding an `{{outlet}}` expression to the template. The following listing shows the updated `notes` template.

Listing 1.11   Adding an outlet to the `notes` template

```
<script type="text/x-handlebars" id="notes">
    <div id="notes" class="azureBlueBackground azureBlueBorderThin">
        {{input valueBinding="newNoteName"}}
        <button class="btn btn-default btn-xs"
            {{action "createNewNote"}}>
            New Note
        </button>

        <div class="list-group" style="margin-top: 10px;">
        {{#each controller}}
            <div class="list-group-item">
                {{#linkTo "notes.note" this}}
                    {{name}}
                {{/linkTo}}
            </div>
        {{/each}}
```

```
        </div>
    </div>
                                        Specifies where to
    {{outlet}}                          render subroutes
</script>
```

After telling the notes template where to render the notes.note route, you can add a template that shows the selected note. Create the new template inside your index.html file with the id notes/note, the contents of which are shown in the following listing.

Listing 1.12 Adding the notes.note template

```
<script type="text/x-handlebars" id="notes/note">          Defines template with
    <div id="selectedNote">                                name notes/note
        <h1>name: {{name}}</h1>
        {{view Ember.TextArea valueBinding="value"}}       Creates text area for
    </div>                                                  viewing and updating
</script>                          Prints name of note      note content
                                  in a header tag
```

Wraps template in div with id selectedNote (annotation)

Although you've only added a small amount of code to allow the user to select a note and view its contents, you now have an application that allows the user to do the following:

- Create a note and add it to the list of notes
- View a list of all notes added to the application
- Select a note, which transitions the user to a new route and updates the URL
- View and edit the contents of the selected note
- Refresh the application while viewing a specific note, which initializes the application and displays the same note to the user

Figure 1.11 shows the updated application.

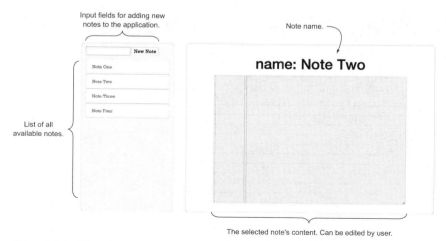

Figure 1.11 The selected note's content appears at the right side of the figure.

Before we move on to the deletion of notes, you'll fix two issues:

- The application doesn't indicate which note is currently selected.
- There's no way to persist changes made to the selected note.

To fix the first issue, use Twitter Bootstrap CSS styling in combination with the addition of a CSS class to the {{linkTo}} expression, as shown in the following listing.

Listing 1.13 Highlighting the selected note

```
<script type="text/x-handlebars" id="notes">
    <div id="notes" class="azureBlueBackground azureBlueBorderThin">
        {{input valueBinding="newNoteName"}}
        <button class="btn btn-default btn-xs"
            {{action "createNewNote"}}>
            New Note
        </button>

        <div class="list-group" style="margin-top: 10px;">
            {{#each controller}}
                {{#linkTo "notes.note" this class="list-group-item"}}
                    {{name}}
                {{/linkTo}}
            {{/each}}
        </div>
    </div>

    {{outlet}}
</script>
```

Removes div and adds CSS class → (annotation pointing to the `{{#linkTo ...}}` line)

That subtle change of removing the div element and adding a CSS class name to the {{linkTo}} expression is enough to successfully highlight the selected note in a blue color. Notice also that this feature works whether you click a note or you enter the notes.note route directly via a URL (or hit refresh).

To fix the second issue, start by adding an Update button to the notes/note template, as shown in the following listing.

Listing 1.14 Adding a button to the notes/note template

```
<script type="text/x-handlebars" id="notes/note">
    <div id="selectedNote">
        <h1>name: {{name}}</h1>
        {{view Ember.TextArea valueBinding="value"}}
        <button class="btn btn-primary form-control mediumTopPadding"
            {{action "updateNote"}}>Update</button><br />
    </div>
</script>
```

Adds button that will trigger the action updateNote on the NotesNoteController → (annotation pointing to the `<button>` line)

Once this button is in place, add an action to the Notes.NotesNoteController to perform the update of the note. Until now, you've managed perfectly OK without overriding the default NotesNote controller that Ember.js created for you. The following listing shows the updated controller in app.js.

Listing 1.15   Adding a `NotesNote` controller to update the note

```
Notes.NotesNoteController = Ember.ObjectController.extend({
    actions: {
        updateNote: function() {
            var content = this.get('content');
            console.log(content);
            if (content) {
                content.save();
            }
        }
    }
});
```

Adds action to catch click of Update button

Creates Notes.NotesNoteController extending from Ember.ObjectController

Saves any changes made

Your application should now look like figure 1.12. Note that the selected note is high-lighted on the left side of the figure, the URL is updated to reflect this, and an Update button now appears below the text area.

You can now move on to the final piece of the Notes application: deleting notes.

1.4.6   Deleting notes

In this section, you'll implement the third and last part of the Notes application.

> **NOTE** The complete source code for this section is available as app3.js in either your source code directory or online at GitHub: https://github.com/joachimhs/Ember.js-in-Action-Source/blob/master/chapter1/notes/js/app/app3.js.

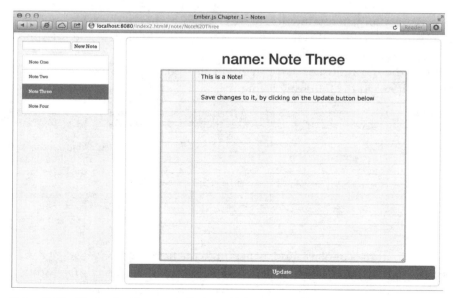

Figure 1.12   The application now indicates which note is selected and saves updates made to the selected note.

To delete notes, add a Delete button to the selected note in the list at left. When the user clicks this button, the Notes application presents a modal panel asking for confirmation before the note is deleted. Once the user confirms that the note deserves to be deleted, the note is removed from the `Notes.NotesController`'s content property and the `selectedNote` property is reset to `null`. To implement this feature, add a modal panel to your application, which is available from the Twitter Bootstrap framework. You also need to add a couple of new actions to the `Notes.NotesController`.

Start by adding the Delete button to the `notes` template, as shown in the following listing.

Listing 1.16   Adding a Delete button to the `notes` template

```
<script type="text/x-handlebars" id="notes">
    <div id="notes" class="azureBlueBackground azureBlueBorderThin">
        {{input valueBinding="newNoteName"}}
        <button class="btn btn-default btn-xs"
            {{action "createNewNote"}}>
            New Note
        </button>

        <div class="list-group" style="margin-top: 10px;">
            {{#each controller}}
                {{#linkTo "notes.note" this class="list-group-item"}}
                    {{name}}

                    <button class="btn btn-danger btn-xs pull-right"
                        {{action "doDeleteNote" this}}>
                        Delete
                    </button>                        ◁─┐  Adds button that fires
                {{/linkTo}}                             doDeleteNote action
                                                        on NotesController
            {{/each}}
        </div>
    </div>

    {{outlet}}
</script>
```

Once you add the button to the user interface, you can add the new `doDeleteNote` action to the `Notes.NotesController`. This time, you pass in `this` to the `doDelete-Note` action to tell the action which note you're attempting to delete. The updated controller is shown in the following listing.

Listing 1.17   Adding the `doDeleteNote` action to the `NotesController`

```
Notes.NotesController = Ember.ArrayController.extend({
    needs: ['notesNote'],

    newNoteName: null,

    actions: {
        createNewNote: function () {
```

Adds new doDelete-Note action to NotesController

Displays the confirmation modal dialog

Stores deleted note in noteForDeletion property on controller

```
        //Same as before
    },

    doDeleteNote: function (note) {
        this.set('noteForDeletion', note);
        $("#confirmDeleteNoteDialog").modal({"show": true});
    },
```

The doDeleteNote action now takes a single parameter. Because you passed in the note you want to delete in the third argument of the {{action}} expression, Ember.js makes sure that this object is passed into your action. At this point, you don't want to delete the note without first making sure that this is what the user wants to do. Before you display a confirmation message to the user, you need to temporarily store which note the user wants to delete. Once that's done, you show the user the modal panel, which you'll create next.

Because the HTML code to render the Twitter Bootstrap modal panel is slightly verbose and you can potentially reuse it in multiple parts of your application, you'll create a new template that renders the modal panel onto the screen. Start by creating a template called confirmDialog inside index.html, as shown in the following listing.

Listing 1.18 Adding a template for the modal panel

Creates div element with id confirmDelete-NoteDialog for modal panel

Adds text to display in header of panel

Adds template named confirmDialog

Adds text to display in body of panel

Creates Cancel button, which fires action doCancelDelete

Creates Delete button, which fires action doConfirmDelete

```
<script type="text/x-handlebars" id="confirmDialog">
    <div id="confirmDeleteNoteDialog" class="modal fade">
        <div class="modal-dialog">
            <div class="modal-content">
                <div class="modal-header centerAlign">
                    <h1 class="centerAlign">Delete selected note?</h1>
                </div>
                <div class="modal-body">
                    Are you sure you want to delete the selected Note?
                    This action cannot be be undone!
                </div>
                <div class="modal-footer">
                    <button class="btn btn-default"
                        {{action "doCancelDelete"}}>
                        Cancel
                    </button>
                    <button class="btn btn-primary"
                        {{action "doConfirmDelete"}}>
                        Delete Note
                    </button>
                </div>
            </div>
        </div>
    </div>
</script>
```

The modal panel is straightforward once you get past the Twitter Bootstrap markup, which in this case is somewhat verbose. The panel includes a header area, a body area, and a footer area. For the Notes application, you add text to the modal panel that prompts the user to confirm that they want to delete the note, and also informs the user that the operation can't be undone. In the footer you add two buttons: one that cancels the deletion and one that deletes the note. The Cancel button calls on its controller's `doCancelDelete` action; the Delete button calls on its controller's `doConfirm-Delete` action.

To display the modal panel, you need to add only one line of code that tells the `notes` template where to render the new `confirmDialog` template. To achieve this, use the `{{partial}}` expression, as shown in the following listing.

Listing 1.19 Rendering the `confirmDialog` template

```
<script type="text/x-handlebars" id="notes">
    <div id="notes" class="azureBlueBackground azureBlueBorderThin">
        //Content same as before
    </div>

    {{outlet}}

    {{partial confirmDialog}}                    ⟵── Renders template
</script>
```

The `{{partial}}` expression finds the template with a name that matches its first argument and renders that template into the DOM.

Your final task is to implement the actions `doCancelDelete` and `doConfirmDelete` on your `Notes.NotesController`. The following listing shows the updated controller.

Listing 1.20 Implementing the `doCancelDelete` and `doConfirmDelete` actions

```
Notes.NotesController = Ember.ArrayController.extend({
    needs: ['notesNote'],                         ⟵── Calls for access to
    newNoteName: null,                                Notes.NotesNoteController

    actions: {
        createNewNote: function() {
            //Same as before
        },

        doDeleteNote: function (note) {
            //Same as before
        },
                                                  Implements
                                                  doCancelDelete
        doCancelDelete: function () {        ⟵──┘
            this.set('noteForDeletion', null);
            $("#confirmDeleteNoteDialog").modal('hide');    ⟵──  Resets
        },                                                       property
                                                                 to null
                                          Implements
                                          doConfirmDelete
        doConfirmDelete: function () {  ⟵──┘
            var selectedNote = this.get('noteForDeletion');
            this.set('noteForDeletion', null);         ⟵──
            if (selectedNote) {
                this.store.deleteRecord(selectedNote);
                selectedNote.save();
```

Hides modal panel ⟶ (points to the `$("#confirmDeleteNoteDialog").modal('hide');` line)

Retrieves note for deletion based on noteForDeletion property ⟶ (points to the `var selectedNote = this.get('noteForDeletion');` line)

If user has a note to delete, deletes note and persists changes into local storage

```
                      if (this.get('controllers.notesNote.model.id') ===
                          selectedNote.get('id')) {
                          this. transitionToRoute('notes');
                      }
                  }
              $("#confirmDeleteNoteDialog").modal('hide');
          }
      }
});
```

If deleted note is currently being viewed, transitions user to notes route →

← **Hides modal panel**

A few things are happening with the code in this example. First, you've implemented the doCancelDelete action. The contents of this action are simple: you reset the controller's noteForDeletion property back to null, and then hide the modal panel.

The doConfirmDelete action is more involved. You first get the note you want to delete from the noteForDeletion property on the controller before you reset the property to null. Next, you ensure that the controller has a reference to an actual note to delete. Once you've confirmed this, tell Ember Data to delete the record from its store. This only marks the note as deleted. To perform the delete operation, you need to call save() on the note object. Once this is done, the note is deleted from the browser's local storage and is also removed from the user's list of notes.

Before you close the modal panel and finish the doConfirmDelete action, you need to consider one more scenario: what should happen if the user is deleting the note currently being viewed? You have two options:

- Notify the user that it's not possible to delete the note that's currently being viewed
- Transition the user back to the notes route

For this application, I felt it more appropriate to do the latter.

If you look at the second line of the controller, you'll see that a needs property has been added. This is one way to tell Ember.js that this controller will, at some point, require access to the instantiated Notes.NotesNoteController. You can then access this controller via the controllers.notesNote property. This allows you to compare the id property of the note being deleted with the id property of the note the user is viewing (if any). If these properties match, transition the user to the notes route via the transitionToRoute()function.

To try out the delete note feature, reload the completed Notes application in your browser and attempt to delete a note (see figure 1.13).

That completes the functionality of the Notes application for this chapter. You'll continue working with the Notes application while delving deeper into the Ember.js core concepts in chapter 2.

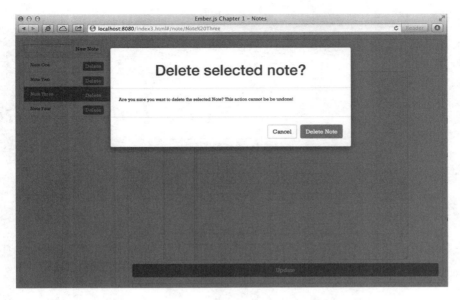

Figure 1.13   The completed Notes application displaying the Delete modal panel

1.5   Summary

This chapter provided an overview of the building blocks that Ember.js is based on and introduced the most important concepts of an Ember.js application. I hope that you gained a better understanding of the Ember.js framework, as well as why it exists and where it's most applicable to you as a web developer.

In this introductory chapter to Ember.js, I guided you through the development process of a simple web application, touching on the important aspects of the framework along the way. The goal of the Notes application was to show you as many of the basic Ember.js features as possible without complicating the application's source code.

Ember.js has a steep learning curve, but the benefits to you, as a web developer, are great, and this chapter has shown some of the power that lies in this advanced framework.

In the next chapter, you'll reuse and extend the code you wrote in this chapter to thoroughly understand the core features that Ember.js provides.

The Ember.js way

This chapter covers

- How bindings work and how they affect your programming style
- Using automatic updating templates
- How and when to use computed properties and observers
- The Ember.js object and class model

This chapter builds on the code that you developed in chapter 1 to explain the most defining aspects of the Ember.js framework in detail. One of the key design goals of Ember.js is to make sane, reasonable, default choices to reduce the amount of boilerplate code that you must write on your own. Ember.js uses default settings that work out of the box with the majority of web applications, and it allows you to override these defaults easily where applicable. Thanks to those sane choices, you can write large web applications without having to constantly consider how your data will get from point A to point B or how your web elements will be updated in a clean and efficient manner, and you can easily integrate with any third-party Java-Script Framework of your choice.

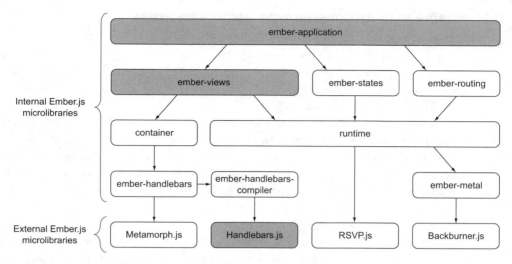

Figure 2.1   The parts of Ember.js addressed in this chapter

If you've worked with other programming environments that use the concept of bindings, such as Objective-C, Adobe Flex, and JavaFX, then you're already familiar with the mindset required to think of your application in terms of observers, bound variables, and automatic synchronization of data across the application. Otherwise, you need to clear out some of your old programming habits to leave room for these essential concepts in Ember.js, because they'll affect how you think about wiring your application together in a big way. Rewiring your development habits to fit into this loosely coupled and asynchronous way of thinking about application code may be the hardest part of learning to user Ember.js efficiently.

Figure 2.1 shows the parts of the Ember.js ecosystem that this chapter examines—ember-application, ember-views, and Handlebars.js.

Throughout the chapter, you'll extend the Notes application created in chapter 1. The changes made affect the index4.html and app4.html files.

> **NOTE**   The source code for this section is available in either your code source directory or online at GitHub: https://github.com/joachimhs/Ember.js-in-Action-Source/blob/master/chapter1/notes/js/app/app4.js.

Let's start with one of the core key features, bindings, which the rest of Ember.js framework builds upon.

The Ember.js framework is based on a couple of related features that hold the whole framework together and form the basis of all the other features offered in Ember.js. Knowing how these core features—bindings, computed properties, and observers—work is essential for any developer using Ember.js.

2.1   *Using bindings to glue your objects together*

One set of tasks that you're most likely to encounter in a repetitive manner when writing web applications is requesting data from a back-end resource, parsing the response to update your controllers, and making sure that your views are up-to-date whenever your data changes.

Then, as the user works with the data, you need to make sure that you update both your in-browser cache and your view in a way that ensures that what's persisted in the in-browser cache matches what the user sees on their screen.

You've probably written code to support that use case hundreds, if not thousands, of times, yet most web applications lack a site-wide infrastructure to handle these interactions in a clean and consistent manner, leaving it up to the developer to reinvent the wheel for each application and each of its layers. A common implementation might look like figure 2.2.

This model assumes that you've thought about how you want to structure your application, and that you've implemented an MVC-like structure in your application. The Ember.js MVC model is slightly different from the MVC models you've become accustomed to when writing web applications, but fear not; the Ember.js MVC model is thoroughly explained in detail in chapter 3.

The problem with the model shown in figure 2.2 is that it leaves it up to the developer to implement a structure that ensures that the data persisted to the server is, in fact, the data presented to the user. Besides the need to implement custom code for each of the six steps listed (steps 3–8), consider the many edge cases:

- What if the server is unable to persist your data?
- What if the server has had updates between the time you loaded the application data (in step 2) and when you persisted it (in step 5)?
- What if the user has created new data and the server needs to generate a unique identifier for that data (steps 3 and 5)?

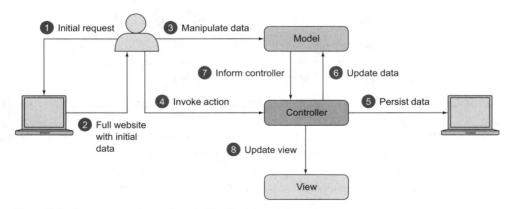

Figure 2.2   A common data synchronization implementation

- If the server changes any of the data persisted, how would the client be notified in order to reflect these changes?
- What happens if the user changes data that has been sent to the server, but a response hasn't arrived yet?
- What happens if the model is updated without the controller being notified of a change?
- What happens if multiple views need to show the same data? How would you synchronize the data so that your user interface is consistent?

These are just a few examples of the decisions that you need to make for every part of your application. If you did your homework and implemented a common solution across your application, good for you; now you know the difficulties involved in synchronizing your application data between views and controllers, between models, and between the client and the server. This is a major area where Ember.js helps you immediately with its complete and robust binding and MVC implementations. Ember.js also offers a complete persistence layer called Ember Data, discussed in chapter 5.

In their simplest form, bindings are a way to tell your application, "Whenever variable A changes, make sure to keep variable B up to date." Bindings in Ember.js can be either one-way or two-way. Two-way bindings work the same as one-way bindings, but they keep two variables in sync regardless of which variable changes. The most common binding type you'll use throughout Ember.js is likely to be the two-way binding because it's the default binding structure in Ember.js, and it's also the type of binding you're most likely to need when writing a client application.

To declare a binding explicitly, use either the `Ember.Binding.twoWay` or `Ember.Binding.oneWay` function calls; you need to do this to create one-way bindings. Most likely, however, you'll use the `Binding` suffix keyword in your objects' property declarations. Ember.js is smart enough in its structure that you'll rarely need to instantiate bindings manually. For this reason, you didn't manually create any bindings within the Notes application developed in chapter 1.

But suppose you want to keep track of which note is selected on your `Notes.NotesController`. You can do this by binding a property, `selectedNote`, to the model object of the `Notes.NotesController`. The following listing shows the updated `NotesController`.

Listing 2.1   Synchronizing two variables using bindings

```
Notes.NotesController = Ember.ArrayController.extend({
    needs: ['notesNote'],
    newNoteName: null,
    selectedNoteBinding: 'controllers.notesNote.model',    ⟵┐ Creates binding
                                                              │ between property
                                                              ┘ and model
    //Rest of controller left unchanged
});
```

```
DEBUG: ————————————————————————                          ember-1.0.0.js:394
DEBUG: Ember.VERSION : 1.0.0                              ember-1.0.0.js:394
DEBUG: Handlebars.VERSION : 1.0.0                         ember-1.0.0.js:394
DEBUG: jQuery.VERSION : 1.10.2                            ember-1.0.0.js:394
DEBUG: ————————————————————————                          ember-1.0.0.js:394
```

Figure 2.3   The console log

If you reload the application at this point and head over to the browser's console log, you should see the display shown in figure 2.3.

Ember.js shows the versions of Ember.js, Handlebars.js, and jQuery that are in use by the application. When Ember.js instantiates your controllers and routes, it puts them into a structure called the *container*. You can ask this container to look up the instantiated `NotesController` and check the value of the `selectedNote` property. Type the following command in the console and press Enter. Figure 2.4 shows the result.

```
> Notes.__container__.lookup('controller:notesNote').get('model')
  null
```

Figure 2.4   Prompting the container for the value of the `selectedNote` property

The `selectedNote` property is returned as undefined. This is the expected result, because you haven't selected any note yet. Now select one of your notes and execute the command again. Figure 2.5 shows the result.

```
> Notes.__container__.lookup('controller:notesNote').get('model')
  ▶ Class {id: "Note Two", store: Class, currentState: (...), _changesToSync: Object, _deferredTriggers: Array[0]…}
> Notes.__container__.lookup('controller:notesNote').get('model.id')
  "Note Two"
```

Figure 2.5   Prompting the container for the value of the `selectedNote` property with a note selected

You can now get hold of the selected note via the `NotesController`'s `selectedNote` property. Note that you were also able to fetch the `id` property of the selected note by calling `get('selectedNote.id')`. Using this dot notation, you can fetch and update values deep within your object hierarchy.

Even though you only added a single statement in listing 2.1, Ember.js helped you create the following features:

- A two-way binding between two controllers, keeping the variables in sync when changes occur.
- A clean separation of concern between the controllers.
- A high degree of testability and application flexibility through a loose coupling between controllers.
- The certainty of only a single definition of which note is the selected one throughout the entire application; knowing that `SelectedNoteController` `.model` will always represent this information enables you to create views that can be automatically updated whenever any change to the selected note occurs.

You'll next add some lines of code to understand how to bind the data all the way out to the view via templates that update automatically.

2.2 Updating templates automatically

By default, Ember.js uses the Handlebars.js template engine. One key aspect of the Ember Handlebars implementation is that whenever you connect your templates to your underlying data, Ember.js sets up two-way bindings between your application layers. You've seen how this works in the Notes application developed in chapter 1.

Consider the code for the `notes/note` template, shown in the next listing.

Listing 2.2   Revisiting the `notes/note` template

```
<script type="text/x-handlebars" id="notes/note">
    <div id="selectedNote">
        {{#if model}}
            <h1>name: {{controller.model.name}}</h1>
            {{view Ember.TextArea valueBinding="value"}}
            <button class="btn btn-primary form-control mediumTopPadding"
                {{action "updateNote"}}>Update
            </button><br />
        {{/if}}
    </div>
</script>
```

Displays content of template only if model defined

Prints name property of model

Binds text area and model values

There are two types of binding going on in this example. First, you have template bindings via Handlebars expressions; second, you're binding properties on a custom view via the `Binding` keyword, similar to what you saw in listing 2.1.

Let's first focus on the Handlebars expression `{{name}}`. Even though this is a simple expression in your template, a lot is going on behind the scenes. The `notes/note` template is injected with a context from its backing controller. In this case, the controller that's driving the data to this template is the `NotesNoteController`.

Behind the scenes, you're working on the `model` property of the `NotesNote-Controller`. This may seem odd at first, but `{{name}}` is shorthand for `{{model .name}}`, which in turn is shorthand for `{{controller.model.name}}`. In fact, you could use either of these expressions to print out the name of the note in the template.

One neat thing about the Ember-Handlebars implementation is that whenever a change occurs in the properties that your template is bound to, Ember.js ensures that your views are kept in sync and automatically updated. For example, if you go into the console and change the name of your note, observers, which are set up by Ember.js, ensure that the view is updated. To try this, launch the Notes application and select a note. Then issue the following command from the console:

```
Notes.__container__.lookup('controller:notesNote')
    .set('model.name', 'New Name')
```

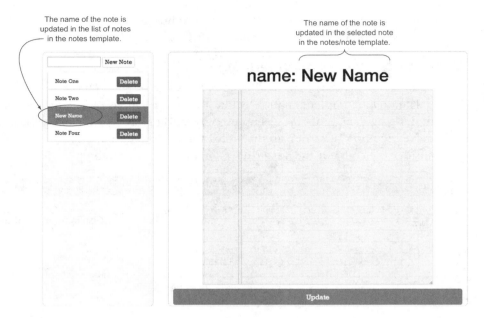

Figure 2.6   Changing the name of a note via the console

You should now see that the name of your note has changed, both in the list of notes at the left and in the header for the selected note. Figure 2.6 shows the result.

To only show the selected note to the user if one is selected, use the Handlebars `if` helper. The statement `{{#if model}}` ensures that the code inside that `if` helper is executed only if the model attribute of the controller is not `null` or `undefined`. With a handful of code lines, Ember.js allows you to implement functionality that you'd otherwise have to handle manually for each of your views:

- Display the selected note only when a note is selected.
- Keep your DOM tree clean. If no note is selected, it keeps the element completely out of the DOM; there's no `display:hidden` in sight.
- Ensure that the user always sees the updated information about the notes in any template that's rendered onto the website.
- Ensure that when the user changes the selected note's value (through the text area), Ember.js will update the underlying Note data.

Now try one more task before we end the automated templates discussion. Create a brand-new `Note` object via Ember Data. You can do this by executing the following command in the browser's console:

```
Notes.__container__.lookup('store:main')
    .createRecord('note', {id: "New Note", "name": "New Note"})
```

Here, you first fetched the Ember Data store from the container, using the keyword `store:main`. Then you created a new note via the `createRecord` function, passing in an `id` and `name` for your note. When you execute this command, notice that the new note is displayed at the bottom of the note list.

At this point, it should be easy to envision how your application would behave if you implemented synchronization of notes between the Notes application and a real back-end server application. Updating the number of notes available in the system, changing which note is selected, and even changing the selected note's data can all be initiated via a push request from the server side. You've written only a handful of code statements, but you've built a rather large list of features into the application, all while keeping the application structure reasonable.

The Ember.js default template engine, Handlebars, has many features that are integrated into Ember.js. Handlebars is thoroughly explained in chapter 4.

You may wonder how you're going to deal with situations in which the data available doesn't exactly match up with the data that you want to display to the user. Similarly, what will you do if the data you're either displaying or dependent on in an `if` helper or `each` helper is complex? Cases like these are where computed properties come into action.

2.3 *Computed properties*

A *computed property* is a function that returns a value derived from other variables or expressions (even other computed properties) in your code. The difference between a computed property and a normal JavaScript function is that Ember.js treats your computed property function as if it were a real Ember.js property. As a result, you can call `get()` and `set()` on your computed properties, as well as bind to them or observe them (more on observers later in this chapter). Normally you find your computed properties on your model object, but every once in a while you need to use them in your controllers or views.

You don't have a computed property in the Notes application yet, but suppose you want to improve the application by showing the first 20 characters of each note's value in the list of notes at the left of the application window. Instead of having to worry about issuing jQuery selectors and injecting/replacing information into a view somewhere, Ember.js allows you to define computed properties.

Next you'll create a computed property named `introduction` on the `Notes.Note` class that returns the first 20 characters of a note's text. The updated `Notes.Note` model class is shown in the following listing.

Listing 2.3 Creating the `introduction` computed property

```
Notes.Note = DS.Model.extend({
    name: DS.attr('string'),
    value: DS.attr('string'),

    introduction: function() {                  Creates normal
        var intro = "";                         JavaScript function
                                                named introduction
        if (this.get('value')) {                If value property of model has value,
            intro = this.get('value').substring(0, 20);   substrings out first 20 characters
        }
```

```
        return intro;
    }.property('value')
});
```

> Adding .property makes introduction
> function a computed property

Ember.js provides you with a great deal of functionality here. First, Ember.js is smart about when and how often it calculates the return value of a computed property. Until a computed property is used, its value isn't calculated at all. This is great for performance, because your application doesn't waste time calculating a lot of properties that may never be rendered onto the user's screen.

Looking at the structure of how you define a function as a computed property should give you a hint as to the second reason a computed property is calculated. Here, `property('value')` means "whenever the `value` property of `this` object changes, recompute the return value of this computed property." Therefore, as you type in the text area to add information to the `value` property of the note, you can see that the user interface is immediately updated to reflect your changes.

Until now, you haven't added the `introduction` computed property to any template. You're going to use it to provide users with a preview of each note in the Notes application. The next listing expands the `notes` template to display the first 20 characters of the `value` property in the list of notes.

Listing 2.4   Showing the `introduction` computed property in the `notes` template

```
<script type="text/x-handlebars" id="notes">
    <div id="notes" class="azureBlueBackground azureBlueBorderThin">
        {{input valueBinding="newNoteName"}}
        <button class="btn btn-default btn-xs"
            {{action "createNewNote"}}>
            New Note
        </button>

        <div class="list-group" style="margin-top: 10px;">
            {{#each controller}}
                {{#linkTo "notes.note" this class="list-group-item"}}
                    {{name}}
                    {{#if introduction}}
                        <br />{{introduction}}
                    {{/if}}

                    <button class="btn btn-danger btn-xs pull-right"
                        {{action "doDeleteNote" this}}>
                        Delete
                    </button>
                {{/linkTo}}

            {{/each}}
        </div>
    </div>

    {{outlet}}

    {{partial confirmDialog}}
</script>
```

Adds introduction computed property to notes template (annotation pointing to `{{/if}}`)

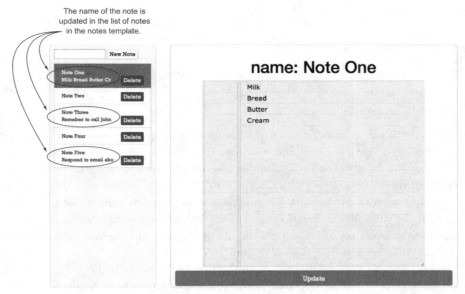

The name of the note is updated in the list of notes in the notes template.

Figure 2.7   The note names now include an additional line that displays the value of the `introduction` property.

You only added a single line of code to your template. This line states that if the `introduction` property of the current `Note` model isn't `null` and has a length greater than 0, print out a new line followed by the content of the `introduction` property itself. Figure 2.7 shows the updated Notes application.

I mentioned that you can also use computed properties as setters. But how do you set a value that's derived from a combination of other properties? In listing 2.5, an object named `Notes.Duration` has a single property, `durationSeconds`. Although it might make sense for a back-end service to store the duration as seconds, it's inconvenient for the user to get the duration presented to them in seconds. Instead, you want to convert the seconds into a string with hours, minutes, and seconds separated by colons.

Listing 2.5   Using computed properties as setters

```
Notes.Duration = Ember.Object.extend({
    durationSeconds: 0,

    durationString: function(key, value) {          ⟵┘ Defines computed property
        if (arguments.length === 2 && value) {         with two arguments
            var valueParts = value.split(":");
            if (valueParts.length == 3) {           ⟵ Verifies that value splits
                var duration = (valueParts[0] * 60 * 60) +  into three parts as expected
                    (valueParts[1] * 60) + (valueParts[2] * 1);
                this.set('durationSeconds', duration);
            }
        }
        var duration = this.get('durationSeconds');   ⟵ Starts getter part
                                                          of computed property
```

Starts setter part of computed property (points to `if (arguments.length === 2 && value) {`)

Updates durationSeconds with new duration (points to `this.set('durationSeconds', duration);`)

```
                    var hours   = Math.floor(duration / 3600);
                    var minutes = Math.floor((duration - (hours * 3600)) / 60);
                    var seconds = Math.floor(duration - (minutes * 60) -
                        (hours * 3600));

                    return ("0" + hours).slice(-2) + ":" +
                        ("0" + minutes).slice(-2) + ":" + ("0" + seconds).slice(-2);
                }.property('durationSeconds').cacheable()
            });
```

Formats return value according to requirements (marginal annotation pointing to the `return` line)

The first thing to notice is that the computed property function now includes two function arguments, a key and a value. You can use these arguments to determine whether the function call is a getter or a setter by checking for exactly two arguments. Depending on your requirements, null might have a logical meaning or not. In this case, you want to update the durationSeconds property only if the input has a valid format. To validate the input value, split it into an array of parts. If the input is valid, start the conversion of the HH:MM:SS string into seconds before updating the object durationSeconds property with the updated value.

The second part of the computed property function is the getter, which, as you might expect, does the opposite of the setter part. It starts by fetching the duration-Seconds property before it generates the durationString and returns it.

As you've probably guessed, it's fairly trivial to use a computed property in this manner to fill out an input field in the GUI via a simple binding to an HTML text field element. Ember.js takes care of automatically formatting the seconds to a human-readable duration and vice versa when the user updates the duration in the text field.

I mentioned that a computed property uses an observer to compute its value, but you've yet to see an observer in action, which brings us to how Ember.js observers work.

2.4   *Observers*

Conceptually, a one-way binding consists of an observer and a setter, and a two-way binding consists of two observers and two setters. Observers go by different names and have different implementations across programming languages and frameworks. In Ember.js an *observer* is a JavaScript function that's called whenever a variable it observes changes. You use an observer in situations where a binding is either not a sufficient mechanism or you want to perform a task whenever a value changes.

To implement an observer, use the .addObserver() method or the inline observes() method suffix. The following listing shows one possible use of an observer: starting and stopping a timer based on the number of items in a controller's content array.

Listing 2.6   Observing the length of a controller to control a timer

```
contentObserver: function() {
    var content = this.get('content');                  ⟵─┐ Gets content array from controller
    if (content.get('length') > 0 && this.get('chartTimerId') == null) {
        var intervalId = setInterval(function() {
            if (EurekaJ.appValuesController.get('showLiveCharts')) {
```

Starts timer (marginal annotation pointing to the `var intervalId` line)

```
                               content.forEach(function (node) {
                                   node.get('chart').reload();
                               });
                           }
                       }, 15000);

                       this.set('chartTimerId', intervalId);
```

Stores intervalld so
you can stop it later

Stops timer

```
               } else if (content.get('length') == 0) {
                   //stop timer if started
                   if (this.get('chartTimerId') != null) {
                       EurekaJ.log('stopping timer');
                       clearInterval(this.get('chartTimerId'));
                       this.set('chartTimerId', null);
                   }
               }
           }
       }.observes('content.length')
```

Observes number of
controller model items

The observer, contentObserver, is a normal JavaScript method. It starts by getting the controller's content array. If there are items in the content array and a timer isn't already started, it creates a new timer that fires every 15000 milliseconds. The timer goes through each of the items in the content array and reloads its data using a custom reload() method. If there are no items in the content array, the code stops any timer that has already been started.

To make this function an observer, append the inline observes() function with the path to the property you want to observe.

It's possible to construct the observer using the addObserver() method instead. The body of the function remains the same, but its declaration looks slightly different, as shown in the following listing.

Listing 2.7 Creating an observer using the .addObserver method

```
var myCar = App.Car.create({
    owner: "Joachim"
    make: "Toyota"
});

myCar.addObserver('owner', function() {
    //The content of the observer
});
```

Creates App.Car object

Observes changes
to owner property

Although it's possible to create observers this way, I find the inline version shown in listing 2.6 to be cleaner and more readable when looking at the source code of my applications. I also like to add the suffix Observer to my observer for added readability, but that isn't required.

Sometimes you may want to observe changes to properties within an array. In the Notes application, the Notes.NotesController has a content array of Ember objects with two properties: name and value. To observe changes to each object's name property, use the @each observer key, as shown in the next listing.

Listing 2.8   Observing changes within arrays using @each

```
Notes.NotesController = Ember.ArrayController.extend({
    content: [],
    nameObserver: function() {
        //The content of the observer          Observes changes to name
    }.observes('content.@each.name')           properties of content array
});
```

All the functionality shown in this chapter is made possible via the Ember.js object model, so let's take a closer look at it.

2.5   *The Ember.js object model*

Ember.js extends the default JavaScript object class definition to build a more powerful object model. In addition, it supports a mixin-based approach to sharing code between modules and between applications.

You may wonder how Ember.js knows that your properties have changed, and how it knows to fire off an observer or a binding. You may also have noticed that Ember.js requires you to use `get()` and `set()` whenever you want to get or update a property from any object that's a subclass of `Ember.Object`. Whenever `set()` is called on any property, Ember.js checks to see if the value you're updating with is different from the value that you already have in your object. If the two are different, Ember.js triggers any bindings, observers, or computed properties derived from the property you're updating.

Even though using `get()` and `set()` may seem awkward when you start using Ember.js, this mechanism is one of the features that enables Ember.js to intelligently batch up observers, bindings, computed properties, and DOM manipulations. In fact, the use of `get()` and `set()` is one of the cornerstones of how Ember.js solves the performance issues involved with multiple DOM updates and bindings.

To create a custom Ember.js object, you generally either extend another Ember.js object and enrich it with custom functionality using the `extend()` method, or you create an instance via the `create()` method. Regardless of which you choose, every object within your Ember.js application extends the `Ember.Object` class in one way or another, and it's this base class that enables Ember.js to provide the functionality discussed throughout this book.

Rather than extending `DS.Model` for the `Notes.Note` model object, imagine that you didn't use Ember Data and you need to provide a `Notes.Note` model yourself, as shown in the next listing.

Listing 2.9   Creating a `Notes.Note` object

```
Notes.Note = Ember.Object.extend({          Creates new Notes.Note
    name: null,                             class definition
    value: null
});
```

Instead of using `Ember.Object.create()` to create an anonymous `Note` instance, you create an explicit `Notes.Note` class by extending the `Ember.Object` class. Notice a couple of things:

- You don't have an instance of the `Notes.Note` class yet because the `extend()` method doesn't return an instance.
- The `Note` class now starts with an uppercase *N* to signal, not only to you, but also to the Ember.js framework, that this is a class definition and not an object instance.

To create a new instance of `Notes.Note`, use the `create()` method:

```
Notes.Note = Ember.Object.extend({          Creates new Notes.Note
    name: null,                              class definition
    value: null
});
```

```
var myNewNote = Notes.Note.create({          Creates new instance
    'name': 'My New Note', 'value': null     of Notes.Note
});
```

At this point you may think you haven't gotten much further than with the anonymous `Ember.Object.create()` implementation. However, it's generally a good idea to explicitly define classes for all your data types and all objects that you use within your Ember.js application. Even though doing so requires more code, you clearly show your intent when you instantiate an object, and you can separate domain model objects from one another cleanly. The resulting code is much easier to read, more maintainable, and easier to test.

Cleanly defining your application's objects also makes it easier to add observers, bindings, and computed properties in the correct place to ensure that the application is as fast as possible. Consider the scenario in which your back-end application changes from supplying the `value` property of each `Note` object as a pure text implementation to encoding the value in Markdown format. As shown in the following listing, with the `Notes.Note` specification in one place in your application, it's easy to add this functionality.

Listing 2.10 Adding a computed property to convert from Markdown to HTML

```
Notes.Note = Ember.Object.extend({
    name: null,
    value: null,

    htmlValue: function() {                               Converts from
        var value = this.get('value');                    Markdown to HTML
        return Notes.convertFromMarkdownToHtml(value);
    }.property('value')
});
```

Once you've successfully implemented the `Notes.convertFromMarkdownToHtml` function, it's trivial to change the view template of the application to use the new computed property `htmlValue` instead of using `value`; simply change the Handlebars template for the view (see listing 2.2) to the following:

```
{{view Ember.TextArea valueBinding="htmlValue"}}
```

Now that you have a working Notes application, let's take a closer look at how Ember.js synchronizes data between the layers in Ember.js's MVC pattern.

2.6   *Data synchronization between layers with Ember.js*

Previously in this chapter, we looked at a data synchronization model that ensured data on both the client and server remained in sync at all times (see figure 2.2). In this model, six out of eight steps in the application required you to explicitly track and make note of your internal application state. Contrast that with how the Ember.js framework uses bindings, controllers, and a clean model layer to automate as much of this boilerplate code as possible. Figure 2.8 shows an updated conceptual model.

The Ember.js approach has fewer steps because you leave more of the boilerplate code up to the Ember.js framework. You're still in full control of how the data flows through your application. The main difference is that the code is now explicit about these operations as close to the source as possible, which is where you tell Ember.js how the application is wired together.

As you'll see throughout this book, Ember.js takes a sane approach to the default operations, while still letting you override these defaults whenever another approach would be a better fit for your specific use case. This lets you get on with doing what you're here for—writing ambitious web applications to power the future web.

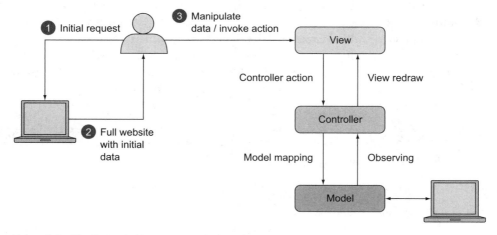

Figure 2.8   The Ember.js data synchronization implementation

2.7 *Summary*

This chapter introduced some concepts that may be unfamiliar to you, or that Ember.js treats differently than you may be used to.

I showed how to use bindings to ensure that the data between your application layers is always up to date and in sync with each other, and you saw how automatically updating templates saves work and ensures that your user interface always reflects the data stored within your model objects.

Once you had the functionality to create, update, and delete Notes, you added a computed property to enrich the UI of your application. Then, we looked at the role of observers and you created one to observe changes to properties within an array on the Notes application.

Next, we looked at the Ember.js object model, and I discussed how it enables you to build complex objects that build on either standard Ember.js objects or customized objects from within your own application.

Finally, I contrasted Ember.js's data synchronization implementation with the common server-side application implementation I introduced in the beginning of the chapter.

I mentioned the Model-View-Controller model a few times, but I haven't yet delved into the details and explained how Ember.js helps you build true MVC applications for the web. That's what the next chapter is all about.

Putting everything together using Ember.js Router

This chapter covers

- Comparing server-side and client-side MVC models
- Exploring the Ember.js MVC model in detail
- Enriching the Ember.js MVC model statecharts
- Binding controllers and views together
- Using the Ember Container

Ember.js attempts to put the developer into a full-featured, client-side Model-View-Controller (MVC) pattern, while also enriching the controller layer with a full-featured statechart implementation called Ember Router. If you're unfamiliar with statecharts, don't worry. I'll touch on the key points of a statechart in section 3.3, and provide a link where you can read the complete specification.

Ember Router allows you to map out each of your application's states into a hierarchical structure containing the relationship between the different states in your application as well as the paths that your user can travel through your application. Implemented correctly, these routes allow you to build a web app with a firm and stable structure with states that are loosely coupled, clearly defined, and highly testable.

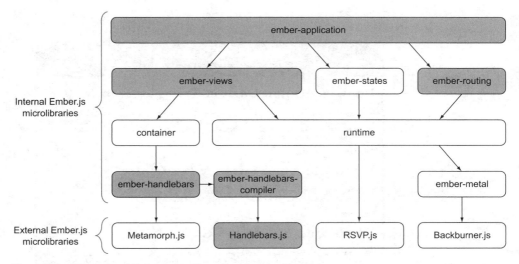

Figure 3.1 The parts of Ember.js you'll work on in this chapter

We'll contrast the Ember.js MVC pattern against a more traditional server-side MVC pattern that has been popular since the early 2000s to show you how Ember Router fits snugly into the center of this picture, connecting your app's parts together to form a uniform user experience. The chapter wraps up with a section explaining how controllers and views are connected and how controllers can be bound together, all via Ember Router.

Figure 3.1 shows the parts of the Ember.js ecosystem this chapter examines: ember-application, ember-views, ember-states, ember-routing, and container.

But before we get into the details of MVC, let's look at the application that you'll build throughout this chapter.

3.1 Introducing the Ember.js in Action Blog

For this chapter, you'll build a simple blog application that retrieves its data from a JSON file located on the file system. In this application, the user is presented with a list of available blog posts. The user can choose to view any of these posts by clicking the Full Article link presented beneath the introduction text of each post. Additionally, the top of the page provides the user with Home and About navigation links. You'll build up the application in three parts:

1 Build the blog index route.
2 Build the blog post route.
3 Define actions.

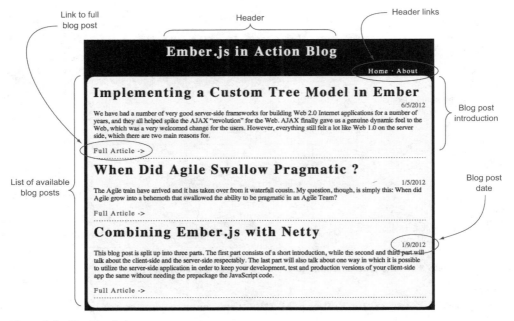

Figure 3.2   The blog index

In the first part, you'll get acquainted with Ember.js's statechart implementation, Ember Router. From there, you'll build up the blog index route. This route, as shown in figure 3.2, presents the user with the following details:

- A header displaying the name of the blog.
- A list of all available posts; each entry includes the blog post title, the opening text, and the published date.
- A link to navigate to the full blog post.

In the second part, you'll extend the router and add a `blog.post` route. This route allows the user to view the selected blog post in its entirety, which you parse from its Markdown format and present to the user in HTML. This route, as shown in figure 3.3, presents the user with the following details:

- The blog post contents, converted from Markdown to HTML
- A link to navigate back to the blog index
- The date the post was published

In the final part, you'll wrap everything up and include actions to navigate back to the index as well as create the About page.

To get started, let's look at what Ember Router consists of. To see where Ember Router fits into the application stack, you first need to understand the Ember.js MVC pattern.

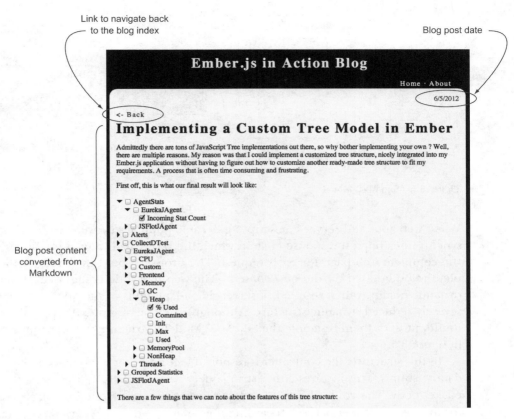

Figure 3.3 The selected blog post

3.2 *The predicament of server-side Model-View-Controller patterns*

Many MVC patterns are available, and they share common design principles and goals. The controller is the object that the user *uses*, and the view is the object that the user *sees*. In terms of implementation details, the controller is an object that accepts actions from the user and knows the data it needs to retrieve or update in the model layer to serve the user's request. The view knows how to use that model to generate the GUI that the user sees. In some MVC implementations, the model layer is reduced to a data-storage layer with dumb objects, whereas other MVC implementations have a rich model layer.

A conceptual and simplified view of the MVC pattern is shown in figure 3.4.

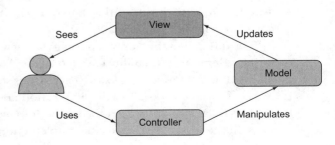

Figure 3.4 Simplified overview of the MVC pattern

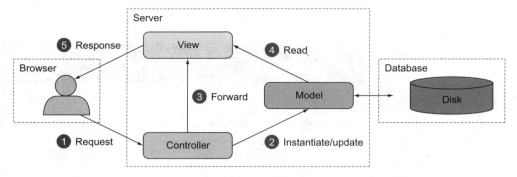

Figure 3.5 Sun MVC Model 2

When web apps and server-side scripting became popular, the web was restricted to a synchronous request-response cycle in which the server had to feed the browser with the complete web page for each request. The browser would then redraw the complete website based on the new content. The web had little going for it in terms of dynamic quality, which resulted in server-side adaptations of the MVC pattern with a severely reduced dynamic structure. Although many server-side MVC patterns can be found, most of them resemble the Sun MVC Model 2 structure in some way, as shown in figure 3.5.

In this structure, the controller is responsible for parsing the request to know what data to supply. This involves either string-query parsing the URL or parsing the HTTP packet body. The controller then updates or instantiates the model objects required for the view to render before forwarding the request to the correct view. The view uses the model objects supplied by the controller to generate the complete website, which it sends back to the user's browser.

This model has a number of strengths and weaknesses. The obvious weakness for any modern web application is that the model has no dynamic parts. After the view is generated and sent to the browser, no mechanism is in place to update the client-side view based on changes to the server-side model.

When Ajax (Asynchronous JavaScript and XML) became mainstream with the Web 2.0 hype, most frameworks solved this problem by increasing the amount of state that the server would need to keep track of for each of the users logged into the system. The server now needed to know not only how to stitch together complicated views but also the intricate details of the state of each user logged in so that it could serve the correct response to an Ajax request.

The difficulties this approach brings along with it in regard to both the application's business logic and scalability have led to the development of powerful client-side JavaScript MVC frameworks that store each user's state where it belongs—in the client.

These frameworks allow the application architecture to scale out more easily as it enables the server to do what the server does best: serve, update, and persist data. Less state on the server also means that implementing a strategy for horizontal scalability is much easier. The client is also left alone to do what it does best: keep state, and render and display websites. Web apps replaced traditional client/server apps, but in many ways, web apps now use the same client/server architecture as the apps they replaced. The major difference is that the client now uses generalized, free, and open technologies to render views, to perform client-side business logic, and to request and receive data, wrapped in a neat, competitive bundle called the browser.

Most modern JavaScript web frameworks rely on a full-featured MVC implementation in the browser to bring back the intended dynamic quality of the MVC pattern, and the Ember MVC pattern is no different.

3.2.1 *The Ember MVC pattern*

The purpose of the MVC pattern is to separate the concerns of your application's logic into clearly defined groups or layers. Each layer has a specific purpose, which makes the application's source code more readable, maintainable, and testable. Let's take a deeper look at Ember.js's controllers, models, and views, as well as how these fit together in the Ember.js ecosystem.

CONTROLLERS

The controller acts mainly as a link between the models and the views. Ember ships with some custom controllers, most notably `Ember.ObjectController` and `Ember.ArrayController`. You use the `ObjectController` if your controller is representing a single object (for example, a selected blog post), and the `ArrayController` if your controller represents an array of items (such as a list of all blog posts). I'll discuss the functionality within these controllers in more detail when you start to use them later in this chapter.

In the examples in this book, I've used Ember Router to enrich the functionality of the controller layer to keep the individual controllers as small and independent as possible. Both are important aspects of scalable web applications.

MODELS

The model layer holds the data for the application. The data objects are specified through a semi-strict schema. The models have little functionality, and the model object is responsible for such tasks as data formatting. The view will bind the GUI components against properties on the model objects via a controller.

I've enriched the model layer with Ember Data, a framework that implements an in-browser cache for the model objects and provides a means to implement Create, Read, Update, and Delete (CRUD) operations on that data via a unified API. We'll discuss Ember Data in detail in chapter 5.

VIEWS

The view layer is responsible for drawing its elements onto the screen. The views hold no permanent state of their own, with few exceptions.

Ember ships with a number of default views, and it's good practice to use these when you need simple HTML elements. For more complex elements in your web app, you can easily create your own custom view or components that either extend or combine the standard Ember views.

The Ember.js view layer is enriched with Handlebars.js templates, which I've used extensively throughout this book as well as in any Ember.js project I've ever come across.

3.2.2   *Putting everything together*

Even though the MVC pattern on the client side has been extended to make the server-side code simpler, the total architecture of your system will be more complex than it was before (as shown in figure 3.4). This added complexity does come with a significant benefit: clean, structured, maintainable, and highly testable client-side code. A complete overview of the Ember.js MVC pattern, along with a typical server-side implementation, is shown in figure 3.6.

As you can see, the client side has been enriched with a complete lifecycle of its own. I've split the complete `model` into three parts (not including the database). Imagine a client application in which the user selects an item from a list in the GUI. That selection (C1) triggers an action on the item's controller (C2) or on the router. This issues a request to the model layer (C3) for the data related to the item being selected (M1). Because that data isn't available in the Ember Data in-browser cache, it must be fetched from the server (M2). While the client waits for the response to come back in an asynchronous manner, Ember Data creates a temporary record representing the item being requested. This record updates the controller via the Ember Observer mechanism (C4). Because the controller's content is bound to the view, the view is

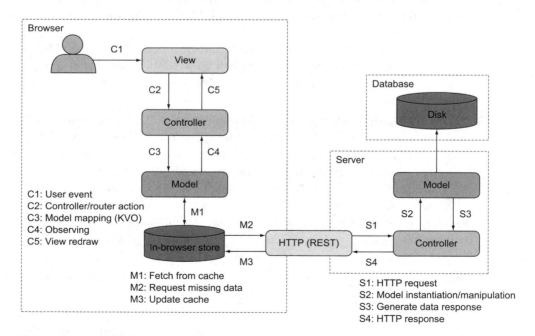

Figure 3.6   Ember MVC model

updated immediately (C5), even if that data currently holds little information—most likely only the identifier of the item selected in C1.

On the server side, the server-side controller receives the HTTP request (S1), generates or manipulates the data required for the request (S2 and S3), and sends an appropriate HTTP response (S4) back to the client application. This HTTP response contains data in a JSON format. When the item is received in Ember Data (M3), Ember Data updates the model (C3), which triggers steps C4 and C5 and updates both the controller and the view. This pattern is built to allow for full dynamic control throughout your application layers, and it works well even with push-style or WebSocket implementations for the data transfer.

Although this approach is more complicated than the Sun MVC Model 2, it's an approach that enables you to deliver what Ember.js promises: the ability to build ambitious web applications that push the envelope on what's possible on the web.

3.3 *Ember Router: Ember.js's take on statecharts*

I mentioned earlier that Ember.js enriches the controller layer with a statechart implementation. This statechart, called Ember Router, is based loosely on the SproutCore statechart implementation called Ki. But unlike Ki, Ember Router is built around the fact that web applications have one important feature that native applications don't—URLs—and it uses this fact to serialize and deserialize the state of the application into the URL.

> ### Learning about statecharts
>
> A thorough explanation of statecharts is out of scope for this book, but if you're interested in reading more about them, you can read David Harel's scientific paper, *Statecharts: A Visual Formalism for Complex Systems* (1987), http://www.wisdom .weizmann.ac.il/~harel/SCANNED.PAPERS/Statecharts.pdf. Keep in mind that Ember Router is in no way a strict implementation of the statechart described by Harel, but the underlying concepts do apply.

Ember Router organizes your application's states into a hierarchical structure that uniquely identifies any given route in your application. Because the relationship between the routes is clear, it's possible to transition from any one route to any other route in your application, and you, as a developer, can be certain that the user interface remains consistent. Separating your application into small, finite states is an important concept that brings power and versatility to Ember.js applications.

Ember Router achieves this organization by making each route responsible for setting up everything required for that state to function as intended upon route entry, as well as for tearing down anything that's specific to that route upon route exit. Because the routes are organized in a hierarchical structure, Ember Router ensures that your routes are initialized in the correct order while constructing your application's complex views and templates.

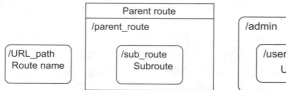

Figure 3.7   A simple route (at left) and a route with a subroute (at right)

Figure 3.8   Visualizing an Ember route with two subroutes

Throughout this book, I'll draw routes as boxes. Because routes can consist of subroutes, each box might have subroutes drawn in it. Figure 3.7 shows a single route at left and a parent route with one subroute at right.

Figure 3.8 shows an Admin route containing two subroutes, User admin and Payment admin.

Each route in the Ember Router has a chain of functions that are called when the user enters and exits a route.

Ember Router has sensible default functionality for these functions, as you'll see throughout this chapter. But, you can override these functions if necessary. Figure 3.9 shows the route's lifecycle and the functions you can override.

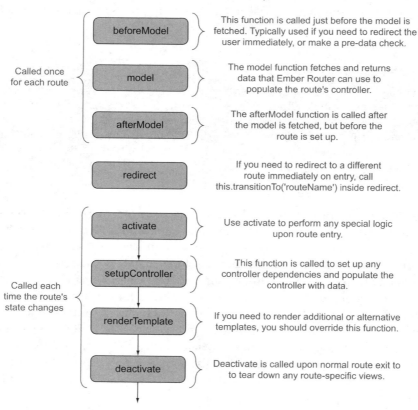

Figure 3.9
The Ember
Router lifecycle

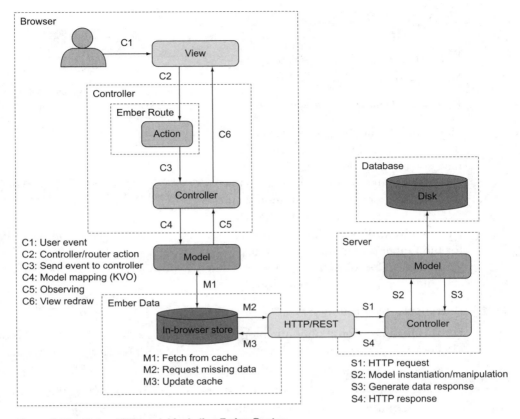

Figure 3.10   Ember MVC model including Ember Router

As I mentioned, Ember Router enriches the controller layer of the application. The final Ember MVC pattern is shown in figure 3.10, which also includes Ember Router.

Now that you know what Ember Router is and how it works, it's time to write an application that uses Ember Router.

3.4   *Ember.js in Action Blog part 1: the blog index*

In this section, you'll build the first part of the blog application.

> **NOTE**   The complete source code for this section is available as app1.js in either the code source or online at GitHub: https://github.com/joachimhs/ Ember.js-in-Action-Source/blob/master/chapter3/blog/js/app/app1.js.

To get started, you'll build up the router for the sample blog application. The blog index has the URL /blog and lists a short summary along with a link to each blog post. When the user clicks an item in the blog index, the application will display that blog post individually via the URL /blog/post/:post_id, where :post_id is the unique

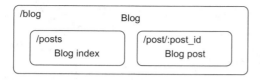

Figure 3.11   Initial application statechart

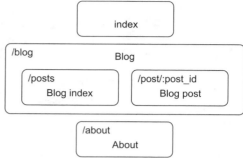

Figure 3.12   The complete Ember.js in Action Blog statechart includes three routes and two subroutes.

identifier of that blog post. When you draw a diagram for the blog route, you have the routes shown in figure 3.11

As the figure shows, the website consists of three routes. In addition, you have the about route with the URL /about and an index route with the URL /. Figure 3.12 shows the complete diagram for the Ember.js in Action Blog router.

Now that you've defined your application's routes and their relationships, you'll start building your Blog application.

3.4.1   Getting the blog router started

For this first part, you'll build the blog index, which lists the introductory text of each blog post. To achieve this, you'll implement a number of features in the application:

- An index route that responds to the / URL
- A router with a single route named Blog that responds to the /blog URL
- An application view and controller
- A blog route, controller, and template
- A way to fetch the blog posts from a JSON file

Running your application

Although you can simply run the Notes application by dragging the index.html file into the browser, I recommend hosting the application in a proper web server. You can use the web server that you are most comfortable with. If you want to start up a small, lightweight web server that will host the current directory you're in, you can use either the asdf Ruby gem or a Python script.

If you have Ruby installed, install the asdf gem by typing gem install asdf into your terminal (Mac or Linux) or command prompt (Windows). Once the gem is installed, you can host the current directory by executing asdf –port 8080 in your terminal or command prompt. Once the gem is started, you can navigate to http://localhost:8088/index.html to load your Notes application.

If you have Python installed, you can execute python -m SimpleHTTPServer 8088 in your terminal or command prompt. Once Python is started, you can navigate to http://localhost:8088/index.html to load your Notes application.

Let's start with the implementation of `Blog.Router`, as shown in the following listing.

Listing 3.1 Application router source code

```
var Blog = Ember.Application.create({});
Blog.Router = Ember.Router.extend({
    location: 'hash'
});

Blog.Router.map(function() {
    this.route("index", {path: "/"});
    this.route("blog", {path: "/blog"});
});

Blog.IndexRoute = Ember.Route.extend({
    redirect: function() {
        this.transitionTo('blog');
    }
});

Blog.BlogRoute = Ember.Route.extend({
    model: function() {
        return this.store.find('blogPost');
    }
});
```

Annotations:
- **Specifies the use of hash-based URLs (default)**
- **Creates new class, extending from Ember.Router**
- **Creates map of routes**
- **Defines route that maps toURL / and /blog**
- **Defines route for index and redirects to /blog route**
- **Creates route for BlogIndex, specifies model objects for controller's content**

This code includes new concepts that we haven't discussed yet. You start by specifying the URLs that the application responds to via the `Blog.Router.map` construct. Inside this construct, you tell Ember.js which routes belong to which URLs in the application. The / URL belongs to the `index` route, but the /blog URL belongs to the `blog` route.

Because you specified `location: 'hash'` (which is the default), Ember Router uses hash-encoded URLs, which means that the URLs are prepended with a hash symbol. A direct URL to a blog post looks like this:

```
/#/blog/post/:post_id
```

You can use the history API instead by specifying `location: 'history'`, in which case the same URL is represented as follows:

```
/blog/post/:post_id
```

Depending on your preference and your back-end server, toggle this option accordingly. Because hash is the default URL pattern, you could omit this declaration of `Blog.Router`, but it's included here to show how this property can be defined.

By specifying the two routes inside `Blog.Router.map`, you tell Ember.js to instantiate three routes, three controllers, and three views using three templates. By default, Ember.js uses a standard naming convention to find and instantiate these objects automatically. If you follow these naming conventions, no extra boilerplate code is required to wire everything together. Ember Router injects the instantiated objects into the Ember Container, which you'll look at near the end of this chapter.

Unless you're doing something specific, you don't need to define any of the objects manually. Ember.js doesn't instantiate them all at once, but Ember Router makes sure that your views are instantiated before they're required. Ember Router also destroys your views when they're no longer needed because the user has navigated away from the route where the view was needed.

Ember Router uses the names of your routes to determine the default names of your routes, controllers, and views. Based on this naming convention, if your route is named `blog`, Ember.js looks up classes named `BlogRoute`, `BlogController`, and `BlogView`. In addition, it assumes that the template used to render the `BlogView` is named `blog`. Unless you have a specific override, you don't have to specify these classes in your code. Ember.js and Ember Router assume that the classes shown in table 3.1 are made available (if not, they're created at runtime).

Table 3.1   **Default class and route names**

Route name	Default classes	Template
application	ApplicationRoute	application
	ApplicationController	
	ApplicationView	
index	IndexRoute	index
	IndexController	
	IndexView	
blog	BlogRoute	blog
	BlogController	
	BlogView	

Because you won't have any content for the `index` route in this application, you redirect to the `blog` route. To do this, implement `Blog.IndexRoute` and specify the `redirect` property. In this case, call `this.transitionTo('blog')` to redirect to the `blog` route automatically when the user enters the `index` route.

The blog state is attached to the URL `/blog`. To tell Ember.js to fetch the blog posts from the server and place them in the `BlogController.model` property, implement the `model()` function. Inside this function, tell Ember.js to find all posts of type `Blog.BlogPost`, via the Ember Data Store using `this.store.find('blogPost')`. When all the posts are found, Ember.js inserts these posts into the `model` property of this route's controller. These few lines of code have a lot going on, so let's break it down to make the process clearer.

`this.store.find('blogPost')` comes from Ember Data. I'll discuss Ember Data in detail in chapter 5, but for now just note that this statement fetches each of the blog posts available from the file `/blogPosts` and stores them in the `model` property of the controller named `Blog.BlogController`.

> **NOTE** Because you don't have any specific functionality that you need to add to `Blog.BlogController`, you don't need to define it. Ember Router instantiates a default `Blog.BlogController`, which will hold a list of blog posts. Ember Router uses the return value in the `Blog.BlogRoute`'s model function to determine whether `Blog.BlogController` should extend `Ember.Object-Controller` or `Ember.ArrayController`.

Ember Router then injects the `blog` template into the `{{outlet}}` expression inside the `application` template.

At this point, you've implemented enough of the Ember Router to satisfy the requirements for part 1 of the blog application, as shown in figure 3.13.

Now that you have the skeleton for your Blog application up and running, it's time to add some views and templates to give the application some content for its users.

Figure 3.13   The Ember Router implementation so far

3.4.2   Adding views and templates

You'll build up the minimum parts that the application must include to work with the router shown in figure 3.13. First, let's recap what you'll provide to Ember Router:

- An `IndexRoute` and a `BlogsRoute`
- An `application` template, an `index` template, and a `blog` template
- A `Blog.BlogPost` model object

You've already seen the two routes, so let's move on to the templates. The following listing shows the implementation of the templates that you need to override to implement the functionality that you want.

Listing 3.2   Application and blog templates

```
<script type="text/x-handlebars" id="application">
    <div id="mainArea">
        <h1>Ember.js in Action Blog</h1>

        {{outlet}}
    </div>
</script>

<script type="text/x-handlebars" id="blog">
    <div id="blogsArea">
        {{#each controller}}
            <h1>{{postTitle}}</h1>
            <div class="postDate">{{postDate}}</div>
            {{postLongIntro}}<br />

            <hr class="blogSeparator"/>
        {{/each}}
    </div>
</script>
```

Annotations:
- **Wraps contents of application in div element** → `<div id="mainArea">`
- **Overrides template and prints header and {{outlet}}**
- **Adds {{outlet}} expression into which any subroutes will be rendered** → `{{outlet}}`
- **Overrides blog template**
- **Prints introduction for each blog post loaded into BlogController's mode**

Notice that you haven't created any view classes for either the application template or the blog template. Because you don't have any specific functionality for these views yet, continue with the default view that Ember.js creates for you.

Ember Router connects the router to the controller, the controller to the view, and the view to the template, as they're needed by the application.

At this point, it should be clear that Ember Router also instantiates your controllers. You might wonder how it knows what type of controller you need for each of your routes. More specifically, how does Ember.js know that your BlogController should be an ArrayController and not an ObjectController? The answer to this lies in the return value of the model() function of the BlogRouter. Because this returns an array, Ember.js knows that it should instantiate the default BlogController as an ArrayController.

The templates are simplistic. The only dynamic element in them is in the application template. Chapter 4 discusses the templates in more detail, but for now think of {{outlet}} as the placeholder where the router injects its subroutes. In the application route, the router will inject the blog template.

You're free to override any of these conventions, but I find it handy that my routes, controllers, and views share a similar nomenclature because I always know which are related based on the name. If I'm currently writing code in the Blog.BlogController, I know that the code for the view for that controller is inside Blog.BlogView, which in turn is using the template blog, and so on.

Next, you need to fetch the blog posts from disk to give the application some content.

3.4.3   Displaying a list of blog posts

For the Ember Data Blog.BlogPost model to work, you need to define the structure of the data and specify a URL from which Ember Data can fetch its data. The following listing shows the Ember Data model definition for your Blog.BlogPost model.

Listing 3.3   BlogPost model structure

```
Blog.BlogPost = DS.Model.extend({          ◁───┐  Properties of
    postTitle: DS.attr('string'),                 each BlogPost
    postDate: DS.attr('date'),
    postShortIntro: DS.attr('string'),
    postLongIntro: DS.attr('string'),
    postFilename: DS.attr('string'),          ┌─  Property that isn't part of
    markdown: null                          ◁─┘  Ember Data model object
});
```

This code introduces several new concepts. The first things you might notice is that you extend from DS.Model, which is the high-level model class from Ember Data, used to clearly define the intended structure of your data models. The Blog.BlogPost model defines four properties of type string and one of type date. All DS.Model classes also define an implicit property named id. The id property serves as the primary key of your data models.

Note also that you have an extra property called markdown. It's not strictly necessary to specify the markdown property here, but I like to include all the properties that each of my model definitions must have. This makes it clear when looking at the source code for the model that the application uses this property. Because the markdown property doesn't have a DS.attr type, Ember Data ignores this property when translating the object to and from JSON.

You use the default DS.RESTAdapter when you fetch data. Both the format of the URL and the data returned from the server must adhere to a specific pattern. For your purposes, Blog.BlogPost maps to the URL /blogPost, and the postTitle property maps to the JSON key postTitle, and so on.

Your Blog.BlogPost object is serialized and deserialized from and to the JSON data, as shown in the following listing

Listing 3.4   JSON structure for the BlogPost model

```
{
    "id": "2012-05-05-Ember_tree",
    "postTitle": "Implementing a Custom Tree Model in Ember",
    "postDate": "2012-05-05",
        "postShortIntro": "Explaining the Client-side MVC model …",
    "postLongIntro": "We have had a number of very good …"
}
```

You'll use the standard DS.RESTAdapter throughout this chapter. Chapter 6 covers how to fetch data without Ember Data, while chapter 5 discusses Ember Data and the RESTAdapter in detail.

Because you're receiving a list of blog posts, you need to wrap your single blog post JSON object into an array and store the contents in a file named blogPosts, the content of which is shown in the following listing. Notice that you add an id property to the JSON as well. Ember Data uses id implicitly, even though it's not specified in the Blog.BlogPost model object.

Listing 3.5   Contents of the blogPosts file

```
{ "blogPosts": [
    {
        "id": "2012-05-05-Ember_tree",
        "postTitle": "Implementing a Custom Tree Model in Ember",
        "postDate": "2012-05-05",
        "postShortIntro": "Explaining the Client-side MVC model ...",
        "postLongIntro": "We have had a number of very good ..."
    }
    ]
}
```

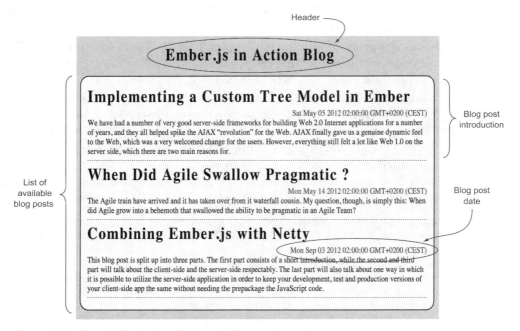

Figure 3.14   Updated Ember.js in Action Blog for part 1

Now you can list the blog posts in your `blogPost` file. If you refresh the application, you should be greeted with an application that looks like figure 3.14.

If you look at the posted date for each of the posts, you'll notice that the date isn't easy to read. You need to format the standard JavaScript date output to something more readable by humans. There are multiple ways to do this. You can bring in a third-party date-formatting library and build a custom Handlebars.js expression to handle the conversion (more about custom expressions in chapter 4). But for your purposes, create a computed property on the `BlogPost` model that returns a properly formatted date. The following listing shows the updated `BlogPost` model.

Listing 3.6   Updated `BlogPost` model

```
Blog.BlogPost = DS.Model.extend({
    postTitle: DS.attr('string'),
    postDate: DS.attr('date'),              ⟵ Changes from
    postShortIntro: DS.attr('string'),         string to date
    postLongIntro: DS.attr('string'),
    postFilename: DS.attr('string'),
    markdown: null

    formattedDate: function() {             ⟵ Adds computed property to format
        if (this.get('postDate')) {             date in human-readable way
            return this.get('postDate').getUTCDay()
```

```
                + "/" + (this.get('postDate').getUTCMonth() + 1)
                + "/" + this.get('postDate').getUTCFullYear();
        }

        return '';
    }.property('postDate')
});
```

⟵ **Calculates computed property based on postdate and updates accordingly**

You've added a computed property to the `Blog.BlogPost` model object called `formattedDate`. This computed property updates whenever the `Blog.BlogPost.postDate` property changes and it prints the date using the formatting `"mm/dd/yyyy"`. Computed properties are a powerful mechanism in Ember.js that lets you add complex computational properties to functions. In addition, computed properties are `bindable` and auto-updatable. In this case, whenever the `postDate` property changes on the `BlogPost` model, the return value for the `formattedDate` also updates. Because the computed property is bindable, any template using the `formattedDate` property will be updated as if `formattedDate` is a normal property. This is an extremely powerful concept.

The only thing you need to update in the template is a single expression. To implement this, introduce a new view and template for the content of the blog post, named `blog`. The following listing shows the new `blog` template.

Listing 3.7   Updated template

```
<script type="text/x-handlebars" id="blog">
    <div id="blogsArea">
        {{#each controller}}
            <h1>{{postTitle}}</h1>
            <div class="postDate">{{formattedDate}}</div>    ⟵
            {{postLongIntro}}<br />

            <hr class="blogSeperator"/>
        {{/each}}
    </div>
</script>
```

Uses formattedDate to print correctly formatted date

You might argue that a library such as moment.js would be better suited for date formatting. Although I agree with that statement, bringing in an extra library is unnecessary in the context of explaining computed properties.

This concludes the first part of the blog application. Next, you'll add links to and display individual blog posts.

3.5   *Ember.js in Action Blog part 2: adding the blog post route*

In this section, you build the second part of the blog application.

NOTE   The complete source code for this section is available as app2.js in either the code source or online at GitHub https://github.com/joachimhs/Ember.js-in-Action-Source/blob/master/chapter3/blog/js/app/app2.js.

The next part involves connecting the blog index to the individual posts. You'll start by updating the `blogPosts` file with some extra entries, as shown in the following listing. I've also updated the contents with real blog posts taken from my company's blog to have real data to work with.

Listing 3.8 Updated `blogPosts` file

```
{ "blogPosts": [
    {
        "id": "2012-05-05-Ember_tree",
        "postTitle": "Implementing a Custom Tree Model in Ember",
        "postDate": "2012-05-05",
        "postShortIntro": "Explaining the Client-side MVC model and how ...",
        "postLongIntro": "We have had a number of very good ..."
    },
    {
        "id": "2012-05-14-when_did_agile_swallow_pragmatic",
        "postTitle": "When Did Agile Swallow Pragmatic ?",
        "postDate": "2012-05-14",
        "postShortIntro": "My question, is simply this: When did Agile ... ",
        "postLongIntro": "The Agile train have arrived and it .."
    },
    {
        "id": "2012-09-03-Combining_Ember_js_with_Netty",
        "postTitle": "Combining Ember.js with Netty",
        "postDate": "2012-09-03",
        "postShortIntro": "Combining Ember.js with Netty ",
        "postLongIntro": "This blog post is split up into three parts. ..."
    }
  ]
}
```

To navigate from the list of blog posts to an individual post, first change the definition of the blog from a route to a resource.

> **NOTE** For each route in your application, Ember Router creates a default template associated with that route. A route that can have subroutes is defined as a *resource*. Each of your resources will automatically have an index route associated with it. Your blog resource will automatically get a `blog.index` route inserted as a subroute, which belongs to the blog/ URL.

Next, add two subroutes to the blog resource, called `index` and `post`. After the routes are in place, add a link in the `blog.index` template to transition out of the `blog.index`

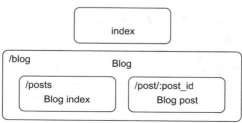

Figure 3.15 Adding the `blog.index` and `blog.post` routes

route and into the `blog.post` route. You also need to make sure that the URL is updated with a dynamic ID that identifies a unique blog post so that users can bookmark a single blog post. But first, let's review the router diagram, shown in figure 3.15.

You've added two new routes. You need the `blog.index` route so you can navigate to both the /blog/ URL and the /blog/post/:post_id URL. You also add an action to transition from the `blog.index` route to the `blog.post` route. The updated `Blog.Router` is shown in the following listing.

Listing 3.9   Adding the blog index and blog post states

```
Blog.Router.map(function() {
    this.route("index", {path: "/"});
    this.resource("blog", {path: "/blog"}, function() {        ◁── Adds and indexes
        this.route("index", {path: '/posts'});                     route to /blog route
        this.route("post", {path: '/post/:blog_post_id'});    ◁──
    });                                                    Moves the blogIndex route so it
});                                                        becomes subroute of blog's route
```

Adds subroute to blog's route (annotation pointing to `});`)

I've already explained the new routes, but you should note two important things. First, because the `blog` route is now defined as a resource, Ember Router automatically creates an `index` route as a direct child of the `blog` route. But because you want to attach the custom URL /posts to the `blog.index` route, you must define it here.

Second, note the URL that you attached to the `blog.post` route, particularly the `:blog_post_id` part of the URL. This part tells Ember Router that you want to have a dynamic part attached to this route. In this case, you want the URL to reflect the blog post that the user is currently viewing. Although this lets your users bookmark and share direct links to individual blog posts, it also specifies to the `blog.post` route which blog post to load and pass on to the `BlogPostController`.

Now that you've added the new routes to the Ember Router definition, let's look at defining the implementation for each of the routes. The following listing shows the updated and new routes.

Listing 3.10   Updated and new routes

```
Blog.BlogIndexRoute = Ember.Route.extend(        ◁── Renames Blog.BlogRoute
    model: function() {                               to Blog.BlogIndexRoute
        return this.store.find('blogPost');
    }
});
                                          Adds BlogPostRoute
                                          for blog.route route
Blog.BlogPostRoute = Ember.Route.extend({    ◁──
    model: function(blogPost) {
        return this.store.find('blogPost', blogPost.blog_post_id);    ◁──
    }
});                                              Uses dynamic part of
                                                 URL to populate
                                                 BlogPostController
```

The `Blog.BlogRoute` is renamed to `Blog.BlogIndexRoute`. In addition, you added a new `Blog.BlogPostRoute`. By overriding the `model()` function of the `BlogPostRoute`, you're able to find the right blog post from Ember Data and pass it on to the `model` property of the `BlogPostController`. Also note that the object that gets passed into the `BlogPostRoute`'s `model()` function has a single property, with a name that matches the name that you gave the dynamic part of the route definition in listing 3.9.

Next, you update the `template` for the blog index so the user can select a blog post, as shown in the following listing.

Listing 3.11 Adding link from `blog.index` template to `blog.post` template

```
<script type="text/x-handlebars" id="blog/index">          Renames blog template
    <div id="blogsArea">                                    to blog.index
        {{#each controller}}
            <h1>{{postTitle}}</h1>
            <div class="postDate">{{formattedDate}}</div>
            {{postLongIntro}}<br /><br />
            {{#linkTo "blog.post" this}}Full Article ->{{/linkTo}}
            <hr class="blogSeperator"/>
        {{/each}}                                   Adds link to blog.post route
    </div>                                           via {{linkTo}} expression
</script>
```

This template has two new details to note. First, you've renamed the template from `blog` to `blog/index`. As the user transfers from the blog index to view an individual blog post, remove the blog index from the document object model and replace it with the `blog.post` route. Because you're no longer implementing a template for the blog route, Ember Router creates a default template for you. This default template contains only a single `{{outlet}}`, which will render the template for its active subroute.

The second detail you've added is a link from the `blog.index` route to the `blog.post` route, using the `{{linkTo}}` expression. This expression takes either one or two parameters, in which the first parameter is the route that you want to link to and the second parameter is a context that you want to pass into the route you're linking to.

Now that you've added a link to the `blog.post` route, it's time to implement the template for this route. You add this template to the index2.html file, as shown in the following listing.

Listing 3.12 Adding the blog/post template

```
<script type="text/x-handlebars" id="blog/post">          Creates new handlebars
    <div id="blogPostArea">                                template with id blog/post
        <div class="postDate">{{formattedDate}}</div>
        <br />{{#linkTo "blog.index"}}&lt; back{{/linkTo}}     Links back to
        {{markdown}}                                            blog.index route with
        <br />{{#linkTo "blog.index"}}&lt; back{{/linkTo}}     {{#linkTo}} expression
    </div>
</script>
```

Wraps contents of template inside div for CSS styling

Displays blog post content

No new concepts are added to the blog.post template. But notice that you're printing out the markdown property of the model. If you remember the BlogPost model definition, you may also remember that you initialize this property to null. In addition, you haven't told the application what goes into this markdown property.

When the user enters the blog.post route, you load the Markdown-based content from the server and place the loaded content into this markdown property. You can do this in multiple ways, but for now, implement an observer on the Blog.BlogPostController that fetches the blog post content and assigns it to the markdown property. The following listing shows the definition of the controller.

Listing 3.13 The `Blog.BlogPostController`

```
Blog.BlogPostController = Ember.ObjectController.extend({          ◁
    contentObserver: function() {                              Extends ObjectController
        if (this.get('content')) {                             as it proxies single
            var page = this.get('content');                    blog post object
            var id = page.get('id');

            $.get("/posts/" + id + ".md", function(data) {     ◁  Fetches blog
                var converter = new Showdown.converter();          post content
                page.set('markdown',
                    new Handlebars.SafeString(converter.makeHtml(data)));   ◁
            }, "text")
            .error(function() {
                page.set('markdown', "Unable to find specified page");
                //TODO: Navigate to 404 state
            });
        }
    }
}.observes('content')          ◁
});
```

Labels pointing to the code:
- **Creates function to listen to changes to content property** → `contentObserver: function() {`
- **Gets id property of controller's content** → `var id = page.get('id');`
- **Initializes converter to convert Markdown to HTML** → `var converter = new Showdown.converter();`
- **Marks function as observer** → `}.observes('content')`
- **Escapes HTML to add HTML and not text to controller** → `new Handlebars.SafeString(converter.makeHtml(data)));`

The code has some things worth noting for the Blog.BlogPostController. You first create a function called contentObserver. By adding the suffix observes('content') to the function, you tell Ember.js that this function will be executed whenever the controller's content property changes. Whenever the user enters the blog.post route to view a different blog post, the contentObserver function is triggered and updates the model's markdown property.

You're using showdown.js to convert the Markdown that's returned from the server into HTML before you assign the generated HTML to the model's markdown property. You could implement this functionality in a number of ways. I chose this method to show how observers work, as well as how to combine Ember Data with standard Ajax.

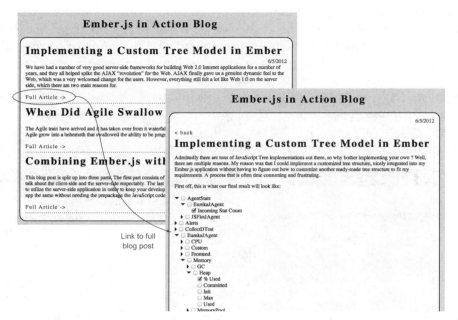

Figure 3.16 Select a blog post and transition into the `blog.post` route.

Now refresh the application and select a blog post to navigate to the `blog.post` route and view the blog post. Figure 3.16 shows what the application looks like.

You can click the Full Article link to transition from the `blog.index` route to the `blog.post` route. In addition, you can click the Back link to transition back into the `blog.index` route.

You do need to fix one thing before moving on. If you click Refresh while inside the `blog.post` route, Ember.js shows an "Error while loading route" exception because you haven't loaded the blog post (it's loaded inside the `blog.index` route). You also haven't supplied the server with a way to provide the blog application with individual blog posts, which Ember Data expects to load from the URL /blogPosts/ :post_id when it enters the `model` function of the `Blog.BlogPost` route.

You can fix this in one of two ways:

- Supply the server with the individual blog posts through the URL /blogPosts/ :post_id.
- Load all the blog posts higher up in the route hierarchy.

Although supplying the server side with a way to respond to the URL /blogPost/ :post_id would be trivial in a real server, it's not straightforward for the simple, file-based server implementation. You solve this issue by loading all the blog posts directly in the `Blog.BlogRoute` instead of in the `Blog.BlogIndex` route. But because you also want access to all the blog posts inside the `Blog.BlogIndex` route (you're listing the blog index from the `blog.index` template), you have to ensure that the blog posts are available in both routes.

You can achieve this in multiple ways. For this example, you'll use the approach that requires the least number of changes to the rest of the application. When we discuss dependency injection and the container at the end of this chapter, we'll discuss the other approaches.

To load the blog posts higher up in the route hierarchy, change the implementation for the `Blog.BlogIndexRoute` route, while also overriding the default implementation of the `Blog.BlogRoute`. The following listing shows the updated routes.

Listing 3.14 Updated `Blog.BlogIndexRoute` and `Blog.BlogRoute` routes

```
Blog.BlogRoute = Ember.Route.extend({                        ◁─┐
    model: function() {                    ◁─┐ Overrides model-function
        return this.store.find('blogPost');     to load blog posts
    }                                                       Introduces
});                                                         definition of
                                                           Blog.BlogRoute

Blog.BlogIndexRoute = Ember.Route.extend({
    model: function() {
        return this.modelFor('blog');   ◁─┐ Ensures model function of Blog.BlogIndexRoute
    }                                       returns same data loaded into Blog.BlogRoute
});
```

Loads all blog posts `└─▷`

If you look closely at the updated routes, you'll notice that you've effectively moved the model definition that you had in the `Blog.BlogIndexRoute` into the `Blog.BlogRoute`. To ensure that you populate the `Blog.BlogIndexController` with the same models that you're loading into the `Blog.BlogController`, use the routes' `modelFor()` function. This function takes the name of a route that's higher up in the route hierarchy and returns the model that's loaded into that route.

Incidentally, you could achieve the same result by having the `model()` function of the `Blog.BlogIndexRoute` return `this.store.find('blogPost')`, as you had before. This option would work in this situation because Ember Data implements an identity map for the data that it has loaded from the server side. We discuss Ember Data in detail in chapter 5.

At this point, you should be able to refresh the application and see that you can now access the application directly at the `blog.post` route, while also supporting the user refreshing the application at this route.

The only thing missing from your application is to implement the About page. I'll leave you to implement this page as an exercise, but I've also provided an implementation for you in the blog posts source code.

I mentioned that we'll discuss Ember Container as well as how dependency injection works in Ember.js, so let's shift gears and examine this central concept.

3.6 Dependency injection and using the Ember Container

You can connect parts of your application in two ways. If you want to connect controllers, you can use the controllers' `needs` property, or you can register and inject objects via dependency injection.

3.6.1   *Connecting controllers through the needs property*

If you want to connect only two controllers, use the needs property of your controller. In the blog application, the blog.index route is dependent on the data that's loaded into the blog route. You solved this earlier by using the modelFor() function inside the model() function of the Blog.BlogIndexRoute.

Another approach is to connect the Blog.BlogIndexController with the Blog.BlogController by using the needs property of the Blog.BlogIndex-Controller. The following listing shows the updated routes and controllers.

Listing 3.15   Using the needs property to connect controllers

```
Blog.BlogController = Ember.ArrayController.extend({      ⟵── Extends ArrayController

});                                                      Creates BlogIndexController
                                                           as ObjectController
Blog.BlogIndexController =  Ember.ObjectController.extend({    ⟵
    needs: ['blog']                             ⟵┐  Specifies that this controller
});                                               │  needs BlogController
```

You might be wondering what the needs property does for your application and how Ember.js uses it to connect the two controllers.

When the BlogIndexController is initialized, Ember.js looks at the needs property of the controller to determine whether the controller is dependent on other controllers. If the controller specifies at least one dependent controller, Ember.js looks up each of the controllers in the Ember Container and injects them into the controller's controllers property.

To get the BlogController from the BlogIndexController, access it through the controller's controllers property. If you're inside the BlogIndexController, you can get the controller via a call to this.get('controllers.blog').

You also must update the blog.index template to reflect this change. The following listing shows the updated template.

Listing 3.16   Updated blog.index template

```
<script type="text/x-handlebars" id="blog/index">
    <div id="blogsArea">
        {{#each controllers.blog}}              ⟵┐  Uses controllers.blog to access
            ...                                   │  the content of the blog controller
        {{/each}}
    </div>
</script>
```

The listing omits the contents of the {{each}} expression because it's the same as before. The only change you've made to the template is inside the {{each}} expression. The logic here is the same as inside the controller. Because you've added the BlogController instance to the BlogIndexController's controller.blog property, you can access it directly via the controllers.blog expression inside the blog.index template.

Although this method uses the Ember Container in the background, its only use case is to connect controllers. If you want to connect other objects, you need to take a close look at the Ember Container.

3.6.2 *Connecting objects via the Ember Container*

The concept of dependency injection is a whole book in itself. In short, the Ember Container allows you to assign objects to common names. After an object is registered, it's possible to inject it into properties on other objects that are also registered into the Ember Container.

Ember Data is an excellent example of a use case that uses the Ember Container to its advantage. The following listing shows the initialization of Ember Data.

Listing 3.17 Ember Data's initialization and the Ember Container

```
Ember.onLoad('Ember.Application', function(Application) {
  Application.initializer({
    name: "store",                              ⟵  Creates application
                                                    initializer named store
    initialize: function(container, application) {
      application.register('store:main', application.Store || DS.Store);
      application.register('serializer:_default', DS.JSONSerializer);
      application.register('serializer:_rest', DS.RESTSerializer);
      application.register('adapter:_rest', DS.RESTAdapter);

      container.lookup('store:main');
    }
  });

  ...

  Application.initializer({          Creates application initializer
    name: "injectStore",         ⟵  named injectStore

    initialize: function(container, application) {
      application.inject('controller', 'store', 'store:main');    Injects container's
      application.inject('route', 'store', 'store:main');         store:main property
      application.inject('serializer', 'store', 'store:main');    into store property of
      application.inject('dataAdapter', 'store', 'store:main');   corresponding object
    }
  });
```

Registers store into container's store:main property (annotation for the `application.register('store:main', ...)` line)

I don't expect you to follow the logic behind the application initializers here. The point of this example is to give you a sense of the power behind the Ember Container. At the top of the listing, you call `application.register()`, which takes two arguments. The first argument is a string that represents the unique name that the object you're registering will be tied to. The second argument is the object or class that you want to register with the container. In this case, you register a `DS.Store` class into the container as `store:main`.

In the second initialize you use `application.inject` to inject one stored property into a property on another registered object. You ensure that whatever you've registered as `store:main` will be injected into the store property of every `controller`, `route`, `serializer`, and `dataAdapter` in your application. This is a big deal, and it's what allows you to call `this.store.find('blogPost')` from within the `model()` functions you've seen in use throughout this chapter.

After something is registered with the container, you'll be able to get these objects via the nonpublic `App.__container__.lookup` function. You shouldn't rely on this in your own application, but it can be quite useful if you need to debug your application via the browser console. The following listing shows a few examples to give you an idea of when this might come in handy.

Listing 3.18   Retrieving registered objects from the container

```
Blog.__container__.lookup('store:main').find('blogPost')        ◁── Finds all blog posts
Blog.__container__.lookup('controller:blog')
    .get('model.length')                                        ◁── Gets number of blog posts
Blog.__container__.lookup('controller:blogPost')
    .get('postTitle')                                           ◁── Gets postTitle of selected blog post
Blog.__container__.lookup('controller:blogPost')
    .set('model.markdown', 'Test')     ◁── Sets markdown property to TEST for selected blog
```

The examples show only a few instances of when being able to interact with objects that are registered in the Ember Container can be useful. Still, they do show how to both retrieve and manipulate the objects that are loaded. Go ahead; load up the blog application and play with the examples provided. It will quickly give you insight into the power that Ember.js provides you as a web application developer, and it will help you understand how it's connected inside your application.

3.7   *Summary*

This chapter represents what will become the heart of your Ember.js application. Your Ember Router implementation represents the way your application is glued together as well as what routes your application can be in and how the user can navigate between these routes. The router also defines the way your controllers are bound together as well as the way data flows between your controllers, and, in extension, between your views.

The benefits of moving the user-specific business logic out to the client, in terms of both the total architecture and the user experience, are clear. Letting the client and the server applications do what they do best allows you to build highly scalable web applications with features that rival native applications, wrapped up with the most powerful distribution channel there is—the web.

Through the sample blog application, I've shown how you can structure your application into logical routes and how a complete Ember.js application is connected.

There's one major piece missing before you can move on to part 2 of the book, so without further ado, let's dive into Ember.js's preferred template engine, Handlebars.js.

Automatically updating templates with Handlebars.js

This chapter covers

- Understanding why you need templates
- Working with Handlebars.js expressions
- Using simple and complex expressions
- Understanding the relationship between Ember.js and Handlebars.js
- Creating your own custom expressions

Ember.js doesn't include a default template library, and you're free to use your favorite JavaScript library. But because the same people who are behind Ember.js are also behind Handlebars.js, Handlebars.js is an especially nice fit for Ember.js applications. Handlebars.js also has all the features that you're looking for in a solid template library. Handlebars.js is based on Mustache, which is a logic-less template library that exists for many programming languages, including JavaScript, Python, Java, Ruby, and most likely your favorite language.

In this chapter, you'll start by getting a clear understanding of what a template is and why you should be excited about using one, before moving on to the features that Handlebars.js provides. In the second half of the chapter, you'll look at how

Ember.js extends the standard Handlebars.js features to provide automatically updated templates for your application. This chapter should leave you with a comprehensive understanding of the template features that are built into Handlebars.js and Ember.js.

4.1   *What's in a template?*

A Handlebars.js template is regular static HTML markup interspersed with dynamic elements called *expressions*. The template library replaces these expressions at runtime to bring you dynamic web applications that update in real time, whenever your underlying data changes.

> **NOTE** The topmost template in Ember.js is called the *application*. By default, this template includes only a single Handlebars.js expression: {{outlet}}. If you need to include anything special in the topmost template, you need to override the application template. Remember, though, that your application template needs to have an {{outlet}} somewhere; otherwise, none of your other templates will be rendered.

Multiple types of template libraries exist. Traditionally, template libraries reside on a server, where they're used to combine a model and a template to generate a view, as shown in figure 4.1.

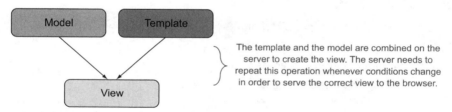

Figure 4.1   The traditional server-side template model

Because Handlebars.js lives on the client side and Ember.js has a rich MVC pattern, Ember.js is able to replace this one-time template compilation with a much more powerful dynamic pattern, as shown in figure 4.2.

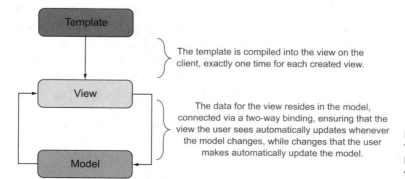

**Figure 4.2
The Ember.js +
Handlebars.js
template solution**

Handlebars.js, like most other template libraries, identifies its expressions by enclosing them in double curly braces. Expressions can either be simple expressions representing dynamic values, or block expressions that also contain logic. You'll start by getting a clear understanding of how simple expressions look and how they work.

4.1.1 Simple expressions

Throughout this chapter, you'll use a simple book-cataloging system that could be used to keep track of books in your home library. For each book, you want to see a few pieces of basic information: the book's title, its author(s), and a short description of the book.

Simple expressions are identifiers that tell Handlebars.js which variable to use to replace the template contents at runtime. Consider the code in the following listing.

Listing 4.1 A simple expression

```
<h1>{{title}}</h1>                    ⟵── Replaces title at runtime
```

When the preceding template is rendered, Handlebars.js looks up the value of the title variable in the current context and replaces the {{title}} expression with the correct value.

You may also use dot-separated paths inside your Handlebars.js expressions. If you have a model object named Book that has three properties—title, author, and text—you may use the Handlebars.js template shown in the following listing to display the book's details.

Listing 4.2 Using dot-separated paths in expressions

```
<h1>{{book.title}}</h1>               ⟵── Displays book's title
<p>By: {{book.author}}<br />                        ⟵── Displays book's author
    {{book.text}}</p>        ⟵── Displays book's text
```

You can use dot-separated paths to access properties in an object in Handlebars.js. You can chain these properties as deep as your object's references go, but whenever you find yourself needing more than three parts in an expression, you'll most likely want to start splitting your templates into smaller, more-specific templates. Also, whenever you have more than three parts in an expression, it might be time to rethink your application structure to see if you're missing a route or a controller.

You'll learn how to split your templates into smaller templates with Ember.js and Handlebars.js later in the chapter, but first let's look at the other type of Handlebars.js expression, the block expression.

4.1.2 Block expressions

A *block expression* has not only a value but also a body that can contain plain markup, simple expressions, or even other block expressions. Handlebars.js identifies a block expression by its prepending pound, or hash, symbol (#). The block expression ends by prepending a backslash (/) to the ending block helper. Anything that's listed between the start and end tag is part of the block expression and builds up the block

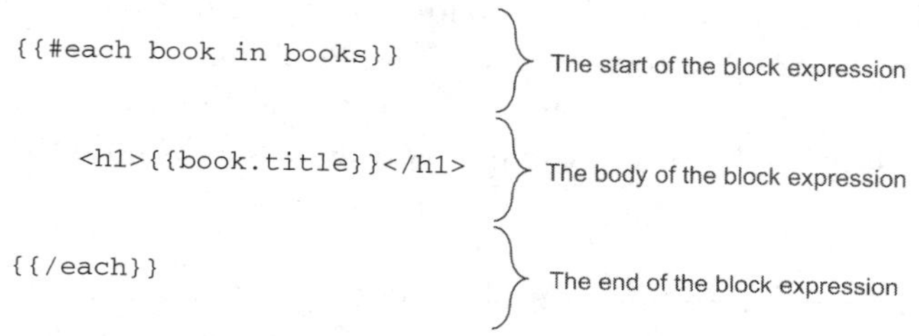

```
{{#each book in books}}                    The start of the block expression

    <h1>{{book.title}}</h1>                The body of the block expression

{{/each}}                                  The end of the block expression
```

Figure 4.3   The {{each}} block expression

expression's body. An example of the structure of the each block helper is shown in figure 4.3.

A block expression also can have a different context than its enclosing template. Let's continue with our book catalog analogy, and assume that you're using the context shown in the following listing.

Listing 4.3   The book catalog context

```
{
    "title": "Books",
    "books": [
        { "title": "Ember.js in Action",
          "author": "Joachim Haagen Skeie",
          "text": "A thorough overview of the Ember.js Framework"
        },
        { "title": "Secret of the JavaScript Ninja",
          "author": "John Resig and Bear Bibeault",
          "text": "A book about mastering modern JavaScript development"
        }
    ]
}
```

You can now create a Handlebars.js template that lists the details of each book inside the books array, as shown in the following listing.

Listing 4.4   Listing each book detail by using block expressions

```
<h1>{{title}}</h1>
{{#each books}}                            Displays page title
    <div class="book">                     Iterates over books array
        <h1>{{this.title}}</h1>            Displays book's title
        <p>By: {{this.author}}<br />       Displays book's author
        {{this.text}}</p>                  Displays book's text
    </div>
{{/each}}                                  Closes each block expression
```

When looking at the code in listing 4.4, you should notice a couple of things. First, you use the built-in each block helper to iterate over the books array. Notice how you can use the keyword this inside the block expression to identify the book you're currently at in the iteration over the books array. The rest of the template is the same as before, except that you make sure to close the {{each}} block at the end of the template.

When this template is rendered with the context from listing 4.3, it results in the following markup.

Listing 4.5 The result of the `{{each}}` block expression

```
<h1>Books</h1>                                              ◁⎯ Main title of page
<div class="book">                             ◁⎯ Contents of first book
    <h1>Ember.js in Action</h1>
    <p>By: Joachim Haagen Skeie<br/>
    A thorough overview of the Ember.js Framework</p>
</div>
<div class="book">                                 ◁⎯ Contents of second book
    <h1> Secret of the JavaScript Ninja </h1>
    <p>By: John Resig and Bear Bibeault<br/>
    A book about mastering modern JavaScript development</p>
</div>
```

I mentioned that a block expression can have a different context than its containing block or template. With the `{{each}}` block expression, you can introduce a context variable that Handlebars.js will use to identify each object in the `books` array. The updated code is shown next.

Listing 4.6 The updated `{{each}}` block

```
<h1>{{title}}</h1>
{{#each book in books}}                              ◁⎯ Creates context-specific variable
    <div class="book">
        <h1>{{book.title}}</h1>                      ◁⎯ Displays book's title
        <p>By: {{book.author}}<br />                 ▷ Displays book's author
        {{book.text}}</p>                            ◁⎯ Displays book's text
    </div>
{{/each}}
```

By using the `{{#each book in books}}` expression, you can create a new variable called `book` at the same time that you declare the `{{each}}` block expression. You can then refer to the `book` variable inside the block statement instead of relying on using `this`.

Handlebars.js has several built-in block expressions. The next section presents each of them and shows examples of how they're used.

4.2 Built-in block expressions

Most of the general block expressions that you're used to from programming languages are built into Handlebars.js and include the following:

- `{{each}}`
- `{{if}}`
- `{{if-else}}`
- `{{unless}}`
- `{{with}}`
- `{{comments}}`

You've just seen how to use the {{each}} block expression to iterate over an array of items and generate a template for each item inside the array, so we'll skip the explanation of the {{each}} block helper here and dive straight into the {{if}} block expression.

4.2.1   The if and if-else block expressions

Whenever you have templates containing options that control whether parts of the template are rendered, you'll most likely use an {{if}} block to express this logic. For example, if you want to render a book only if it has an author assigned to it you could use the template shown in the following listing.

Listing 4.7   The {{if}} block expression

```
{{#if book.author}
    <h1>{{book.title}}</h1>
    <p>By: {{book.title}}<br />{{book.text}}</p>
{{/if}}
```
◁──┐ **Conditionally renders
    book's details**

The {{if}} block expression takes a single parameter, the value that it will evaluate to determine whether the body of the expression will be rendered. In this case, the book's details won't be rendered if book.author evaluates to null, undefined, 0, false, or any other *falsy* value.

But what if you want to include a simple error message in the template for a case when the book's author isn't defined yet? Luckily, Handlebars.js supports {{else}} as well. The following listing shows how {{if-else}} is defined.

Listing 4.8   The {{if-else}} block expression

```
{{#if book.author}}
    <h1>{{book.title}}</h1>
    <p>By: {{book.title}}<br />{{book.text}}</p>
{{else}}
    <p>{{book.title}} does not have an assigned author</p>
{{/if}}
```
│ **Completes {{if-else}}
◁─┘ expression**

You're using {{else}} to specify the section that's added to the rendered template if book.author returns a falsy result. Notice that the {{else}} expression doesn't start with a hash symbol because that expression is part of the {{if}} expression.

4.2.2   The {{unless}} block expression

Sometimes you're interested in rendering a block only if its condition is falsy. You use the {{if}} block expression whenever you want to say, "If this is true, I want to…." In contrast, you use the {{unless}} block expression if the opposite is the case and you want to say, "If this is false, I want to…."

Instead of having to specify an empty if section to an {{if-else}} block expression, Handlebars.js includes the {{unless}} block expression, shown in the next listing.

Listing 4.9 Using the {{unless}} block expression

```
{{#unless book.bookIsReleased}}
<p>{{book.title}} is not released yet.</p>
{{/unless}}
```

◁─┐ **Specifies only else
   part of {{if-else}}**

Here you've added the property bookIsReleased to your books. In this case, you want to include a notice in the rendered template only if a book has yet to be released. The {{unless}} block is a nice fit in these situations.

4.2.3 The {{with}} block expression

Even though Handlebars.js supports using paths in its expressions, it can sometimes be handy to be able to shorten a long path (for example, book.author.address .postcode) by using the {{with}} block expression to shift the context for a subsection of the template. Consider the following code, which is an updated version of listing 4.6.

Listing 4.10 Using {{with}} to shift the context for the book subsection

```
<h1>{{title}}</h1>
{{#each book in books}}
    {{#with book}}
        <div class="book">
            <h1>{{title}}</h1>
            <p>By: {{author}}<br />
            {{text}}</p>
        </div>
    {{/with}}
{{/each}}
```

◁─┐ **Shifts context
   of its body**

Using the {{with}} block expression shortens the paths for each of the expressions inside the {{with}} block. This can prove handy when you need to use complex and long paths in your expressions.

4.2.4 Handlbars.js comments

Because any logic you put inside your templates will be part of your Handlebars.js expressions, you might sometimes want to annotate your code with comments to explain in more depth what's happening. Handlebars.js uses the {{! }} notation to indicate a comment. An important note, though, is that comments won't be part of the generated markup. If you'd like to include them in the generated HTML, you should instead use standard HTML comments. The following listing shows how comments are used.

Listing 4.11 Using Handlebars.js comments

```
<div class="comments">
    {{! A Handlebars comment that won't be part of the rendered markup}}
    <!-- An HTML comment that will be part of the rendered markup -->
</div>
```

So far you've looked at Handlebars.js simple and complex expressions, as well as the built-in expressions that are part of the library. You've seen that each expression has a context and that the library uses this context to generate each template's output. But you haven't seen how Handlebars.js fits into Ember.js, how Ember.js controls the context of each of the templates, and how to split complex templates into smaller, more manageable templates. So let's dive into these issues in the next section.

4.3   *Using Handlebars.js with Ember.js*

Ember.js extends Handlebars.js and enriches it with the powerful features that you've come to expect from your Ember.js applications. After you tell Ember.js to render a Handlebars.js template, you can rest assured that Ember.js will keep your view up-to-date whenever your application models change, without you having to specifically implement any logic to perform these updates.

To know what part of the DOM tree to update when your application models change, Ember.js injects Metamorph tags before and after each expression's content. You'll review Metamorph later in the chapter.

You'll look at how Ember.js extends Handlebars.js, which new expressions it adds, and how Ember.js views are tied into Handlebars.js. But first, let's look more closely at how to define templates in an Ember.js application. You'll truly learn to love writing applications in this way.

4.3.1   *Defining templates inside index.html*

Handlebars.js supports defining your templates inside index.html, which can serve as a convenient and easy-to-get-going alternative. Keep in mind, though, that placing all your templates inside this one file quickly becomes inconvenient.

But if you do choose to define your templates inside your index.html file, your templates will be inside a `script` tag with the type `text/x-handlebars`. You can define your application template inside your `body` tag by creating an anonymous `script` tag, as shown in the following listing.

> **Listing 4.12   Creating the application template**

```
<html>
    <head><title>My Book Catalog Page</title></head>
    <body>
        <script type="text/x-handlebars">
            Welcome, {{user.fullName}}!          ◁──┐ Defines application
        </script>                                    │ template inside body tag
    </body>
</html>
```

The application template is displayed on the page by your application's router. Refer to chapter 3 to read more about Ember Router.

Obviously, having only one application template won't do you any good. Each of your additional templates needs to be defined inside the `head` element and have a unique name applied to it via either the `data-template-name` attribute or the `id` attribute, as shown in the following listing.

Listing 4.13 Creating the `books` template

```
<html>
    <head>
        <title>My Book Catalog Page</title>

        <script type="text/x-handlebars" id="books">     ⟵┐  Defines named template
            <div class="books">Book Catalog</div>            │  in head element
        </script>
    </head>
    <body>
        <script type="text/x-handlebars">
            Welcome, {{user.fullName}}!
        </script>
    </body>
</html>
```

You'll most likely use some sort of build tool to manage all your application's assets, including precompiling your Handlebars.js templates and making them available to your Ember.js application. Build tools are covered in more detail in chapter 11.

Because this approach quickly becomes less than practical, throughout this book you'll define your templates in separate *.hbs files that you'll bring into your application via either build tools or AJAX calls. You have a third option, though, which is to define your templates directly in the `Ember.TEMPLATES` hash.

4.3.2 *Defining templates directly in the Ember.TEMPLATES hash*

When an Ember.js application initializes, it will read through the index.html file and place any templates that it finds inside the `Ember.TEMPLATES` hash. You can compile your templates directly into this hash. This approach is OK during development, but it quickly gets ugly because you constantly have to manage string concatenation. The following listing shows how you can name and compile the templates from listing 4.13 into the `Ember.TEMPLATES` hash.

Listing 4.14 Compiling your templates into `Ember.TEMPLATES`

```
Ember.TEMPLATES['application'] = Ember.Handlebars.compile('' +
    'Welcome, {{user.fullName}}!'
);                                                    ⟵┐  Defines application
                                                         │  template
Ember.TEMPLATES['books'] = Ember.Handlebars.compile('' +
    '<div class="books">' +
        'Book Catalog' +
    '</div>'                     ┌ Defines books
);                               └ template  ⟵
```

This approach has two advantages: it's easier to split your templates into multiple files, and it keeps your templates out of your index.html file. If you aren't using any build tools, you have to constantly juggle your single and double quotes. If you want to keep your templates nice and formatted, you also need to use string concatenation to combine the code lines in your templates.

> **NOTE**   The drawbacks of using this approach should be evident. In the long run, you would be better off defining your templates either inside index.html, or as separate *.hbs files that you can compile in your build tools. This approach is covered in chapter 11.

After defining your templates, you can create views that will use those templates to define their rendered content, which is covered in the next section.

4.3.3   Creating Handlebars.js template-backed Ember.js views

Ember.js views are created by either extending or instantiating a class of type `Ember.View`. In this case, you want to create a new view that uses the template `books` from listing 4.14, so you'll create a view that uses this template. The code is shown in the following listing.

Listing 4.15   Creating a template-backed view

```
App.BookView = Ember.View.extend({          ⊲─┐ Creates new view that
    templateName: 'book'    ⊲─┤ Defines view's template    extends Ember.View
});
```

You start by creating a new view, `App.BookView`, that extends `Ember.View` via the `extends` keyword. Further, you specify that this view uses a template whose name is defined in the `templateName` property.

So far, so good, but Ember.js also lets you define your templates inline, directly inside your views, instead of referring to an external template via its name.

Whenever you have views that you want to use in multiple parts of your application, you might want to create a reusable custom view. Whenever I create views that are reusable, especially if they are reusable across applications, I tend to inline the template. The following listing shows how `App.BookView` could be written using an inline template via the `template` property.

Listing 4.16   Creating a view with an inline template

```
App.BoookView = Ember.View.Extend({
    template: Ember.Handlebars.compile('' +
        '<div class="books">' +          ⊲─┐ Creates inline
            'Book Catalog' +             template
        '</div>')
})
```

Notice that you need to call `Ember.Handlebars.compile` to compile your Handlebars.js template into the `template` property of the view. I generally use inline templates when I am creating custom reusable views and the templates are rather simple and small. If my template stretches over many lines of code and has multiple block expressions, I specify them separately from the view and refer to the template via the `templateName` property.

I mentioned earlier that Ember.js provides additional Handlebars.js expressions, so let's go ahead and look at those.

4.4 Ember.js-provided Handlebars.js expressions

Ember.js extends Handlebars.js with additional expressions that you'll likely use often throughout your application. Ember.js provides the following additional expressions:

- `{{view}}`
- `{{bind-attr}}`
- `{{action}}`
- `{{outlet}}`
- `{{unbound}}`
- `{{partial}}`
- `{{link-to}}`
- `{{render}}`
- `{{control}}`
- `{{input}}`
- `{{textarea}}`
- `{{yield}}`

In this section, you'll review each of the Ember.js-provided expressions and see how they're used.

4.4.1 The {{view}} expression

As you might have guessed by its name, the `{{view}}` expression is used to add a view into a Handlebars.js template and it's often used to inject self-contained views into a template. You'll create a view for your book catalog example called `App.BookDetails-View` and inject this view into the application template from listing 4.14. The combined result is shown in the next listing.

Listing 4.17 Injecting a view with the `{{view}}` expression

```
Ember.TEMPLATES['bookDetails'] = Ember.Handlebars.compile('' +          ◁──┐
    '<div class="book">' +
        '<h1>{{title}}</h1>' +                      Adds bookDetails template
        '<p>By: {{author}}<br />' +                 into Ember.TEMPLATES hash
        '{{text}}</p>' +
    '</div>'
);                                                  Adds books template to
                                                    Ember.TEMPLATES hash
Ember.TEMPLATES['books'] = Ember.Handlebars.compile('' +      ◁──
    '{{#each book in books}} ' +
        '{{view App.BookDetailsView valueBinding="book"}}' +
    '{{/each}}'
);
```

```
App.BookDetailsView = Ember.View.extend({
    templateName: 'bookDetails'
});
```
◁— **Creates App.BookDetailsView to use bookDetails template**

Injects anonymous view into application template
```
Ember.TEMPLATES['application'] = Ember.Handlebars.compile('' +
    '<h1>Welcome, {{user.fullName}}!</h1>' +
    '{{view Ember.View templateName="books"}}'
);
```
◁— **Adds application template to Ember.TEMPLATES hash**

Notice here that you're compiling your templates directly into the `Ember.TEMPLATES` hash to demonstrate how this works. You're creating two new templates, `books` and `bookDetails`. Together these two views represent the list of books as well as the details for each book. You're also creating a new view, `App.BookDetailsView`, that uses the `bookDetails` template. Finally, you're using an anonymous view inside the application template to render the `books` template.

Even though it's possible to create anonymous views in this manner, my experience is that creating anonymous views only works for small and simple views. For anything more complex than the preceding view, you'd be much better off creating a proper `Ember.View` instance, like the `App.BookDetailsView`, and using that instead. But sometimes you only need to bring up a simple view to render a template, and in this case anonymous views will serve that purpose quite well. After all, it's fairly easy to refactor the anonymous view later. Another approach to render a template without having to define a view for it is to use the `{{partial}}` expression, which we'll discuss later.

4.4.2 The {{bind-attr}} expression

Whenever Ember.js renders an expression, it injects Metamorph `script` tags into your code so as to be able to re-render each expression when the underlying model changes. Metamorph works almost anywhere in your HTML code, except for when you bind your model to HTML element attributes. To amend this situation, Ember.js also includes the `{{bindAttr}}` expression to use bindings to also update your HTML element attributes. Consider the HTML code in the following listing, which specifies the `src`, `height`, and `width` attributes of the HTML `img` tag.

Listing 4.18   Binding HTML tag attributes to a backing model

Binds width attribute
```
<script type="text/x-handlebars" id="image-template">
    <img {{bind-attr src=imageUrl}}
        {{bind-attr height=imageHeight}}
        {{bind-attr width=imageWidth}} />
</script>
```
◁— **Binds src attribute**
◁— **Binds height attribute**

Whenever you want to bind your model object to an HTML tag attribute, you need to use the `{{bind-attr}}` expression, which is always a simple expression. The expression takes one argument, which specifies the HTML tag attribute to render. The value of the argument specifies which property to bind to in the current context.

You can also use `{{bind-attr}}` with a Boolean value. The Boolean result specifies whether the attribute will be included in the rendered markup. Consider the code in the following listing.

Listing 4.19 Using `{{bind-attr}}` with a Boolean value

```
<script type="text/x-handlebars" id="image-template">
    <input type="checkbox" {{bind-attr disabled=canEdit}} />     ◁──┐ Toggles tag
</script>                                                              attribute
```

If the result of `canEdit` resolves to `true`, Ember.js renders the template with the disabled attribute included: `<input type="checkbox" disabled />`. If `canEdit` resolves to `false`, Ember.js omits it: `<input type="checkbox" />`.

> ### Metamorph
>
> For Ember.js to know what DOM elements to update whenever your application models a change, it injects special `script` tags into your DOM before and after your Handlebars.js expressions. These tags have a type defined as `text/x-placeholder` and indicate the area where Ember.js will replace the contents.
>
> For each expression in your templates, Ember.js surrounds the generated HTML markup with `script` tags, as shown here:
>
> ```
> <script id="metamorph-30-start" type="text/x-placeholder"></script>
> <!-- The Contents of the convMarkdown expression -->
> <script id="metamorph-30-end" type="text/x-placeholder"></script>
> ```
>
> Ember.js does all the bookkeeping necessary to know which Metamorph script it will use to update your views whenever your model changes. Most of the time, you won't notice that Ember.js injects these Metamorph tags, but you still need to know that they exist because they do add elements to the DOM tree that can affect your CSS styling.

4.4.3 The {{action}} expression

The `{{action}}` expression is, as its name indicates, used to fire DOM actions on HTML elements. The action is forwarded into the template's `target`, which will most likely be the current route's controller. The `{{action}}` expression takes three arguments: a name, a context, and a set of options. Any event triggered via the `{{action}}` expression will have `preventDefault()` called on it.

Consider the following code, which creates a link with an appropriate action.

Listing 4.20 Using the `{{action}}` expression

```
<script type="text/x-handlebars" id="bookDetails">
    <div class="book">
        <h1>{{title}}</h1>
        <p>
```

```
                      By: {{author}}<br />
                      {{text}}<br />
                      <button {{action "editBookDetail" this}}>Edit Book</button>
                 </p>
            </div>
</script>
```

Triggers action when button is clicked

This template renders a standard HTML button tag for each of your books. When the user clicks this button, the action `editBookDetail` fires. The first parameter to the `{{action}}` expression is the name of the action. Ember.js uses the action name to trigger an action on the template's `target`, and it expects to find a function with the exact same name as the action name. If you haven't supplied a target, Ember.js assumes you want to send the event to the current route's controller.

The second argument is the context (data), which it will supply to the invoked function—in this case, the current `book`.

You can supply various options to the `{{action}}` expression:

- The DOM event type
- A target
- A context

SPECIFYING THE DOM EVENT TYPE

By default, the DOM event type used by the `{{action}}` expression is the `click` event. You can override this by specifying the `on` option with a supported event name. `Ember.View` specifies 28 supported event names, which are grouped in five categories, as shown in table 4.1.

Table 4.1   The DOM event types associated with Ember views

Mouse events	Keyboard events	Touch events	Form events	HTML5 drag-and-drop events
click	keyDown	touchStart	submit	dragStart
doubleClick	keyUp	touchMove	change	drag
focusIn	keyPress	touchEnd	focusIn	dragEnter
focusOut		touchCancel	focusOut	dragLeave
mouseEnter			input	drop
mouseLeave				dragEnd
mouseUp				
mouseDown				
mouseMove				
contextMenu				

If you want to specify that the Edit Book button's action triggers on double-click, you specify `on="doubleClick"` as the option argument to the `{{action}}` expression. The following listing provides an example of this.

Listing 4.21 Specifying a DOM event type

```
<script type="text/x-handlebars" id="bookDetails">
    <div class="book">
        <h1>{{title}}</h1>
        <p>
            By: {{author}}<br />
            {{text}}<br />
            <button {{action editBookDetail this on="doubleClick"}}>Edit
    Book</button>                                          ◁
        </p>                                                         Specifies DOM
    </div>                                                           event type
</script>
```

SPECIFYING A TARGET

If you're using Ember Router in your application (refer to chapter 3 for a detailed overview of Ember Router), the default target for your `{{action}}` expression will always be the current route's controller. If you haven't defined your action inside this controller, the action will bubble up to the current route and up the route hierarchy until it finds the action.

If you need your action to go anywhere else, you must manually override the `target` option, as shown in the following listing.

Listing 4.22 Overriding the `target` option of the `{{action}}` expression

```
<script type="text/x-handlebars" id="bookDetails">
    <div class="book">
        <h1>{{title}}</h1>
        <p>
            By: {{author}}<br />
            {{text}}<br />
            <button {{action "editBookDetail" this
                target="App.editBookController"}}>
                Edit Book
            </button>                              ◁        Overrides default target
        </p>
    </div>
</script>
```

When this target is invoked by clicking the link, Ember.js tries to invoke the `editBook-Detail` function of the `App.editBookController` instance.

You can also specify a path relative to the current view by using `target="view"`.

SPECIFYING A CONTEXT

If you specify a context as the second argument to the `{{action}}` expression, you can pass data along to the invoked action method. Considering the `{{action}}` expressions from listings 4.20 through 4.22, the `editBookDetail` method is called with a single parameter containing the `book` object as its context.

The following listing shows how you can use the context that you pass in via the `{{action}}` expression.

Listing 4.23   Retrieving the `action` context

```
App.EditBookController = Ember.Route.extend({
    actions: {
        editBookDetails: function(book) {
            console.log(book.get('name'));
        }
    }
});
```

Specifies action method with context provided

Retrieves book and prints name

4.4.4   The {{outlet}} expression

The `{{outlet}}` expression is simply a placeholder in your templates where your controllers can inject a view. Whenever the current controller's `view` property changes, Ember.js makes sure to replace the outlet with the new view. Using Ember Router, update the controller's `view` property via the `renderTemplate` method. The following listing shows how you can use `renderTemplate` to update the outlet.

Listing 4.24   Using `renderTemplate` to update the outlet

```
Ember.TEMPLATES['application'] = Ember.Handlebars.compile('' +
    '{{outlet books}}' +
    '{{outlet selectedBook}}'
);

App.BooksRoute = Ember.Route.extend({
    renderTemplate: function() {
        this.render('books', { outlet: 'books'});

        var selectedBookController = this.controllerFor('selectedBook');

        this.render('selectedBook', {
            outlet: 'selectedBook',
            controller: selectedBookController
        });
    }
});
```

Adds outlet for selected book

Adds outlet for list of books

Renders list of books into book's outlet

Renders selected book into selectedBook outlet

In the preceding code, you start by defining two outlets in your application template: one for a left-hand menu containing the books, and one for the selected book. Then, in your `App.BooksRoute` route, you use the `renderTemplate` function to render your views into the outlets via `this.render()`.

This example is a bit contrived. Normally, you'd solve this problem via Ember Router, having one route named `books` and one route named `books.book`. That way, you could use the `{{outlet}}` expression without any arguments in the book's template to tell it where to render the `books.book` template.

4.4.5 The {{unbound}} expression

The {{unbound}} expression allows you to output a variable to the template without using the binding capabilities of Ember.js. Note, though, that the contents of this expression won't be automatically updated whenever your model objects change. The following listing shows how to use the {{unbound}} expression.

Listing 4.25 Using the `{{unbound}}` expression

```
<script type="text/x-handlebars" id="book">
    '<div>{{unbound book.name}}</div>'
</script>
```
◁— Specifies one-time evaluated variable

4.4.6 The {{partial}} expression

The {{partial}} expression allows you to render another template in the current template. This lets you easily reuse your templates. Consider the following code.

Listing 4.26 Using the `{{partial}}` expression

```
<script type="text/x-handlebars" id="books">
    {{#each book in books}}
        {{partial "book"}}
    {{/each}}
</script>
```
◁— Injects another template

```
<script type="text/x-handlebars" id="book">
    Title: {{title}}<br />
    Author: {{author}}<br />
</script>
```
◁— Indicates book template to inject

Using the {{partial}} expression, you can easily embed another template into the current template. But I still find it more convenient and cleaner to create routes that represent these templates.

4.4.7 The {{link-to}} expression

The {{link-to}} expression is used whenever you want to create an HTML link that will take the user from one route to the next. Consider the following router, taken from chapter 3.

Listing 4.27 The blog router

```
Blog.Router.map(function() {
    this.resource('index', {path: '/'}, function() {
        this.resource('blog', {path: '/blogs'}, function() {
            this.resource('posts', {path: '/posts'}, function() {
                this.route('index, {path: '/'};
                this.route('post', {path: '/:blog_post_id'});
            })
        })
    });
    this.route('about');
});
```

The posts.index route you want to link from —▷

The posts.post route you want to link to ◁—

Whenever you're in the `blog.index` route, you want to provide the user with a link that can be clicked for each blog post and that will fetch the selected blog post content and transition the user to the `blog.post` route. This can be done via the `{{link-to}}` expression, as shown in the following listing.

Listing 4.28 Using the `{{linkTo}}` expression

```
<script type="text/x-handlebars" id="blogIndex">
    {{#each blog in blogs}}
        {{#link-to "posts.post" blog}}View Post{{/link-to}}    ◁─┐ Adds link to
    {{/each}}                                                      posts.post route
</script>
```

As you can see, you're using the `{{link-to}}` expression with two parameters. The first parameter is the name of the route to transition to when the link is clicked, and the second parameter is the context, which you'll pass into the route's `setup-Controller` function.

Until now, you've seen how to use the built-in expressions from Handlebars.js, as well as the additional expressions that Ember.js includes. You might wonder how you can create your own expressions, which is what you'll look at in the upcoming section about Handlebars.js helpers.

4.4.8 The {{render}} expression

Whereas the `{{partial}}` expression is used to render a template using the current context, the `{{render}}` expression is used to render a template that's backed by its own singleton controller and view. As a result, if you render a template named `header`, you also instantiate a new singleton `HeaderController` and a `HeaderView`. This is important if you want to have a template that isn't tied directly into the current controller context. But note that the `{{render}}` expression will render the template belonging to the current route, meaning that actions inside the template will bubble up through your route hierarchy.

The following listing shows an example of how the `{{render}}` expression can be used.

Listing 4.29 The `{{render}}` expression

```
<script type="text/x-handlebars" id="books">
    {{render "header"}}                           ◁─ Renders header template backed by
    <ul>                                             singleton HeaderController and HeaderView
        {{#each book in books}}
            <li> {{partial "bookDetails"}} </li>  ◁─ Renders template
        {{/each}}                                    bookDetails via
    </ul>                                            {{partial}} expression
</script>
```

Using the `{{render}}` expression enables you to render the same template in multiple parts of your application. Because the controller and the view that the render template will be connected to are singletons, had you rendered multiple header templates, each of these would share the same controller and thus the same data.

Sometimes, though, you don't want your templates to share their controllers and views, which is where the {{control}} expression comes in.

4.4.9 The {{control}} expression

Unlike the {{render}} expression, the {{control}} expression is backed by its own controller and view. Consider the following code.

Listing 4.30 The {{control}} expression

```
<script type="text/x-handlebars" id="books">
    {{render header}}                              ◁── Renders header template backed by
    <ul>                                                singleton HeaderController and HeaderView
        {{#each book in books}}
            {{control "bookDetails" book}}         ◁── Renders template
        {{/each}}                                        bookDetails via
    </ul>                                                {{control}} expression
</script>
```

This code is similar to listing 4.29, with one significant difference. Instead of using the {{partial}} expression to render the bookDetails template, you're now using the {{control}} expression. As a result, each bookDetails template that you render will have its own BookDetailsController and BookDetailsView. In addition, you can inject the current book into the {{control}} expression, which then serves as the context for each of the templates. The {{control}} expressions have been replaced by Ember Components, covered in chapter 7.

4.4.10 The {{input}} and {{textarea}} expressions

I'm bundling the {{input}} and {{textarea}} expressions together because they serve a similar purpose. The {{input}} expression simply renders an HTML input tag into the DOM, and the {{textarea}} expression renders an HTML textarea tag into the DOM.

An {{input}} without a type or a type="text" renders as a standard HTML text-field. The {{input}} expression has the following attributes:

- type
- value
- size
- name
- pattern
- placeholder
- disabled
- maxlength
- tabindex

The {{textarea}} expression has the following attributes:

- value
- name

- rows
- cols
- placeholder
- disabled
- maxlength
- tabindex

When the attributes on either the {{input}} or the {{textarea}} expression are set with quotes, their values are directly inserted into the DOM as strings. If the attributes are set without quotes, they're bound to the current context. The following listing shows examples of both.

Listing 4.31   Using the {{input}} and {{textarea}} expressions

```
App.AwesomeController = Ember.Controller.extend({
    userCanEdit: true,
    placeholder: "Enter a value",
    fieldLength: 20,
    defaultValue: "Food"
});
<script type="text/x-handlebars" id="awesome">
    {{input type="text" value="Groceries" size="25"}} <br/>

    {{input type="text" value=defaultValue size=fieldLength}} <br/>
    {{textarea value="My text area text"}} <br/>

    {{textarea value=defaultValue}}

</script>
```

Renders textfield with attributes bound to controller

Renders textarea with values bound to controller

Renders textfield with values outputted as string directly

Renders textarea with values outputted as strings directly

The difference between bound and unbound attributes should be clear to you by now. The way these two expressions are set up gives you full control of how these expressions are rendered onscreen and whether or not attributes are bound to the context.

4.4.11   The {{yield}} expression

The {{yield}} expression is of limited use in Ember.js, and is applicable only for views that have a layout attached to them, and for Ember.js components. If you have a view that uses a layout, use the {{yield}} expression to tell the view's layout where to render the view's template. In this case, you can think of the {{yield}} expression as doing the same as the {{outlet}} expression does for routes. The following listing shows how to use the {{yield}} expression from within a view that has a layout.

Listing 4.32   Using the {{yield}} expression

```
App.MyLayoutView = Ember.View.extend({
    layout: Ember.Handlebars.compile('' +
        '<div class="layoutClass">{{yield}}</div>'),
    templateName: 'viewsTemplate'
});
```

Creates layout this view will use

Defines where to render view's template inside layout

`App.MyLayoutView` does, in essence, have two templates. One template controls the layout, and you use the `{{yield}}` expression to tell the layout where to draw the template into the layout template.

Even though Ember.js does pack a large number of expressions that you can use in your application, sometimes you need to use an expression that's not built in. Luckily, Ember.js allows you to create your own expressions as well.

4.5 Creating your own expressions

Internally, Handlebars.js calls expressions *helpers*. You use the `registerHelper` method to register your own custom helpers, which can then be invoked from any of your Handlebars.js templates. In the following listing, you'll create and register a new helper called `convMarkdown` that uses the `Showdown` library to convert text from Markdown format to HTML.

Listing 4.33 Creating a helper to convert from Markdown to HTML

```
Ember.Handlebars.registerHelper('convMarkdown',          ◁─┐  Registers new expression
        function(value, options) {                            convMarkdown

Creates new
Showdown ─▷    var converter = new Showdown.converter();
converter
        return new Handlebars.SafeString(converter.makeHtml(value));    ◁─┐

});                                                         Returns converted markup
                                                            via Handlebars.SafeString
```

You start by registering a new helper via the `Handlebars.registerHelper` method, passing in the name that you want your new expression to have. In the callback function, you get the value of the passed-in function name before using the contents of this value to convert its Markdown markup to HTML. But Handlebars.js will escape any HTML markup contained in its returned value. To return the actual HTML markup, return a new `Handlebars.SafeString` object instead. You can now use this new expression in any of your applications' Handlebars.js templates, as shown in the following listing.

Listing 4.34 Using a custom expression

```
{{convMarkdown markdownProperty}}       ◁─┤  Using newly created convMarkdown expression
```

4.6 Summary

This chapter serves as a summary of the built-in template library Handlebars.js. Even though you're free to use your favorite template library, Handlebars.js will most likely have the functionality you're after in your web application. If you require additional logic, Handlebars.js makes it easy to create custom expressions that provide your application with the specific logic that your application needs.

We've reviewed the expressions built into Handlebars.js and shown examples of using each of them. As Ember.js extends the core Handlebars.js features, we've also shown how you can use the Ember.js-specific expressions in your application, as well as how you can create your own.

This chapter concludes part 1 of this book. As you move along to part 2, you'll be introduced to a real open-source Ember.js application, Montric. Montric appears in examples throughout the rest of this book and is used to explain the finer details of how you can interact with your server side, build complex custom components, and assemble and test your Ember.js application.

Part 2

Building ambitious web apps for the real world

Part 1 guided you through the core Ember.js features and functionality, while familiarizing you with the conventions used throughout Ember.js applications. Part 2 shifts the focus slightly so you can explore how to make Ember.js applications come alive.

Part 2 introduces the case study that forms the basis for most of this book's sample code, Montric. Montric is an open source tool for monitoring application performance. Its front end is written in Ember.js. Its back end is Java-based, running on top of a horizontal scalable database, Riak.

You start by learning how to integrate server-side communication via Ember Router, first using Ember Data beta 2 in chapter 5, and then moving on to rolling your own model layer in chapter 6.

After sorting out the server-side communication options, you move on to another important core feature of Ember.js: custom components. Although self-contained components were added late in the development toward Ember.js v1.0.0, this feature is powerful and much-needed. Chapter 7 discusses Ember.js's approach to self-contained components by first introducing a few simple components and then combining them into new, more-complex components.

Before leaving part 2, you take an in-depth look at testing your Ember.js application. Chapter 8 shows you how to use QUnit and Phantom.js to build a complete testing strategy.

Bringing home the bacon— interfacing with the server side using Ember Data

5

This chapter covers

- An introduction to Ember Data and core concepts
- Using Ember Data models and model associations
- Using the built-in `RESTAdapter` to interface with your server
- Customizing the `RESTAdapter`

Distilled down to a single statement, Ember Data is the Object Relational Mapping framework for the web. Ember Data lets you interact with your server side in a straightforward and intuitive manner, while keeping the required code to a minimum. If you can also customize the format that your server provides its data in, you'll be up and running on your client side with a minimal amount of code.

But not everyone can adapt the back-end application to fit with the standard REST-based API that Ember Data expects out of the box. For these situations, Ember Data offers pluggable adapters and serializer APIs so that your Ember.js application can understand your specific server-side data APIs.

99

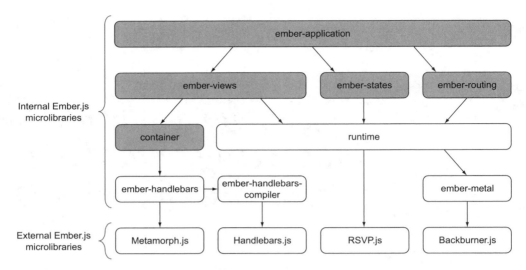

Figure 5.1   The parts of Ember.js you'll work on in this chapter

This chapter starts with the basic building blocks and patterns that make up the core of Ember Data before it delves into how you can use the built-in `RESTAdapter` and `RESTSerializer` to get data in and out of your Ember.js application. It wraps up with an overview of how you can implement custom adapters and serializers so that Ember Data works with the server-side API that you already have in place.

Figure 5.1 shows the parts of the Ember.js ecosystem that this chapter examines—ember-application, ember-views, ember-states, ember-routing, and container.

NOTE   At the time of writing, the newest version of Ember Data is 1.0.0-beta.2. As a result, this book covers Ember Data beta 2 throughout.

Now, let's roll up our sleeves and get going.

5.1   Using Ember Data as an application cache

Ember Data is effectively a caching layer inside your web application. Whenever you load data from your server to your client, you populate this cache with data. To maintain a rigorous structure to your cache, you need to define model objects for your models. Before we go into how the Ember Data cache works, let's quickly go over what an Ember model object is.

5.1.1   Defining Ember Data models

Ember Data model objects serve as class definitions for your data and tell Ember Data what attributes each model object has and what type each attribute has.

The following listing shows the `MainMenu` object from the Montric project.

Listing 5.1   The `MainMenu` object

Specifies name
attribute as
type string.

Model object can
have one chart
associated with
it of type
Montric.Chart.

```
Montric.MainMenu = DS.Model.extend({          ◁——  Extends DS.Model object.
    name: DS.attr('string'),
    nodeType: DS.attr('string'),                     If model object has parent, it's
    parent: DS.belongsTo("mainMenu"),         ◁——   of type Montric.MainMenu.
    children: DS.hasMany("mainMenu"),
    chart: DS.belongsTo("chart"),                                        ◁——

    isSelected: false,          ◁——  Neither isSelected nor        Model object can have
    isExpanded: false,                isExpanded is an Ember       zero, one, or more
});                                   Data attribute.              children of type
                                                                   Montric.MainMenu.
```

Note that the model here doesn't specify an `id` property because the `id` property is implicit for `DS.Model` objects. Ember Data automatically adds an `id` property, and it raises an error if you attempt to specify one yourself. Ember Data uses this `id` property to keep track of all your loaded objects. You created two properties, `name` and `nodeType`, that are both of type `string`, which you specify via `DS.attr()`. Ember Data uses this information to automatically serialize data to and from your back end via the specified serializer. `DS.attr` supports the attributes `string`, `number`, and `date`, but as you'll see later in this chapter, you can specify your own attributes.

Getting your data in and out of your application isn't the only strength of Ember Data, because it also supports one-to-one, one-to-many, and many-to-many relationships between your data. In listing 5.1, both the `parent` and the `chart` properties specify a one-to-one relationship using `DS.belongsTo`, whereas the `children` property specifies a one-to-many relationship using `DS.hasMany`. Relationships are explained in more detail later in this chapter.

You also specify two properties that aren't backed by Ember Data. These properties, `isSelected` and `isExpanded`, aren't strictly necessary to define in the class definition of `Montric.MainMenu`, but you can include them to make it clear that the rest of the application expects to find and use these properties. They are purely for human readability, because they have no Ember.js-specific meaning.

One of the major features of `DS.Model` objects is that they're also `Ember.Object` objects. You can therefore combine the model object with the core features of Ember.js itself, which include bindings, observers, and computed properties.

Often you want to know if a specific `Montric.MainMenu` has children or if it's a leaf node. The following listing shows how you can add computed properties to achieve this functionality across the application in one easy-to-find place.

Listing 5.2   Adding computed properties to the `MainMenu`

```
Montric.MainMenu = DS.Model.extend({
    name: DS.attr('string'),
    nodeType: DS.attr('string'),
    parent: DS.belongsTo('mainMenu'),
    children: DS.hasMany('mainMenu'),
    chart: DS.belongsTo('chart'),
```

```
    isSelected: false,
    isExpanded: false,
                                                          ┌──────────────────────────────┐
    hasChildren: function() {                             │ Returns true if number of    │
        return this.get('children').get('length') > 0;  ◄─┤ children is greater than 0   │
    }.property('children').cacheable(),                   └──────────────────────────────┘
                                                          ┌──────────────────────────────┐
    isLeaf: function() {                                  │ Returns true if number       │
        return this.get('children').get('length') == 0; ◄─┤ of children is 0             │
    }.property('children').cacheable()                    └──────────────────────────────┘
});
```

I'm sure you can see the huge advantage of enriching your model objects with computed properties in this manner. In fact, you can chain computed properties together to create complex properties, and you can bind to these computed properties right out to the templates.

5.1.2   *Ember Data is an identity map*

A common problem with JavaScript-based web applications that fetch their data via a JSON- or a REST-based interface is that they tend to store that data right in the DOM tree itself. Although this may be a quick way to update the web application's views, it's also error-prone because the developer needs to ensure that the old data isn't still displaying somewhere on the web page.

Ember Data solves this issue by implementing its data store as an identity map. Ember Data does the bookkeeping necessary to keep one and only one copy of your data in the cache. This copy is the master data that the rest of your application refers to. Whenever your application requests a specific model by asking for it with the model's unique id, Ember Data makes sure that the object instances you receive are the same each time you request a model of the same type and id. It doesn't matter if you get the data via a direct query by your model's id or if you iterate through a list of models. Each time you encounter a model object with the same id, you're working on the same instance of that object.

Figure 5.2 shows how Ember Data manages its data and how an identity map implementation works.

In this example, you begin with an empty cache. You then request a model with the id "ABC" of type Model. Because Ember Data doesn't have a model object with the id "ABC," it creates one. The only information Ember Data knows about your model at this time is the id, which means that it creates a new object of type Model and assigns its id property the value "ABC". Next, it synchronously returns that model object back to the controller. At the same time, it asynchronously reaches out to the server to fetch the rest of the model.

This asynchronous feature enables your application to set up the views that may be necessary for displaying your model object while you wait for the data to be returned from the server side, often making your application feel snappier. When the asynchronous response comes back from the server, Ember Data ensures that it updates the

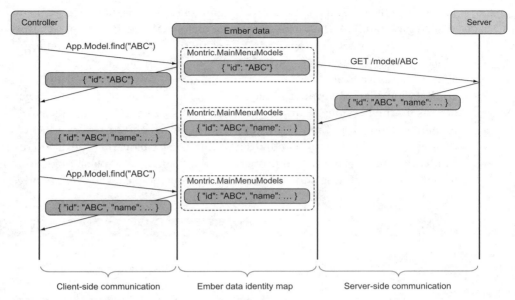

Figure 5.2 **The data flow of the Ember Data identity map**

object in the identity map before notifying the rest of the application that it's finished loading the model.

Because a binding is in place between the model in the identity map and a property in the controller, and bindings are also between the property on that model and the templates in the view, any changes occurring on the model object propagate through the controller and out to the template automatically.

Later, when you issue a new request to Ember Data of a model of type `Model` with id "ABC," Ember Data will already have the model cached in its identity map. An important concept of an identity map is that you'll receive the same object instance in return. This is important to keep your data updated and in sync throughout your application.

The fact that your data store is an identity map is something that Ember Data builds upon throughout its implementation. Ember Data is also smart enough to know when you need to run a query against your back end and serve the results in an asynchronous manner, and when it can serve your request in a synchronous manner straight from the identity map.

Sometimes, though, you need to refresh your data after it's been loaded in the cache. Luckily, Ember Data has built-in support for this as well.

5.1.3 *Relationships between model objects*

Ember Data knows that your data can be messy, intertwined, connected, and nonstandard, and it does a good job of providing features and integration points that enable you to structure that data in a sensible manner. Ember Data comes preloaded with a `RESTAdapter` and a `RESTSerializer` that expect JSON data to adhere to a specific contract. It also allows you to override any of these defaults, either by telling the `REST-Adapter` how to interpret your JSON keys or by implementing your own custom adapter and serializer.

Relationships on Ember Data are implemented using the `ids` of your model objects. In the previous example, the `Montric.MainMenu.children` property is a one–to-many relationship. Ember Data expects your back end to return a JSON array containing the `ids` of each of the children in this one-to-many relationship. This relationship is also made using the `id` property of the `Montric.MainMenu` object that it refers to. The following listing shows an example of how the JSON data is structured to comply with the `RESTAdapter`.

Listing 5.3   JSON data for the `Montric.MainMenu`

```json
{
    "mainMenus": [                                    ◁── Returns data in JSON array
        {
            "id": "JSFlotJAgent",                     ◁── Each model object returned has unique id property for this data type
            "name": "JSFlotJAgent",
            "children": [                             ◁── List of children; each element refers to id property of child model
                "JSFlotJAgent:Agent Statistics",
                "JSFlotJAgent:CPU",
                "JSFlotJAgent:Custom",
                "JSFlotJAgent:Frontend",
                "JSFlotJAgent:Memory",
                "JSFlotJAgent:Threads"
            ],
            "nodeType": "chart",
            "chart": "JSFlotJAgent",
            "parent": null                            ◁── Top-level menu items have no parent menu item attached
        },
        {
            "id": "JSFlotJAgent:Agent Statistics",    ◁── Child menu item
            "name": "Agent Statistics",
            "children": [
                "JSFlotJAgent:Agent Statistics:API Call Count"
            ],
            "nodeType": "chart",
            "chart": "JSFlotJAgent:Agent Statistics",
            "parent": "JSFlotJAgent"                  ◁── Child menu item refers back to parent via parent_id property
        }
    ]
}
```

Unless you specify otherwise, the `RESTAdapter` expects you to send in a list of objects and also expects the name of this list to be derived from the model object that it's going to map this data to. The default `RESTAdapter` and `RESTSerializer` expect your keys to be in camelized form, meaning they start with a lowercase letter and subsequent words in the key start with an uppercase letter. Whenever you return a list of items, the key is suffixed with an "s," indicating that the value for that key is plural.

If you look closer at the JSON data, you'll notice that the array provided for the key `children` is a list of strings and not real objects. This list of strings represents the `ids` of each of the objects that the `children` property is associated with. In this case, `children` refers to a list of zero or more `Montric.MainMenu` objects.

This is also true for the `chart` relationship. Even though this relationship is one to one, the JSON returned from the server for the `MainMenu` model also represents the `id` for the object that the `chart` property is associated with. As you may have guessed, Ember Data uses these `ids` to wire your models together correctly.

Ember Data won't, however, materialize your associations ahead of time. What this means is that Ember Data won't try to connect and load in your associations before your code requires them. When you call `MainMenu.get('chart')`, Ember Data looks up that `id` in its identity map and returns a result synchronously if it has a model of the correct type with that `id`. If the model object isn't loaded yet, it synchronously returns an empty record with only the `id`. It won't attempt to fetch the `chart` object from the server before you access a non-`id` property. You can rely on Ember Data to do the right thing most of the time. If you're not accessing any data that Ember Data hasn't stored in its cache, you can be certain that your application won't fetch data from your server before the user requests that data.

Although you can set up your views while you're awaiting a response from the server side, you may want to hold off rendering certain parts of your view until you're sure that the models that you're going to render have arrived safely in Ember Data, which leads us to take a closer look at the states an Ember Data model can be in.

5.1.4 *Model states and events*

Because most of the data you bring to your application via Ember Data is loaded in an asynchronous manner, each Ember Data model has a built-in state manager that keeps track of the state that your model objects are in at any given point in time. Ember Data uses this information internally to know how to provide your application with the data it receives from the server, but you can also use this information when you build your application. For example, this information comes in handy when you want to implement loading indicators, or when you want to ensure that your GUI doesn't update until a certain amount of (or all) your data is loaded properly.

> **NOTE** Ember.js version 1.2.0 includes specific loading and error subroutes that handle scenarios when your data is loading and when you receive errors from the back-end server.

To provide your application with this information, each model object that extends `DS.Model` has built-in convenience functions you can use both in your controllers and

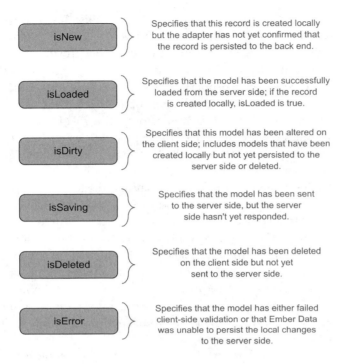

Figure 5.3   The states that an Ember Data model object can have

also in your templates. Each model object comes with the state properties shown in figure 5.3.

Note that these state properties aren't mutually exclusive. A model can have both isDirty and isDeleted return true, meaning that the model was deleted locally but not yet persisted, or both isDirty and isSaving return true, meaning that the model was updated locally and sent to the server side but that the server side hasn't responded with a status update.

Sometimes you need your controllers to be notified whenever your models change or when they enter a specific state. Each Ember Data model allows your controllers to subscribe to events. The valid events are shown in figure 5.4.

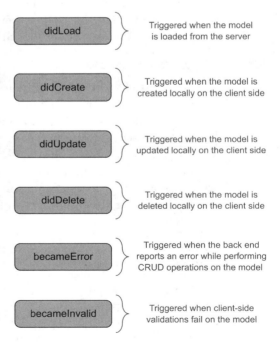

Figure 5.4   The model events

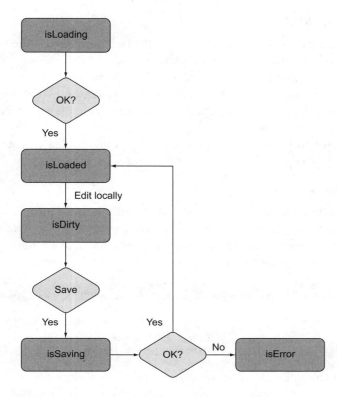

Figure 5.5 The most common Ember Data states that your models will be in

You can subscribe to all of these events within your code. If you want to perform an action when a model is loaded, you can use the on function on the model object in order to be notified when your model has finished loading:

```
model.on('didLoad', function() {
  console.log("Loaded!");
});
```
⟵ **Uses on function to subscribe to didLoad event**

As you've probably guessed, Ember Data models follow a lifecycle in which they can transition from one state to another. In fact, models have a hierarchical structure. Figure 5.5 shows the topmost states that a model can be in. This figure isn't complete, but it does contain the states that your data is most likely to be in.

A model usually starts out in the isLoading state. After the back end returns the model, it transitions to the isLoaded state. If the model gets modified locally, either via a user action or another client-side process (such as a timer), the model transitions to the isDirty state, where it remains until it's saved. When save() is called on a model, it transitions into the isSaving state. If the back end returns an OK response (HTTP 200, for example, and possibly an updated model), the model is brought back to the isLoaded state. If Ember Data fails while trying to persist the model to the server, or if the server returns a non-200 HTTP status code, the model transitions to the isError state.

5.1.5   Communicating with the back end

The default `RESTAdapter` uses XML HTTP Request (XHR) to integrate with the server, but you can provide your own adapter implementation. You may want to use a different type of integration, for example, or you may need to adapt Ember Data to work with an existing API. Building in support for either LocalStorage or WebSockets is made possible and approachable in Ember Data. As discussed in chapters 1 and 2, you use a third-party LocalStorage adapter.

You're probably eager to learn how you can integrate Ember Data in your own application, so let's get started.

5.2   Firing up Ember Data

To use Ember Data, you need to be using a store. You can think of the store as an in-memory cache that Ember Data uses to retrieve and store its model objects. In fact, the store is also responsible for fetching data from your back-end server. To get started, you need to define a store for your application, as shown in the following listing.

Listing 5.4   Creating a store

```
Montric.Store = DS.Store.extend({        ◁── Defines new store for application
    adapter:  "Montric.Adapter"     ◁── Defines which adapter to use when
});                                       interfacing with server side
```

You create the store in the same manner you create any other Ember object; in this case, by extending a new `DS.Store` object. When Ember Data is initialized, it initializes a new store object and registers it with the Ember Container as `store:main`. You may have an API that's different from each data type that the server returns. Ember Data supports per-type adapters and serializers precisely for this purpose. We'll look at custom adapters and serializers later in this chapter.

You also need to specify which adapter to use. In this case, use a custom adapter called `Montric.Adapter`, shown in the following listing.

Listing 5.5   The `Montric.Adapter`

```
Montric.Adapter = DS.RESTAdapter.extend({     ◁── Extends from default DS.RESTAdapter
    defaultSerializer: "Montric/application"  ◁── Uses default serializer
});                                               Montric.ApplicationSerializer
```

You're creating a new `Montric.Adapter` that extends the standard `DS.RESTAdapter`. For now, use the standard functionality inherited from this adapter. The only piece you override is the default adapter, telling `Montric.Adapter` to rely on the adapter named `Montric.ApplicationSerializer`. The code for this serializer is shown in the following listing.

Listing 5.6 The `Montric.ApplicationSerializer`

```
Montric.ApplicationSerializer = DS.RESTSerializer.extend({});
```

> Extends default
> **DS.RESTSerializer**

You may wonder why you bothered creating your own implementation of the REST-Adapter and the RESTSerializer, because you aren't overriding any functionality in either of these two classes. The reason I'm showing you this now is twofold. First, I want to show you early how you can define a custom adapter and serializer for your application. Second, you'll make use of this later on in this chapter.

Now that you've initialized Ember Data, it's time to fetch some data from your server.

5.2.1 Fetching data from your models

You can load data from Ember Data (and, in turn, from your back end) in two ways. You can either call `store.find('model')` to load all your models of a specific type, or you can pass in an `id` to load a specific model object.

Consider the code shown in this listing.

Listing 5.7 Fetching data from your models

```
Montric.MainChartsRoute = Ember.Route.extend({
    model: function() {
        return this.store.find('mainMenu');
    }
});
```

> **Uses model function to specify which model object to load for this route**

> **Returns all instances of Montric.MainMenu**

As you learned in chapter 3, the model function specifies which model objects will be populated to a route's controller. If you use the Ember Router, this will become the most common way that you'll load models from Ember Data to your controllers. `this.store.find('mainMenu')` is how you tell Ember Data to fetch all objects of type `Montric.MainMenu`. Ember Data then looks at its internal cache and returns any objects it has there. If the cache for that model type is empty, it goes out to the back-end server and asks it for the data. Ember Data does this by issuing an HTTP GET XHR to the URL /mainMenus, which it derived automatically from the model's class name.

Likewise, if you instead called `this.store.find('main Menu', 'JSFlotJAgent')`, Ember Data would look at its cache to see if it had an object of type `Montric.MainMenu` with an `id` of `JSFlotJAgent`. When the server side returns, it then populates the cache with the updated data. Ember.js's observers and bindings take care of moving that data out all the way to the DOM. (See figure 5.2 for a schematic of this process.)

5.2.2 Specifying relationships between your models

You've loaded all the `Montric.MainMenu` objects from the server to the Ember Data identity map. But before we go over the relationships, let's review what you'll use the

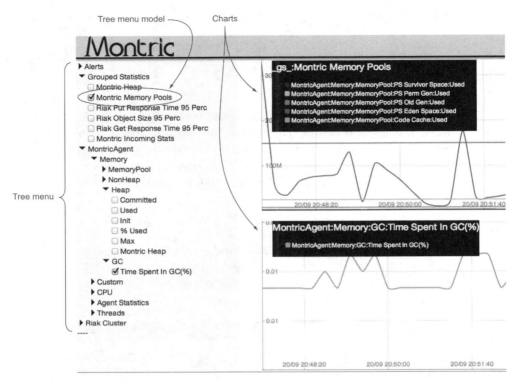

Figure 5.6 **The use case for the models you've defined**

data for. Figure 5.6 shows the types of models that you have in the Montric application.

Each of these `Montric.MainMenu` model objects represents a single element in the tree structure on the lefthand side. We'll call the top-level elements `rootNodes`. Each of the nodes in the tree can have zero or more `children` nodes. The `children` nodes are also of the `Montric.MainMenu` model type. If a node has `children`, a disclosure triangle is displayed at the left of the node's name. Users click this triangle to expand it and reveal its `children` nodes.

Users can expand the nodes until they reach a node that has zero children. This node is called a leaf node. Leaf nodes are selectable. By clicking the checkbox to the left of the leaf nodes, users can select which nodes they want to show charts from. After at least one chart is selected, the area to the right of the tree menu displays each of the selected charts. Each `Montric.MainMenu` node has a `chart` property that Montric follows to load the chart for each selected node.

You've already seen the `MainMenu` model, so before moving on to the relationships present, let's go through the `Montric.Chart` model, which is shown in the following listing.

Listing 5.8 The `Montric.Chart` model

Name property is of type string

```
Montric.Chart = DS.Model.extend({          ⟵    Extends DS.Model
  name: DS.attr('string'),
    series: DS.attr('raw')                  ⟵   Series property is of
});                                              custom type "raw"
```

The Chart model is fairly simple. It has two properties, a name and a series. The name property is a string, but the series property is of type raw. The raw property type isn't something that's supported directly in Ember Data but is rather a custom transformation that's specific to the Montric application. We'll get back to this custom transformation later in the chapter, but for now you can think of this property as holding a plain JavaScript array and not an extension of an Ember.Object.

Before explaining the different relationship types that Ember Data offers, let's review the relationships that you've set up in the Montric.MainMenu and Montric.Chart models. Figure 5.7 shows the relationships.

The MainMenu model is related to exactly one other MainMenu model via the parent property, whereas it's related to zero or more MainMenu models via the children property. Each item in the menu will have exactly one parent item, while it can have multiple child items. In addition, the MainMenu model is related to exactly one Chart model via the chart property. With this in mind, let's explore the different relationship types that are built in to Ember Data.

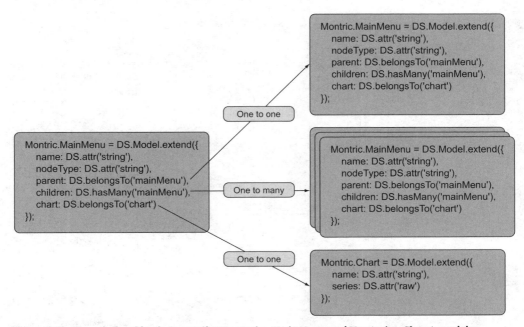

Figure 5.7 The relationships between the `Montric.MainMenu` and `Montric.Chart` models

5.3   *Ember Data model associations*

Ember Data supports a number of different types of associations, each with its own assumptions as to how it expects the data to be returned from the server by default. Ember Data lets you override these default assumptions and expectations. However, it's useful to know which associations are available as well as their default behavior and server API expectations.

5.3.1   *Understanding the Ember Data model relationships*

Out of the five association types that are available for models in Ember Data, three of them can be considered true types, while the remaining two association types can be considered derivations, or special cases. The available Ember Data model relationships are shown in figure 5.8.

The names of the relationships are similar to the names of the relationships in relational database systems, except that the relational model doesn't distinguish between a

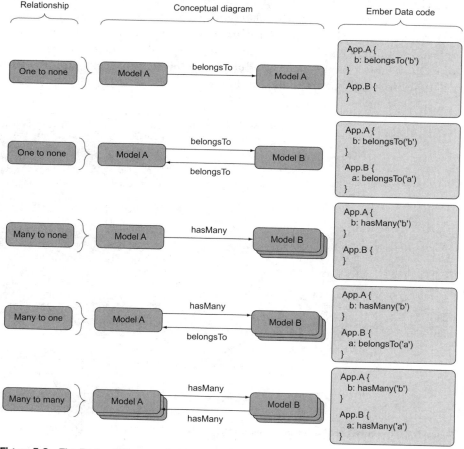

Figure 5.8   The Ember Data associations that allow you to specify relationships between models

`*-to-none` and a `*-to-many` relationship. Relationships are defined in Ember Data models either via the `belongsTo()` function or the `hasMany()` function. These functions tell Ember Data both how to wire your data together and also how it asks the server for the data as well as the format it expects the return to be in. Figure 5.9 shows

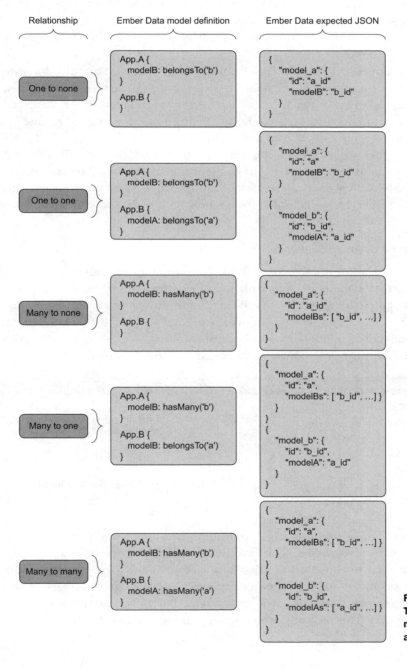

**Figure 5.9
The Ember Data JSON mappings that are available by default**

how Ember Data and the default `RESTAdapter` expect the data to be returned from the server.

Keep in mind one important naming convention. Whenever you create a relationship via either `belongsTo()` or `hasMany()`, the string value you pass in must be the same as the name of the model class you're setting up the relationship to. This string value has the standard Ember.js camelized form that you've become used to. Other than that, the name of the properties directly reflects the expected keys in the JSON hash coming from the server.

I've mentioned that Ember Data employs a lazy loading structure for your data. For the Montric application, the data for a chart won't be loaded before the application requests access to either the `name` or the `series` property of the `Montric.Chart` model. This is fine for this use case, because you're only loading charts one at a time when the user selects a chart from the tree menu.

But for other types of data, this can lead to a significant number of AJAX calls between the client and the server. To tackle this issue, Ember Data supports embedding and sideloading data in the JSON hash returned from the server. Embedding works slightly differently than standard relationships, so let's take a look at embedded records.

5.3.2 Ember Data sideloaded records

To optimize for a low number of requests between the client and the server, Ember Data supports the ability to both embed and sideload records in the response from the server. Sideloading works by adding multiple top-level hashes in the JSON returned from the server. For this to work, the `id` of each of the hashes needs to map with the camelized model names. Because Montric doesn't have any sideloaded records, consider the one-to-many relationship in the following listing.

Listing 5.9 One-to-many association

```
Blog.Post = DS.Model.extend({
    name: DS.attr('string'),                    Each Blog.Post has zero
    comments: DS.hasMany('comment')         ⊲─┘ or more Blog.Comments.
});

Blog.Comment = DS.Model.extend({
    text: DS.attr('string'),                    Each Blog.Comment belongs
    post: DS.belongsTo('post')              ⊲─┘ to a single Blog.Post.
});
```

This code is from a common blog application in which each blog post has a set of comments associated with it. The two model objects `Blog.Post` and `Blog.Comment` form a standard one-to-many relationship. If you followed the normal path, you'd most likely begin by fetching all or a couple of blog posts from the server. When the user chooses to view a blog post, you'd then fetch that blog post's comments to display them to the user. The exchange would go something like figure 5.10.

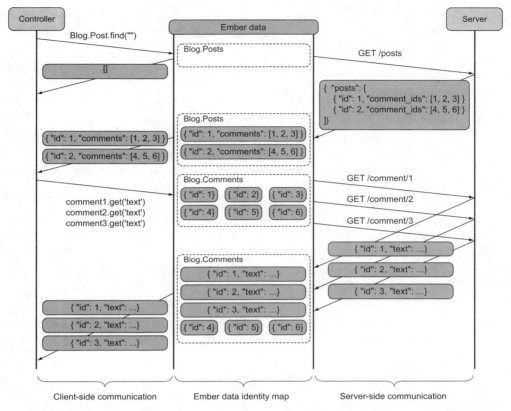

Figure 5.10 The data flow for loading posts and comments using the standard Ember Data control flow through associations

Multiple requests go from Ember Data to the server, one to fetch a list of `Blog.Post` models and then one request to fetch each comment for the blog post with `id 1`. Depending on your application, data, and requirements, this can become inefficient if the data is sufficiently large. We'll look at the possibility of sideloading the comment information in the initial XHR GET to /post.

One possible solution is to sideload the comments to the same response as the post they belong to. The following listing shows the JSON for sideloading the comments.

Listing 5.10 The JSON for sideloading `Blog.Comment` records

```
{
  "posts: [
    {"id": 1, "comments": [1, 2, 3]},
    {"id": 2, "comments": [4, 5, 6]}
  ],
  "comments"; [
```

Post's hash is included as before

Post with id I is related to comments with ids I, 2, and 3

Post with id 2 is related to comments with ids 4, 5, and 6

Comments are sideloaded in same response

```
    {"id": 1, "text": "Comment 1", "post": 1},
    {"id": 2, "text": "Comment 2", "post": 1},
    {"id": 3, "text": "Comment 3", "post": 1},
    {"id": 4, "text": "Comment 4", "post": 2},
    {"id": 5, "text": "Comment 5", "post": 2},
    {"id": 6, "text": "Comment 6", "post": 2},
  ]
}
```

Comments with ids 1, 2 and 3 are related to post with id 1

Comments with ids 4, 5, and 6 are related to post with id 2

Here, when you load the `Blog.Post` models, instead of having the server return only the data for the `Post` model objects, you also append an array with the key `comments` that contains the comments associated with your two blog posts. By including a JSON hash with the correct `ids`, Ember Data loads the two posts and the six comments into its identity map in one big swoop. Additionally, it's not necessary to tell Ember Data that it has to accept sideloaded objects.

Figure 5.11 shows the updated data flow when sideloading data. The advantage to the sideloading approach should be clear; you've effectively reduced the number of XHRs from a total of seven down to one, while you've also reduced the total number of bytes sent from the server, even if you were to disregard the time required to negotiate for the seven XHR connections as well as the extra bytes for the six HTTP headers that you've removed.

The downside is that the server needs to send data to the client that potentially will never be displayed to the user (if the user never visits the blog post with `id 2`, for

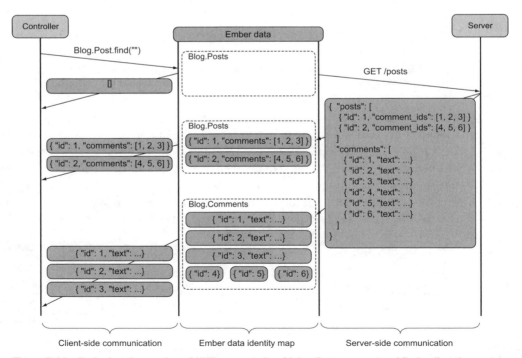

Figure 5.11   Reducing the number of XHR requests by sideloading comments while loading the posts

instance). You should therefore consider the implications of sideloading before you implement this in your applications.

I've mentioned that it's possible to override many of the default assumptions that the RESTAdapter has toward the JSON that it receives from the server. Before we conclude this chapter, let's look at the customizations that the adapter and the serializer have.

5.4 *Customizing the adapter and serializer*

Because Ember Data supports both default and per-type adapters and serializers, you can support any of the following scenarios:

- Write a separate adapter and serializer to support applications for which the server-side API has no common standard across data types
- Write a separate adapter and serializer to support data types that differ from the server-side API that your server specifies
- Write a separate adapter but keep the default serializer in cases where the URL patterns or top-level JSON keys for a specific type differ from the server-side API that your server specifies

Let's get started with a specific example from Montric that illustrates the third scenario: creating a custom adapter for the Chart model to customize the URL that Ember Data calls the server with.

5.4.1 *Writing a custom adapter but keeping the default serializer*

In Montric, when the user selects a chart to view from the main menu, Ember Data looks up which chart to load via the chart property of the Montric.MainMenu node that the user selected. It then notices that this is a one-to-one relationship. Because Montric won't have the chart loaded in its cache initially, it reaches out to the server via the adapter's find() method.

But because the user can select the time period that the chart will be based on from elsewhere in the application, you need to also tell the server side the timespan that you wish to view the chart for. If the user hasn't made a selection, the timespan will be set to 10 minutes. The user interface where the user selects the chart timespan is shown in figure 5.12.

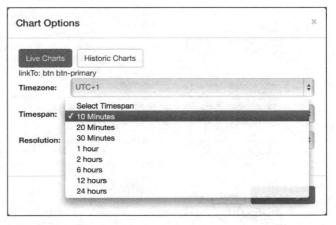

Figure 5.12 Selecting how long the charts will be displayed

Next, you need to add a new custom adapter for the Chart model. You can do this by implementing a new class called Montric.ChartAdapter:

```
Montric.ChartAdapter = DS.RESTAdapter.extend({
    //contents omitted at this point
});
```

Here, you create a new class that extends the default RESTAdapter. The name of the adapter tells Ember.js to use this adapter whenever it needs to either get or persist Chart models. This follows the naming convention that you've become accustomed to while using Ember.js, and it's nicely implemented for custom adapters, too.

When you create a custom adapter, you can override a few things from the default RESTAdapter to customize its behavior. Figure 5.13 shows the methods you can override and their responsibilities.

For your purpose, you only need to override a single function, the find() function, to append a query string to the URL whenever you fetch single Montric.Chart models.

Now that you've identified which function to override, update the ChartAdapter as shown in listing 5.11.

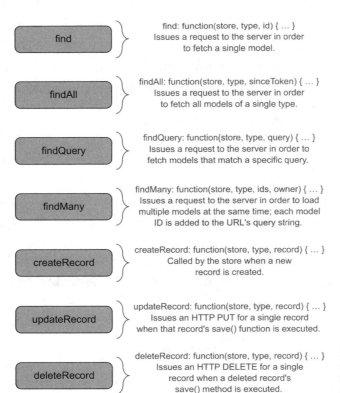

find: function(store, type, id) { ... }
Issues a request to the server in order
to fetch a single model.

findAll: function(store, type, sinceToken) { ... }
Issues a request to the server in order
to fetch all models of a single type.

findQuery: function(store, type, query) { ... }
Issues a request to the server in order to
fetch models that match a specific query.

findMany: function(store, type, ids, owner) { ... }
Issues a request to the server in order to load
multiple models at the same time; each model
ID is added to the URL's query string.

createRecord: function(store, type, record) { ... }
Called by the store when a new
record is created.

updateRecord: function(store, type, record) { ... }
Issues an HTTP PUT for a single record
when that record's save() function is executed.

deleteRecord: function(store, type, record) { ... }
Issues an HTTP DELETE for a single
record when a deleted record's
save() method is executed.

Figure 5.13   The methods available in the Ember Data adapter that you can override to create a custom adapter

Listing 5.11 The updated `Montric.ChartAdapter`

```
Montric.ChartAdapter = DS.RESTAdapter.extend({
    find: function(store, type, id) {
        return this.ajax(this.buildURL(type.typeKey, id), 'GET');
    },

    buildURL: function(type, id) {
        var host = Ember.get(this, 'host'),
            namespace = Ember.get(this, 'namespace'),
            url = [];

        if (host) { url.push(host); }
        if (namespace) { url.push(namespace); }

        url.push(Ember.String.pluralize(type));
        if (id) { url.push(id); }

        url = url.join('/');
        if (!host) { url = '/' + url; }

        var queryString = this.buildQueryString();

        return url + queryString;
    },

    buildQueryString: function() {
        var queryString = "?tz=" + Montric.get('selectedTimezone');
        if (Montric.get('showLiveCharts')) {
            queryString += "&ts=" + Montric.get('selectedChartTimespan');
        } else {
            queryString += "&chartFrom=" +
    Montric.get('selectedChartFromMs');
            queryString += "&chartTo=" + Montric.get('selectedChartToMs');
        }
        queryString += "&rs=" + Montric.get('selectedChartResolution');

        return queryString;
    }
});
```

Copy of default code from DS.RESTAdapter → points to `find` function

Overrides DS.RESTAdapter's buildURL function to append query string ← points to `buildURL`

Builds queryString → points to `var queryString = this.buildQueryString();`

Returns URL and queryString as URL to use against server ← points to `return url + queryString;`

Custom function builds up query string → points to `buildQueryString: function() {`

You don't have to be able to follow all the code in this listing. Most of the code is taken straight from the DS.RESTAdapter code. The only thing you add is a function that builds up the query string and appends it to the URL. Previously, the URLs to retrieve Chart models from the server looked like this:

```
/charts/_gs_:Montric%20Heap
```

Now, the URLs look like this:

```
/charts/_gs_:Montric%20Heap?tz=2&ts=10&rs=15
```

Now that you've seen how to implement a custom adapter to query the server with nonstandard URLs, let's look at how to add a serializer to parse JSON that doesn't follow the RESTAdapter's conventions.

5.4.2 *Writing custom adapters and serializers*

When a user logs in to Montric, the application issues a find() to the currently logged-in user. An example of a nonstandard (in regards to the RESTSerializer) JSON hash is shown in this listing.

Listing 5.12 A nonstandard JSON hash for the Montric.User model

```
{
    "user_model": {
        "id": joachim@haagen-software.no,
        "user_name": "joachim@haagen-software.no",
        "account_name": "Haagen Software",
        "user_role": "root",
        "firstname": "Joachim Haagen",
        "lastname": "Skeie",
        "company": "Haagen Software AS",
        "country": "Norway"
    }
}
```

Nonstandard
JSON keys

The three keys user_name, account_name, and user_role are all nonstandard with regard to the RESTSerializer. In addition, the key for the user object, user_model, doesn't follow the RESTSerializer standard. You can sort this out by creating a new class, Montric.UserSerializer. When you write a custom serializer, you can override a few functions to customize how the serializer works with the JSON data (figure 5.14).

Incoming JSON transformations (from server to Ember.js)

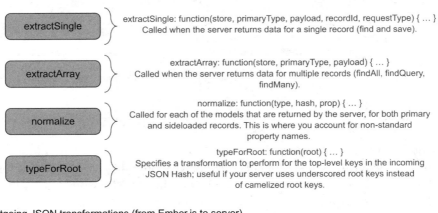

Outgoing JSON transformations (from Ember.js to server)

Figure 5.14   The methods you can override to build a custom serializer

To work with the JSON returned for each of the top-level keys, override two functions: one that lets you specify the format of the top-level keys and one that lets you account for nonstandard property names. For this example, you need to override `typeForRoot` to tell the adapter to use `user_model` as the top-level key. You also need to implement `normalize` to support the three property names `user_name`, `account_name`, and `user_role`. The following listing shows the `Montric.UserSerializer`.

Listing 5.13 The `Montric.UserSerializer`

```
Montric.UserSerializer = DS.RESTSerializer.extend({
    typeForRoot: function(root) {                          ⟵ Strips away last
        return root.slice(root.length-6, root.length);        six characters
    },                                                        of top-level key

    normalize: function(type, hash, property) {           ⟵ Creates new object that you'll build
        var json = {};                                         up with correct property keys
        for (var prop : hash) {                            ⟵ Iterates over each property in original hash
            json[prop.camelize()] = hash[prop];           ⟵ Adds new camelize property
        }                                                      with value from original hash

        return this._super(type, json, property);         ⟵ Calls normalize function
    }                                                          in super class
});
```

This code is extremely specific to this use case. You strip away the last six characters of each of the top-level keys, which works for this one use case, but if you find yourself needing to implement the `typeForRoot` function, you might be better off implementing something more sophisticated.

The `normalize` function, however, is more robust. It creates a new object (`json`) before it iterates over each of the properties for the current hash. For each property in the hash, it adds a new property to the `json` object, of which each key is camelized. The function ends by calling the `normalize` function of the super class `DS.REST-Serializer`. This is important for the rest of the serialization to work.

Now that you've seen how you can create both custom adapters and serializers, let's move on to see how to customize the URLs that your application uses when it contacts the server.

5.4.3 Custom URLs

By default, Ember Data expects to reach its data with a URL that lives at the root of the domain where the application runs. All the URLs are prefixed with a /, followed by the decamelized and underscored model name.

Some back ends have special requirements that make this naming convention either inconvenient or impossible for different reasons. In these cases, you have two options: you can either specify a namespace to prepend a specific path to where the back end responds or you can specify a new URL. Both approaches are shown here:

```
Montric.Adapter = DS.RESTAdapter.extend({
    defaultSerializer: "Montric/application",
```

Prepends URL by updating url property

```
        namespace: 'json/v1',
        host: 'http://api.myapp.com'
});
```

Prepends /json to URL by updating the namespace property

Normally, when you call `this.store.find('mainMenu')`, you issue an XHR `GET` to the URL `/mainMenus`. In this example, you add both a namespace and a host to the application default adapter. This causes that call to issue an XHR `GET` to the URL http://api.myapp.com/json/v1/mainMenus instead.

5.5   *Summary*

This chapter serves as an introduction to Ember Data and the built-in `RESTAdapter`. You started out learning how you can implement models that extend the Ember Data model object to represent the data that your application uses. You then looked at how Ember Data is structured as an identity map to ensure that your application is consistent by ensuring that only one copy of the data lives in Ember Data.

Models in Ember Data follow a strict lifecycle, and you looked at how that affects how you use the data in your application and how you can use this fact when you write your own application.

Ember Data provides powerful built-in relationships between model types. You looked at how you can use these relationships to build complex structures between your data. In addition, you saw how the lazy loading of relationships can have a negative effect on performance and how you can use sideloading to amend these issues by reducing the number of XHRs that are required to fetch data from the server.

Finally, this chapter wraps up by explaining the customization that the REST-Adapter supports and how you can build your own adapters and serializers.

Thus far, we've covered most of the features that are offered in Ember Data beta 2. Sometimes, though, Ember Data is more than you need for your applications. In the next chapter, you'll look at how to use Ember.js without the help of Ember Data.

Interfacing with the server side without using Ember Data

This chapter covers

- Learning what Ember.js expects from your data layer
- Defining a generic model object that acts as the model layer for the application
- Fetching, persisting, and deleting data using jQuery Ajax calls
- Integrating your model layer with Ember Router through the web application used for the Ember Fest conference

Ember Data will become a remarkable product; however, it's not ready for production use at the time I'm writing this. Even though you can interact with the server side in the same way you're used to with jQuery, Ember.js does require some extra thought before implementing a sane strategy for retrieving and persisting data between your Ember.js application and the server side.

In some situations, Ember Data may not be suitable for your particular use case. For example, if you're dealing with a simple data structure, you may prefer to

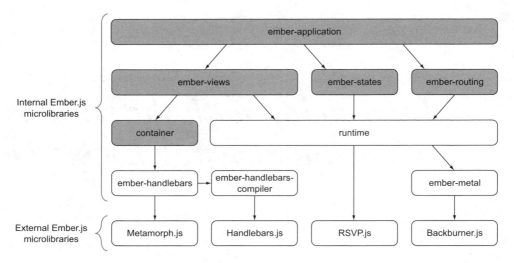

Figure 6.1   Parts of Ember.js you'll work on in this chapter

implement something less complex than Ember Data to fetch the data from the back end. Ember Router makes it easy to write your own integration layer. That being said, though, once your application grows, you'll most likely need to find solutions to a lot of issues that Ember Data solves out of the box for you. Regardless, learning how to use Ember Router to communicate efficiently with any back end you might have or are building, comes in handy when you have a nonstandard API to interact with or when you want to implement something quick for some (or all) of your model objects.

This chapter examines the assumptions that Ember.js has about your client-to-server-side strategy, as well as an implementation strategy used in a real-world application.

Figure 6.1 shows the parts of Ember.js that you'll look at in this chapter.

Let's start by taking a quick look at the application you're developing parts of before diving into where you'll plug your data layer into your application.

6.1   Introducing Ember Fest

In this chapter, you'll develop the data model layer of the web application for the European Ember.js Conference, Ember Fest. This application is fairly straightforward with limited functionality. Figure 6.2 shows the GUI of three routes in the Ember Fest application.

> **NOTE**   The 2013 version of the Ember Fest website was built on top of the concepts taught in this chapter. The 2014 version of the Ember Fest website is built on top of the Conticious CMS, using Ember Data. The code represented in this chapter is contained within a branch on the project's website: https://github.com/joachimhs/EmberFestWebsite/tree/Ember.js-in-Action-branch.

The application is a set of pages, with each page representing a single route in the application. The application highlights the current route in the navigation bar as the

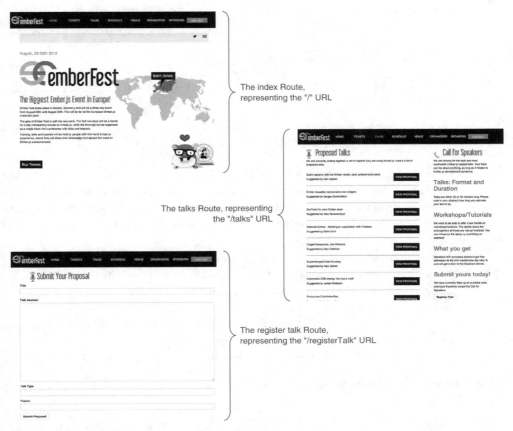

The index Route, representing the "/" URL

The talks Route, representing the "/talks" URL

The register talk Route, representing the "/registerTalk" URL

Figure 6.2   Three routes in the Ember Fest application

user navigates through the application. At the top, the user can log in or create a new account, which is provided via Mozilla Persona in this application. Authentication is covered in more detail in chapter 9.

You'll look at how to use Ember Router as an integration point into the model layer, and then you'll look at the way you use each route's `model()` hook to fetch data into the Ember Fest controllers.

6.1.1   Understanding the application router

The router is the glue that holds your Ember.js application together, so it's not surprising that the router plays a significant role in your data layer strategy as well.

The router for this application is shown in the following listing.

Listing 6.1   Ember Fest router

```
Emberfest.Router = Ember.Router.extend({
    location: 'history'
});
```

```
Emberfest.Router.map(function() {

    this.route('tickets');                                    talks route displays
    this.resource('talks', function() {                       all submitted talks.
        this.route('talk', {path: "/talk/:talk_id"});
    });                                                       talks.talk subroute
    this.route('schedule');                                   displays current
    this.route('venue');                                      selected talk.
    this.route('organizers');
    this.route('sponsors');
    this.route("registerTalk");
});
```

As the listing shows, each of the application's routes is defined in a flat structure with little hierarchy. Because each route effectively replaces the contents of the application (not including the header and footer), this is an appropriate and simple router definition. Note, though, that the `talks.talk` route is defined as a subroute of the `talks` route.

Throughout this chapter, you'll concentrate on three routes. You'll take a closer look at both the `talks` route and the `talks.talk` route while also taking a closer look at the `registerTalk` route, which is responsible for allowing logged-in users to register new talks for the conference.

You'll use the `model()` hook for the `talks` and the `talks.talk` routes to tell the application's data layer to fetch data from the server.

Let's look at these routes before moving on to the data model implementation.

6.1.2   Using the model() hook to fetch data

You'll fetch all talks in the Ember Fest application and store them in the `Talks-Controller`. You can accomplish this task in many ways; however, some of these approaches will lead you down the path of duplicated data, missing data, and missed updates.

Ember.js was built to support complex data with complex associations, and it can help you toward an efficient data layer implementation. The key to Ember Router's way of handing loading data from the back end into the Ember.js application is the `model()` function in each of your routes' definitions.

The following listing shows how to use the `model()` function to fetch the application's talks and load them into the `Emberfest.TalksController`.

Listing 6.2   TalksRoute

```
Emberfest.TalksRoute = Ember.Route.extend({
    model: function() {                           Hooks in data layer
        return EmberFest.Talk.findAll();
    }                                             Returns result of fetching
});                                               all talks from server
```

The code looks pretty simple, right? As it should! You return the result of fetching all the talks from the server from the `model()` function. Ember Router injects this data into the `content` property of the correct controller, in this case the `Talks-Controller`.

Ember.js calls the `model()` function when the `talks` route is created. This prevents additional calls to the `findAll()` function and reduces the traffic between the client and the server.

To ensure that you don't end up with duplicate data for your application, you'll implement an identity map in the model layer. But first let's look at the `TalksTalk-Route`, shown in the following listing.

Listing 6.3   `TalksTalkRoute`

```
Emberfest.TalksTalkRoute = Ember.Route.extend({
    model: function(id) {
        return Emberfest.Talk.find(id.talk_id);        ◁──┐  Returns a single talk
    }
});
```

The `TalksTalkRoute` is similar to the `TalksRoute`, but notice that you pass the `id` parameter to the `model()` function to fetch a single `Emberfest.Talk` object from the data layer.

You may remember from the discussion of the router in chapter 3 that when you enter the `TalksTalkRoute` via a direct URL, Ember.js sets up the `TalksRoute` before setting up the `TalksTalkRoute`. Both `Emberfest.Talk.findAll()` and `Emberfest.Talk.find(id)` are called one right after the other. To account for both methods being called, you'll design your data layer intelligently enough not to query the server twice, because the communication between your client application and the server application is most likely the slowest part of your system by at least one order of magnitude.

6.1.3   *Implementing an identity map*

Several approaches are available to avoid multiple server queries. For this application, I chose an identity-map-like implementation. (For a discussion of identity maps, see chapter 5.) You'll implement an in-browser cache, ensuring that there's only one object of each type and `id`. After data is loaded into the identity map, only one object of each of the talks will remain.

This ensures that whenever you call `Emberfest.Talk.find(id)`, you retrieve the same instance of that object, and the cache contains no duplicate data. Figure 6.3 shows the role of the identity map in this setting.

Now that you've seen the structure of Ember Fest and you have a better understanding of how an identity map works, let's look at the implementation.

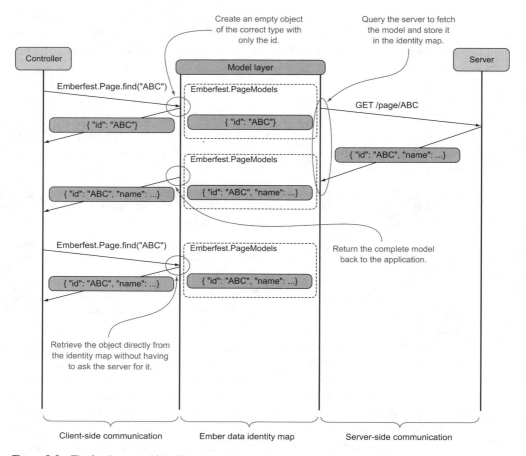

Figure 6.3   The implemented identity map

6.2   *Fetching data*

For the Ember Fest application, it's sufficient to always fetch all items from the server because you're storing a small amount of data for each individual data type. For instance, only a handful of submitted talk proposals are entered into the Ember Fest application. You only have to implement Ajax calls from within the findAll() function.

You first implement the find() function before you implement the data fetching in the findAll() function. After you see how you can fetch data from both the local identity map and the server, you'll look at an abstract implementation of a shared model class, which keeps code duplication to a minimum.

Let's look at the find() function.

6.2.1   *Returning a specific task via the find() function*

Because some of your controllers require only a single item, you support fetching single items from your identity map. When the user enters the talks.talk route, Ember.js calls the find() function for the talks.talk route to locate the specific talk that the user selected from the identity map. But because the talks.talk route is a subroute of the talks route, Ember.js also calls the findAll() function of the talks route to load all talks. The object that's returned from the find() function must be the same as the one that will be included in the list of objects from the findAll() function. This is an important concept that's central to the implementation of an identity map.

The following listing shows the implementation of the find() function.

Listing 6.4 The find() function

```
Emberfest.Model = Ember.Object.extend();              Defines new class

                                                      Reopens class definition
Emberfest.Model.reopenClass({                         to add class methods
    find: function(id, type) {                              Implements find
        var foundItem = this.contentArrayContains(id, type);   function, taking id
                                                               and type parameter
        if (!foundItem) {
            foundItem = type.create({ id: id, isLoaded: false});
            Ember.get(type, 'collection').pushObject(foundItem);
        }
                                                      If object isn't loaded,
        return foundItem;        Returns found item or  creates new object and
    }                            item with only an id   sets id and isLoaded
});
```

Checks whether object of this type and id is already loaded

Pushes new object into identity map of this type

The code defines a new class type called Emberfest.Model. This is the top-level model type for your application, and it's not intended to be instantiated into an object directly. Next, you reopen the class definition to add the find() class method. You add this method inside reopenClass to avoid having to instantiate the class into an object. This is similar to static methods from other languages such as Java and .NET.

The find() function takes two parameters: an id and a type. The function calls the contentArrayContains() function to check whether an object of that type and ID already exists in the identity map. If so, you return that item directly; if not, you create a new object of the correct type. In this case, you create a new instance of the type you passed into the function. The only thing you know about the object at this point is the ID, because you passed this into the find() function. In addition to setting the ID of the newly created object, you also set its isLoaded property to false so that the rest of the application can see whether the object is fully loaded or created locally. Finally, you add the newly created object to the collection property by using pushObject.

Next, you'll implement the findAll() function to fetch the data from the server.

6.2.2 Returning all talks via the findAll() function

The findAll() function calls the server side to fetch data and load it into your cache. To fetch data, pass the function three parameters:

- A URL
- The data type that you expect to get in return
- The hash key that identifies the data retrieved from the server side

As you'll see later, you'll tell the `Emberfest.Talk.findAll()` function to fetch data through the /abstracts URL and get a collection of `Emberfest.Talk` objects in return.

The following listing shows the implementation of the `findAll()` function.

Listing 6.5   The `findAll()` function

```
findAll: function(url, type, key) {          ◁──┐ Takes URL, type, and        Fetches data
    var collection = this;                        key used to fetch data        from URL
    $.getJSON(url, function(data) {            ◁─                               passed in
        $.each(data[key], function(i, row) {   ◁──┤ Iterates over result from server
            var item = collection.contentArrayContains(row.id, type);   ◁─┐
            if (!item) {                                                   Checks whether
                item = type.create();                                     current
                Ember.get(type, 'collection').pushObject(item);           object exists
            }
            item.setProperties(row);          ◁──┐ Updates properties
            item.set('isLoaded', true);            on page object
        });
    });

    return Ember.get(type, 'collection');     ◁──┘ Returns collection
}
```

- **Takes URL, type, and key used to fetch data**
- **Fetches data from URL passed in**
- **Creates reference to object used from within callbacks**
- **Iterates over result from server**
- **If it doesn't exist, creates new object and pushes it to collection**
- **Checks whether current object exists**
- **Updates properties on page object**
- **Marks item as loaded**
- **Returns collection**

The `findAll()` function calls the server with the URL provided. Here, you use the jQuery `$.getJSON` call, passing in the URL as well as a callback that's executed when the server responds.

Once the JSON has been successfully retrieved from the server, use the key to get the data array and iterate over the contents of this array. Once inside the iteration, see if this object is already loaded into the hash. If it's not, create a new instance and push it into the `collection` property.

Next, pass the current row into the item's `setProperties()` function. This updates the item object and sets the properties retrieved from the server before setting the `isLoaded` property to `true`, telling the rest of the application that this model object has finished loading properly. Finally, return the entire collection to the calling function.

Now that you've implemented a generic strategy to fetch data from the server, it's time to look at the `Emberfest.Talk` class.

6.2.3   *Implementing the Emberfest.Talk model class*

Each talk in the Ember Fest application shares a set of common properties. These properties indicate the ID, title, content (`talkText`), related topics, type, the person who suggested the talk, and metadata that tells the Emberfest application whether this talk is suggested by the currently logged-in user.

The following listing shows the data for the talks as it's returned from the server.

Listing 6.6   The JSON retrieved from the server

```
{"abstracts": [          ◁──┤ Returns array of abstracts
    {                                        ◁──┤ Defines key values
```

- **Returns array of abstracts**
- **Defines key values**

```
"id": "05D5D5122DBA0C9E",
"talkTitle": "Query params …",
"talkText": "An introduction to Ember Query…",
"talkTopics": "querystring, router, pushState",
"talkType": "20 or 35 minute talk",
"talkByLoggedInUser": false,
"talkSuggestedBy": "Alex Speller"
        }
    ]
}
```

Uniquely identifies the talk in application (annotation pointing to the top lines)

Indicates simple string values (annotation pointing to the right)

As you would expect, the data format between the client and the server is standard JSON, with a list of talks specified as an array named `abstracts`.

Because you aren't implementing anything special in your model layer, the properties that Ember Fest receives from the server become real properties when the `Emberfest.Talk` model is instantiated by the `findAll()` function. It's the server side that mandates which properties are available to the Ember Fest application.

The data that the server returns is loaded into separate `Emberfest.Talk` models, as shown in the following listing. Because you're doing most of the work in the generic `Emberfest.Model` class, the implementation for the `Emberfest.Talk` model is quite simple.

Listing 6.7 The `Emberfest.Talk` model

```
Emberfest.Talk = Emberfest.Model.extend();        ◁── Creates model class

Emberfest.Talk.reopenClass({                       ◁── Reopens class definition to
    collection: Ember.A(),                              add find and findAll functions

    find: function(id) {              ◁── Fetches talk from cache
        return Emberfest.Model.find(id, Emberfest.Talk);
    },                                                ◁── Delegates call to
                                                          Emberfest.find, including
                                                          model type to get returned
    findAll: function() {
        return Emberfest.Model.findAll('/abstracts,
            Emberfest.Talk, 'abstract');              ◁── Delegates call to
    }                                                     Emberfest.Model; adds URL,
});                                                       model type, and name of hash
```

Initializes collection of pages (annotation pointing to `collection: Ember.A()`)

You define a new class called `Emberfest.Talk`, which extends from the `Emberfest.Model` class you defined previously (see listing 6.4). To add `find()` and `findAll()` as class methods, reopen the class by using the `reopenClass()` construct. To have one collection that's unique for each data type, initialize a `collection` variable. Here, for simplicity, you specify that the `collection` property is an Ember.js array by using `Ember.A()`.

The `find()` function takes a single parameter, which is the `id` element of the model you wish to find. You delegate to the `Emberfest.Model.find()` function, but you tell it the type of class that you expect to get in return from `Emberfest.Model.find()`.

The findAll() function is similar, only here you specify the URL, '/abstracts', that Emberfest.Model.findAll()fetches the data from, as well as the type you expect in return (Emberfest.Talk) and the name of the array in which you expect to find data for the pages ('abstracts').

Using this approach, it's easy to reuse the Emberfest.Model class for different model objects. The following listing shows the implementation of the Emberfest.User model.

Listing 6.8 The Emberfest.User model

```
Emberfest.User.reopenClass({
    collection: Ember.A(),

    find: function(id) {
        return Emberfest.Model.find(id, Emberfest.User);
    },

    findAll: function() {
        return Emberfest.Model.findAll('/user, Emberfest.User, 'users');
    }
});
```

Returns Emberfest.User objects ➙ (annotation pointing to find function)

Returns data based on specified URL, hash key, and object type ➙ (annotation pointing to findAll)

The talk and user model objects are quite similar, so it's easy to scale this approach out to support additional model objects that your application might need. You create a new EMBERFEST.YourModel class for each of the model objects that your application needs to support.

Because the model object implementations are so similar, you could take this one step further and standardize on the URL and hash keys, too.

Figure 6.4 shows the result of loading all talks from the server.

Figure 6.4 Showing all talks registered in the application in the talks.index route

Now that you've seen how you can create a strategy for fetching data, let's look at how to implement data persistence via `create` and `update`.

6.3 Persisting data

To allow users to submit new talk proposals to the Ember Fest application, you implement persisting of data. You extend the strategy you've created by adding a few extra features to your setup.

Because the keyword `create` is reserved for creating new objects in Ember.js, you implement persistence via the two methods `createRecord()` and `updateRecord()`.

6.3.1 Submitting a new talk via the createRecord() function

To create a new `Emberfest.Talk` object on the client side (as opposed to the server side), you use the `createRecord()` function. This function instantiates a new model object of the given type and serializes the model to JSON before it sends the data to the server via an Ajax call. The following listing shows the contents of `Emberfest .Model.createRecord()`.

Listing 6.9 Implementing the `createRecord()` function

```
Emberfest.Model.reopenClass({
    createRecord: function(url, type, model) {
        var collection = this;
        model.set('isSaving', true);
        $.ajax({
            type: "POST",
            url: url,
            data: JSON.stringify(model),
            success: function(res, status, xhr) {
                if (res.submitted) {
                    Ember.get(type, 'collection').pushObject(model);
                    model.set('isSaving', false);
                } else {
                    model.set('isError', true);
                }
            },
            error: function(xhr, status, err) {
                model.set('isError', true);
            }
        });
    },
});
```

Annotations:
- **Takes URL, type, and model to persist** → `createRecord: function(url, type, model) {`
- **Creates local variable you can refer to in Ajax callback** → `var collection = this;`
- **Indicates object is being saved** → `model.set('isSaving', true);`
- **Persists new model objects** → `$.ajax({` / `type: "POST",`
- **Sends model's string representation as data to server** → `data: JSON.stringify(model),`
- **Adds new talk to collection array and resets isSaving to false** → `Ember.get(type, 'collection').pushObject(model);` / `model.set('isSaving', false);`
- **If anything goes wrong, updates isError to true** → `model.set('isError', true);`

If you compare the `createRecord()` function to the `findAll()` function, you'll notice that they have quite a few similarities. The function gets a local reference to `this`, which you'll use later inside the Ajax callback. To indicate to the users that the model they're currently watching has been sent to the server but still awaiting a response, you set the model's `isSaving` property to `true` before you issue the call to the server. You're creating a new object, so you call the server by using the HTTP `POST` method. If the server responds with a successful response message, you push the newly created model onto the `collection` array and set the `isSaving` property back to `false`. If the Ajax call fails or the server responds with an unsuccessful response, you update the model's `isError` property to `false`.

After this abstract function is implemented on the `Emberfest.Model` class, you'll add a `createRecord()` function to the `Emberfest.Talk` class, which is the class that the Ember Fest application uses, similar to the `find()` and `findAll()` functions you added previously. The following listing shows the result of adding this function to the `Emberfest.Talk` class. The `createRecord` method takes a model object as its only input parameter and delegates to `Emberfest.Model`, adding the URL and the object type you're persisting.

Listing 6.10   Adding `createRecord` to `Emberfest.Talk`

```
Emberfest.Talk.reopenClass({
    collection: Ember.A(),

    find: function(id) {
        return Emberfest.Model.find(id, Emberfest.Talk);
    },

    findAll: function() {
        return Emberfest.Model.findAll('/abstracts',
            Emberfest.Talk, 'abstracts');
    },

    createRecord: function(model) {                      ⟵── Adds createRecord function
        Emberfest.Model.createRecord('/abstracts',
            Emberfest.Talk, model);
    }
});
```

You delegate the call down to the `Emberfest.Model` class. In addition to the model you're persisting, you also pass in the type of model you're persisting, as well as the URL that `Emberfest.Model.createRecord()` will call.

When users of the Ember Fest website submit a talk to the system, they navigate to the `registerTalk` route, where they're presented with a form in which they enter the details of their talk and submit it to the system. After the talk is submitted, the users are forwarded to the `talks.talk` route, where they can view all talks submitted to the system so far. Figure 6.5 shows the flow.

At this point, everything is set up for you to create a new talk and submit it to the server side. The following listing shows an excerpt from the `Emberfest.Register-TalkController.submitAbstract()` function that demonstrates how to use the newly created `createRecord()` function. You're expecting the validation of the user input to be `true`. For each failed validation, update `validated` to `false`.

Figure 6.5   Submitting a new talk

Listing 6.11   Using the `createRecord()` function

```
submitAbstract: function() {
    var validated = true;

    //Validation omitted from this listing

    if (validated) {
        var talkId = Math.uuid(16, 16);
        var talk = Emberfest.Talk.create({
            id: talkId,
            talkTitle: this.get('content.proposalTitle'),
            talkText: this.get('content.proposalText'),
            talkType: this.get('content.proposalType'),
            talkTopics: this.get('content.proposalTopics')
        });

        Emberfest.Talk.createRecord(talk);
        this.transitionToRoute('talks');
    }
}
```

If user input is validated, persists talk to server

Redirects user to talks route

Calls EMBERFEST.Talk.createRecord() to send model to server

After the user input has been validated, you create a new `Emberfest.Talk` model object and initialize it with the input from the user. To persist the talk to the server, call `Emberfest.Talk.createRecord(talk)`.

> **NOTE** Because you're dealing with user input, you must validate that the input adheres to the rules that you've defined for the system's talks/abstracts. The validation itself is omitted in this code listing but is available in the project's source code on GitHub.

After the proposed talk has been persisted, transition the user to the talks route to show the complete list of talks submitted to the system. Redirect the user to the talks route via the `transitionToRoute` function.

Next we'll look at the `updateRecord()` function.

6.3.2   *Updating a talk's data via the updateRecord() function*

The `updateRecord()` function is implemented in a similar style as the `create-Record()` function. The difference between them is that you don't add the model to the `collection` array, because it should already be there when you issue an update. The following listing shows the implementation of the `updateRecord()` function.

Listing 6.12   Implementing `updateRecord()` on `Emberfest.Model`

```
Emberfest.Model.reopenClass({
    updateRecord: function(url, type, model) {          Creates local variable to refer
        var collection = this;                          to within Ajax callback
        model.set('isSaving', true);
        console.log(JSON.stringify(model));
        $.ajax({                                        Uses HTTP PUT method for
            type: "PUT",                                updating new model object
            url: url,
            data: JSON.stringify(model),                Sends model's string
            success: function(res, status, xhr) {       representation as
                if (res.id) {                           data to server
                    model.set('isSaving', false);
                    model.setProperties(res);
                } else {
                    model.set('isError', true);
                }
            },                                           If anything goes
            error: function(xhr, status, err) {          wrong, updates
                model.set('isError', true);              isError to true
            }
        })
    }
});
```

- **Sets model's isSaving property to true**
- **If Ajax call is successful, resets isSaving back to false**
- **Updates model object with response from server**

The `updateRecord()` function has many similarities to the `createRecord()` function. The `updateRecord()`function first finds a local variable reference to `this`, which you'll use inside the Ajax callback. Because you want to tell the user that you've sent the request to the server but are awaiting a response, set the model's isSaving property to true before issuing the Ajax call.

The standard HTTP method to use for updating is PUT, so be sure to specify this method to the Ajax call. If the response from the server is successful and it contains the data of the updated model object, update the isSaving property by resetting it to false before updating the model via the setProperties() function.

If the Ajax call fails or the server doesn't return the updated model object, update the isError property to true to indicate to the rest of the application that something went wrong while updating the model on the server. This alerts the user that you were unable to persist the proposed talk.

Once this function is implemented on the EMBERFEST.Model class, add a function to the EMBERFEST.Talk class the way you did earlier with the createRecord() function, as shown in the following listing. The updateRecord() method takes a model object as its only input parameter and delegates to Emberfest.Model, adding the URL and the object type you're persisting.

Listing 6.13 Adding updateRecord() on Emberfest.Talk

```
Emberfest.Talk.reopenClass({
    collection: Ember.A(),

    find: function(id) {
        return EMBERFEST.Model.find(id, EMBERFEST.Talk);
    },

    findAll: function() {
        return EMBERFEST.Model.findAll('/abstracts', Emberfest.Talk,
     'abstracts');
    },

    createRecord: function(model) {
        EMBERFEST.Model.createRecord('/abstracts', Emberfest.Talk, model);
    },

    updateRecord: function(model) {
        EMBERFEST.Model.updateRecord("/abstracts", Emberfest.Talk, model);
    }
});
```

Here you're delegating the call down to the Emberfest.Model class. In addition to the model you're persisting, you also pass in the type of model you're persisting, as well as the URL Emberfest.Model.updateRecord() will call.

The users can edit a talk that they've submitted. Once inside the talks.talk route, they can click an edit button that will present a talk edit form. When the users update the talk, they are forwarded to the talks route, showing all the talks submitted to the application. Figure 6.5 shows the flow of this action.

Figure 6.6   Editing a talk

Figure 6.6 shows the process the user follows to edit the proposed talk.

At this point, everything should be ready for the user to update a talk and submit it to the server side. Listing 6.14 shows an excerpt from the `Emberfest.TalksTalkController`'s `submitTalk()` function that shows how you can use the newly created `Record()` function.

You expect the validation of the user input to be `true`. For each failed validation, update `validated` to `false`. If the user input is validated, persist the talk to the server. When the new `Emberfest.Talk` model is instantiated, call `Emberfest.Talk.updateRecord()` to send the model to the server.

Listing 6.14   Using the `updateRecord()` function

```
submitTalk: function() {
    var validated = true;                              ◁───  Indicates input
                                                             expected to be true
    //Omitting the validation from the code listing

                                                             If user input is validated,
    if (validated) {                                   ◁───  persists talk to server
        var talk = this.get('content');
        EMBERFEST.Talk.updateRecord(talk);
    }
```
Sends model to server ─▷ (points to `EMBERFEST.Talk.updateRecord(talk);`)

```
        this.transitionToRoute('talks');      ◁──┐  Redirects user
    }                                              │  to talks route
}
```

When the user input has been validated, you get the `content` property of the `Emberfest.TalksTalkController` (which contains a single `Emberfest.Talk` instance) and pass this along to `Emberfest.Talk.updateRecord()`.

> **NOTE** Again, because you're dealing with user input, you must validate that the input adheres to the rules you defined for the system's talks/abstracts. The validation itself is omitted from the code listing but is available in the project's source code on GitHub.

To display the complete list of talks submitted to the system, transition the user to the `talks` route via the `transitionToRoute()` function.

Now that you've seen how to create, update, and read data from the server, there's only one operation missing. The next section shows how to implement deletion.

6.3.3 *Deleting a talk via the delete () function*

The site administrator of the Ember Fest website can delete proposed talks. These could be talks that were submitted in error or any type of spam. The administrator is presented with a Delete button alongside the list of talks. When the Delete button is clicked, the Ember Fest application calls on the server to delete the talk.

Implementing deletion is similar to the functions you created previously in this chapter. You use the standard `HTTP DELETE` method when sending the Ajax call to the server, and you remove the deleted object from the collection array once the server has indicated that the item has been successfully deleted, as shown in the following listing.

Listing 6.15   Implementing `delete()` on `Emberfest.Model`

```
delete: function(url, type, id) {
    var collection = this;                     ◁──┐  Creates local variable you
    $.ajax({                                       │  can refer to in Ajax callback
        type: 'DELETE',                              ← Uses HTTP DELETE method
        url: url + "/" + id,                       ◁──┐  Formats URL, adds ID
        success: function(res, status, xhr) {         │  of deleted model
            if(res.deleted) {
                var item = collection.contentArrayContains(id, type);   ← Fetches object from collection array
                if (item) {
                    Ember.get(type, 'collection').removeObject(item);   ◁──┐  Removes deleted item
                }                                                            │  from collection array
            }
        },
        error: function(xhr, status, err) {
            alert('Unable to delete: ' + status + " :: " + err);   ← If anything goes wrong, displays alert to user
        }
    });
}
```

The `deleteRecord()` function has many similarities to the `updateRecord()` function. The function finds a local variable reference to `this`, which you use inside the Ajax callback.

The standard `HTTP` method to use for deletion is `DELETE`, so you'll specify this method to the Ajax call. If the response from the server is successful, fetch the item from the `collection` array and remove it. If the Ajax call fails, display an alert to the user.

After this function is implemented on the `Emberfest.Model` class, add a function to the `Emberfest.Talk` class as you did with the `updateRecord()` function. The following listing shows the result of adding this function to the `Emberfest.Talk` class. The `delete()` method takes a model `id` as its only input parameter and delegates to `Emberfest.Model`, adding the URL and the object type you're persisting.

Listing 6.16 Adding `delete()` on `Emberfest.Talk`

```
Emberfest.Talk.reopenClass({
    collection: Ember.A(),
                                              Delegates to Emberfest.Model,
                                                 adding URL and object type

    delete: function(id) {
        EMBERFEST.Model.delete('/abstracts', Emberfest.Talk, id);
    }
});
```

Here you're delegating the call down to the `Emberfest.Model` class. In addition to the model `id` you're deleting, you also pass in the type of model you're persisting, as well as the URL `Emberfest.Model.delete()` will call.

At this point, everything should be set up for an admin user to delete a talk and submit it to the server side. The following listing is an excerpt from the `Emberfest.TalksIndexController`'s `deleteTalk()` function that shows how to use the newly created `delete()` function.

Listing 6.17 Using the `delete()` function

```
deleteTalk: function(a) {
    Emberfest.Talk.delete(a.get('id'));        Deletes model
}
```

The `deleteTalk()` function responds to the user clicking a Delete button in the application. This action function gets the model object that the user clicked as its only parameter and it passes the `id` property of this model object along to `Emberfest.Talk.delete()`.

This concludes the implementation of the server-side communication for the Ember Fest website.

6.4 Summary

This chapter examined one strategy for creating Create, Read, Update, and Delete (CRUD) functionality in your Ember.js application. This approach is similar to the

CRUD operations of any rich web application, but it's adapted to fit into the Ember.js lifecycle. Because Ember.js might issue calls to the `find()` method before `findAll()`, depending on the route through which the user enters the application, it helps to implement an identity map inside the application to minimize the number of Ajax calls that you issue to the server.

You've also seen how to create and update models on the client side and how to issue Ajax calls to the server to persist them. The approach taken here will be familiar to you if you have experience with writing Ajax-bound web applications. The deletion of models is also similar to what you might expect.

In this chapter, you created a simple approach to data persistence. Many improvements could be made to this implementation to make it more robust and easier to use. But this approach does work well for smaller applications in which a large-scale framework such as Ember Data might bring in too much overhead. Overall, the chapter has gone through the expectations that Ember.js has for your data layer implementation. In addition, after implementing a model layer yourself, you should have a clearer understanding of where data layer frameworks such as Ember Data, Ember Persistence Framework, and Ember Model are coming from and what kind of scenarios they're built to solve.

In the next chapter, you'll look at how to create custom components for your application.

Writing custom components

This chapter covers

- An introduction to writing custom components
- Implementing a selectable-list component
- Implementing a tree-view component
- Integrating Ember.js with Twitter Bootstrap

The ability to write custom components is a key feature in most GUI frameworks because it allows you to build parts that can be reused in the same application as well as across applications. Most applications have components that share a similar functionality throughout. Features such as selectable lists, buttons that integrate with Twitter, and tree-based components are a few examples of situations in which implementing custom components can make sense in your application.

Ember.js's use of Handlebars.js templates, easy integration of third-party Java-Script libraries, and strong binding system make it an excellent framework for building custom components. This chapter presents a few of the custom components that have been written for the Montric project and discusses how they're structured to achieve different goals in your application. When combined, some of these components work together to form complex functionality. You'll structure

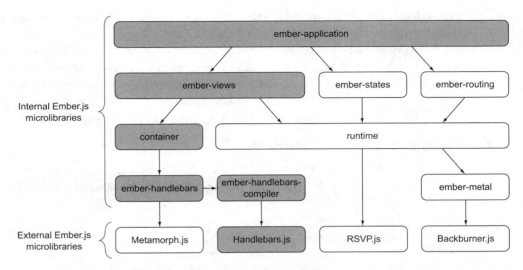

Figure 7.1 The parts of Ember.js you'll work on in this chapter

your components to be as small and specific as possible so that you can reuse them individually as well as combine them as building blocks to create components that are more complex.

Figure 7.1 shows the parts of the Ember.js ecosystem this chapter examines—ember-application, ember-views, container, ember-handlebars, ember-handlebars-compiler, and Handlebars.js.

You'll begin by creating a `selectable-list` component, which is similar to the selectable list you implemented in chapter 1 for the Notes application. This time, however, you'll split the functionality of the selectable list into three different self-contained components. Next, you'll learn how to create a hierarchical tree-based component in which the leaf nodes (the nodes without subnodes) are selectable via a check box.

7.1 About Ember custom components

The technical description of a component would be something along the lines of "an identifiable part of a larger program that provides a particular function or a group of related functions." You can think of a component as an independent part of your application that you can reuse in multiple places of your application without modification. If you do build your components generally enough, they may also serve a purpose outside of your initial application.

When Ember components were built in the later-release candidates of Ember.js, it consolidated a group of functions that would otherwise be directed at custom view, handlebars templates, and custom handlebars expressions. Now, your components generally consist of two items: a handlebars template and a component class. In fact, only a template is necessary for the simplest of components.

If you're used to large, server-side frameworks like JavaServer Faces or Microsoft ASP.NET MVC, you'll be surprised that your Ember.js custom components are built with relatively little code and with few moving parts. This is a true testament to the power that Ember.js provides you as a web developer!

Let's get started with your first custom component, the selectable list.

7.2   *Implementing a selectable list*

The `selectable-list` component works as a list from which the user can select an item. In addition to selecting an item, the user can delete an item via a handy Delete button.

The component displays a list of items, and each item appears in a separate row. The component, with no item selected, is shown in figure 7.2.

When the user clicks a row with the mouse, you want to highlight the selected row. The component with an item selected is shown in figure 7.3.

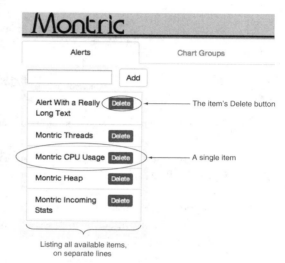

Figure 7.2   The resulting view of the `selectable-list` component with no item selected

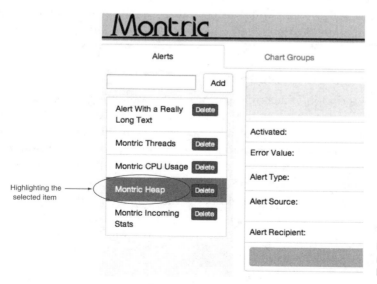

Figure 7.3   Selecting a row in the selectable list highlights the item.

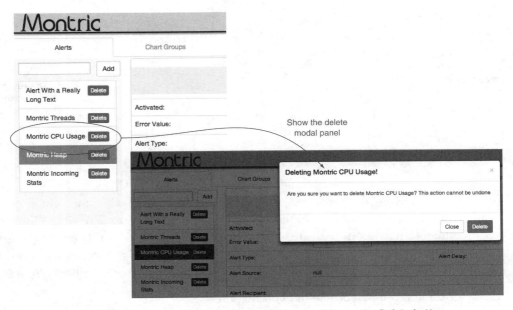

Figure 7.4 Showing the `delete-modal` panel when the user clicks on the Delete button

This component has one more part. When the user clicks the Delete button, you want to show a modal panel that prompts the user to confirm the deletion. The `delete-modal` panel is shown in figure 7.4.

As I mentioned previously, you build your components as small and specific as possible. In fact, the functionality that you've seen in the previous three figures consists of a total of three components:

- A `selectable-list` *component*—Displays the list of items from which the user can select and is rendered using Twitter Bootstrap's List Group CSS markup
- A `selectable-list-item` *component*—Displays each individual item in the list and is also rendered using Twitter Bootstrap's List Group CSS markup
- A `delete-modal` *component*—Displays the modal panel that prompts the user to confirm the item's deletion

Now that you have a clearer picture of the components you're building, you'll begin by implementing the `selectable-list` component. But before moving on, it's useful to review the Montric router definition in the following listing to note which route is involved.

Listing 7.1 The Montric router definition

```
Montric.Router.map(function () {
    this.resource("main", {path: "/"}, function () {
        this.resource("login", {path: "/login"}, function () {
```

```
        });
        this.route('charts');
        this.resource("admin", {path: "/admin"}, function() {
            this.resource('alerts', {path: "/alerts"}, function() {
                this.route('alert', {path: "/:alert_id"});
            });
            this.route('chartGroups');
            this.route('mainMenu');
            this.route('accessTokens');
            this.route('accounts');
            this.route('alertRecipients');
        });
    });
});
```

The route we will add a selectable-list to

The route we want to transition into from selectable-list

You add your `selectable-list` component to the `alerts` route, which means that you add it to the alerts.hbs file. When the user selects a node from the list (an alert), the user transitions to the `alerts.alert` route. The URL is updated, allowing the user to bookmark and get direct access to a selected alert. Now that you know where your component will be used inside your application, you can begin the implementation.

7.2.1 Defining the selectable-list component

An initial implementation of the `selectable-list` component is shown in the following listing.

Listing 7.2   The components/selectable-list template

```
<div class="list-group mediumTopPadding" style="width: 95%;">
    {{#each node in nodes}}
        <div class="list-group-item">{{node.id}}</div>
    {{/each}}
</div>
```

Prints list of node ids

Creates list-group div element

Renders selectable-list-item component for each node

The first thing to notice in this listing is the path and the name of the template. Any components must start with components/. In addition, the name of the component must contain a dash (-) character.

Why the strange naming requirement?

The use of the dash has a logical explanation. To prevent a name clash with the future and final WebComponents specification (to be ratified by the TC39), the Ember.js team decided to require that Ember.js components contain a dash in their names.

You may have noticed that the code in this listing looks like a standard Handlebars.js template, and you're absolutely right. This is one of the key strengths of Ember components. But, whereas a standard Handlebars.js template is backed by an Ember.js view that has access to the current context in the application (like the controller and the route), a component can be considered a special kind of view that has no access to the context in which it lives. Ember.js won't inject the current controller into a component. This is what helps make Ember components behave like standalone, complete pieces of reusable functionality.

Currently, your component doesn't do much other than iterate over each of the elements in the node property and print out each node's id property. But let's examine how to use this brand-new component in your application. When your application initializes, Ember.js finds all components in the components/directive and sets up custom Handlebars.js expressions for them. In this case, the component is accessible via the {{selectable-list}} expression, as shown in the next listing for your component from the alerts.hbs file.

Listing 7.3   Using the `{{selectable-list}}` component

```
{{selectable-list nodes=controller.model}}
```
⊲ **Using our component from the alerts.hbs file**

That was easy enough. To use your selectable-list component, use the {{selectable-list}} Handlebars.js expression. But because the component won't have access to the current context, you need to pass any data to it manually. In this example, you pass the controller's model property to the component's nodes property. That's all you need to create a component.

You've implemented the first part of your component, and you can now list each of your nodes. Figure 7.5 shows your progress so far.

Next up, you'll add the functionality to select an item in the list and transition from the alerts route to the alerts.alert route.

Figure 7.5   Listing each of the alerts registered for the logged-in account

7.2.2   *The selectable-list-item component*

To separate the concerns between the selectable list and each of the items in the list, create a new component whose sole responsibility is to render a single list item. The following listing shows the updated selectable-list component template.

Listing 7.4   Selecting a node and transitioning to the `alerts.alert` route

```
<div class="list-group mediumTopPadding" style="width: 95%;">
    {{#each node in nodes}}
        {{#if linkTo}}
            {{#linkTo linkTo node tagName=div
                classNames="list-group-item"}}
                {{selectable-list-item node=node action="showDeleteModal"
```

Links to route specified by linkTo and makes link a div element

Checks whether linkTo property is defined

```
                    param=node textWidth=textWidth}}
              {{/linkTo}}
          {{/if}}
      {{/each}}
</div>
```

Prints each node via
selectable-list-item

This `selectable-list` component template has a few new concepts. First, if the component has a `linkTo` property, you want to link to the route that this property specifies. You use the standard `{{#linkTo}}` Handlebars.js expression to achieve this. In addition, you use the `{{#linkTo}}` expression's `tagName` property to specify that you want the link to be rendered as a `div` element and the `classNames` property to specify the Twitter Bootstrap `list-group-item` CSS property.

The most important point is that you've moved the rendering of each of the nodes to a second component named selectable-list-item. The reason for this will become apparent soon, but let's go ahead and look at the implementation of this component template. The following listing shows the `selectable-list-item` template code.

Listing 7.5   The `components/selectable-list-item` component

```
<div {{bind-attr width=textWidth}} {{bind-attr maxWidht=textWidth}}>
   {{node.id}}
</div>
```

Prints id

Adds div element with
attributes width and maxWidth

You print out a `div` element with the attributes `width` and `maxWidth` set, and you print out the `id` property of the `node` element.

For your component to work as intended, you need to tell the `selectable-list` component the width of the text inside the component as well as which route to link to, as shown in the next listing.

Listing 7.6   Adding `linkTo` and `textWidth` properties to the `selectable-list` component

```
{{selectable-list nodes=controller.model textWidth=75
  linkTo="alerts.alert"}}
```

Adding linkTo and
textWidth properties

After you add these two new properties, you can click an item in the list to select it. When an item is selected, the user transitions to the `alerts.alert` route and the application displays the selected alert at the right of the selectable list.

Figure 7.6 shows the progress so far.

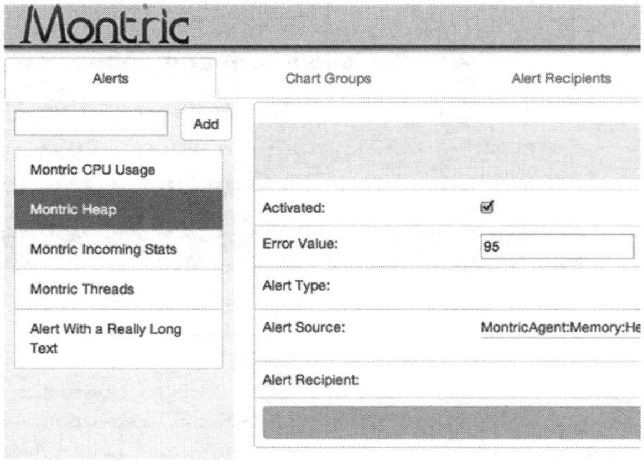

Figure 7.6   Selecting an item to transition to the `alerts.alert` route

You've created a component that has no actions added to it. Next, you'll add a Delete button to your `selectable-list-item` component that you can click to delete the item. To achieve this, you create a new component called `delete-modal`.

7.2.3 *The delete-modal component*

The `delete-modal` component is responsible for showing a Twitter Bootstrap modal panel. This panel prompts users to confirm that they're interested in deleting the node. As you would expect, the modal panel has two buttons; the Close button cancels the deletion, and the Confirm button confirms the deletion.

The `delete-modal` component template is shown in the following listing.

Listing 7.7 The `delete-modal` component template

```
<div class="modal-dialog">
    <div class="modal-content">
        <div class="modal-header">
            <button type="button" class="close" data-dismiss="modal"
                aria-hidden="true">&times;</button>
            <h4 class="modal-title">Deleting {{item.id}}!</h4>
        </div>
        <div class="modal-body">
            <p>Are you sure you want to delete {{item.id}}?
                This action cannot be undone</p>
        </div>
        <div class="modal-footer">
            <button type="button" class="btn btn-default"
                data-dismiss="modal">Close</button>
            <button type="button" class="btn btn-danger"
                {{action "deleteItem"}}>Delete</button>
        </div>
    </div><!-- /.modal-content -->
</div><!-- /.modal-dialog -->
```

Displays id of item being deleted in header of modal panel

Displays id of item being deleted in body of modal panel

Adds Close button to cancel deletion

Adds Delete button to confirm deletion

Most of the code here is standard Twitter Bootstrap code. If you're unfamiliar with the structure presented here, head over to the Twitter Bootstrap project website to get an explanation of the HTML markup.

> **NOTE** Twitter Bootstrap is a common GUI library found on many websites across the world. You can read more or download Bootstrap at the project's website, http://getbootstrap.com

The `delete-modal` component has one property named `item` that triggers the action `deleteItem` when the user clicks the Delete button. But because the component won't have access to the outer context that it's part of, you may be wondering where you can catch this action to perform the deletion.

For each of your component templates, Ember.js automatically instantiates a default `Component` object for you. To catch the `deleteItem` action, you need to override the default `DeleteModalComponent` class. The code for the `Montric.Delete-ModalComponent` is shown in the following listing.

Listing 7.8   The `Montric.DeleteModalComponent` class

Adds Twitter Bootstrap modal and fade CSS class names

Called when user clicks Delete button

Closes modal panel

Creates new DeleteModalComponent that extends Ember.Component

Implements action's hash to catch deleteItem action

Deletes record via Ember Data

If item is defined, deletes it

```
Montric.DeleteModalComponent = Ember.Component.extend({
    classNames: ["modal", "fade"],

    actions: {
        deleteItem: function() {
            var item = this.get('item');
            if (item) {
                item.deleteRecord();
                item.save();
                $("#" + this.get('elementId')).modal('hide');
            }
        }
    }
});
```

The `Component` class follows the naming convention you've become accustomed to in Ember.js. The name of the class is the same as the component template, but each of the dashes in the template name is removed. The name is then camelized, and the string "`Component`" is added to the end of the name. It's also important to note that any component extends the `Ember.Component` class, which ensures that the component won't get passed in the outer scope from the application.

After the component class is created, you can catch the component action as you would inside a controller or a route via the action's hash. Here, you implement a function named `deleteItem` that's triggered whenever the Delete button is clicked and the `deleteItem` action is fired. Inside the `deleteItem` function, you ensure that the component has an `item` property and that it contains a non-null value before deleting it. After the item is deleted, you close the modal panel.

To wrap up the functionality of your three components, you still need to complete the following:

- Add a Delete button to the `selectable-list-item` component template
- Tell the `delete-modal` component which item to delete

7.2.4   Deleting an item using the three components

Before you can delete an alert from Montric, you need to add a Delete button to the `selectable-list-item` component template. The updated template is shown in the following listing.

Listing 7.9   Adding a Delete button to the `selectable-list-item` component template

```
<button class="…" {{action "showDeleteModal"}}>Delete</button>
<div {{bind-attr width=textWidth}} {{bind-attr maxWidht=textWidth}}>
    {{node.id}}
</div>
```

Adds Delete button

You've added an action to the `selectable-list-item` component template. Now you need to create a `Montric.SelectableListItemComponent`, as shown in the following listing.

Listing 7.10 The `Montric.SelectableListItemComponent`

```
                                                          Creates new SelectableListItemComponent,
                                                               extending Ember.Component
Montric.SelectableListItemComponent = Ember.Component.extend({       ◄──
    actions: {
        showDeleteModal: function() {          ◄──   Implements showDeleteModal action
            $('#deleteAlertModal').modal('show');      ◄──┐  Shows modal
            this.sendAction('action', this.get(node));    │  panel
        }
    }
});
```

Implements action's hash to catch any actions the component fires → `actions: {`

Sends action with context → `this.sendAction('action', this.get(node));`

The code for this component is similar to the delete-modal component, but one important concept has been added. Notice that you get the `node` property and pass that to the `this.sendAction()` function. The `sendAction()` function is how a component sends actions out of the component and to the outside application. You use this so the `selectable-list-item` component can send an action to the outside application. Because the `selectable-list-item` component is defined inside the `selectable-list` component, this is where your action is sent. But before you can catch the `showDeleteModal` action in the `selectable-list` component, you need to update the `selectable-list` template slightly. The updated template is shown in the following listing.

Listing 7.11 The updated `selectable-list` component template

```
<div class="list-group mediumTopPadding" style="width: 95%;">
    {{#each node in nodes}}
        {{#if linkTo}}
            {{#linkTo linkTo node tagName=div
              classNames="list-group-item"}}
                {{selectable-list-item node=node action="showDeleteModal"
                  textWidth=textWidth}}
            {{/linkTo}}
        {{/if}}

    {{/each}}
</div>

{{delete-modal id="deleteAlertModal" item=nodeForDelete}}
```

Adds action to selectable-list-item expression → `{{selectable-list-item node=node action="showDeleteModal"`

Adds delete-modal expression to selectable-list component → `{{delete-modal id="deleteAlertModal" item=nodeForDelete}}`

You've added two new things to the `selectable-list` component template: an action property to the `selectable-list-item` expression and a `delete-modal` expression that renders the `delete-modal` panel.

Inside the `action` property, you refer to the action that the `selectable-list-item` fires whenever the `sendAction('action')` function is called in that component.

Note that you give the `delete-modal` an `id` as well as an `item`. You haven't seen the `nodeForDelete` property yet, but when you implement the action `showDeleteModal` for the `selectable-list` component, you'll see where this property comes from. The following listing shows the new `Montric.SelectableListComponent`.

Listing 7.12   The `Montric.SelectableListComponent`

```
Montric.SelectableListComponent = Ember.Component.extend({        ◁  Creates SelectableListComponent
    nodeForDelete: null,                                              that extends Ember.Component

    actions: {                         Implements action's
        showDeleteModal: function(node) {       ◁  Passes node selected by user
            if (node) {
                this.set('nodeForDelete', node);   ◁  Assigns node to component's
            }                                          nodeForDelete property
        }
    }
});
```

Implements action's hash to catch any actions the component fires

You now see where the `nodeForDelete` property comes from. Whenever the user clicks the Delete button of a node, the `selectable-list-item`'s `showDeleteModal` action is triggered. This, in turn, fires the `showDeleteModal` action on the `selectable-list` component, setting the node the user wanted to delete in the `selectable-list` component's `nodeForDelete` property. Because the `nodeForDelete` property is

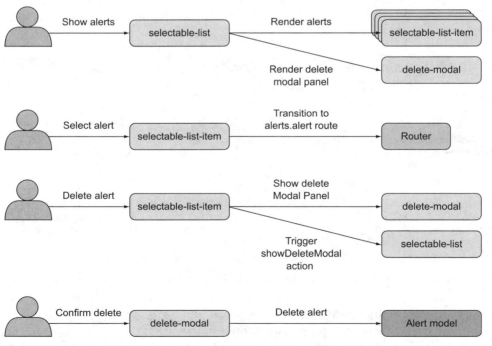

Figure 7.7   An overview of the three components, their relationships, and actions triggered

passed in and bound to the `delete-modal` component's `item` property, the modal panel can show the user which item will be deleted when the Delete button is clicked. The `deleteItem` action of the `delete-modal` component deletes the item and closes the modal panel.

This is a good time to recap what you've implemented. Figure 7.7 shows the relationships and the actions that are called for each of your three components.

Now that you've seen how to create three components and combine them to create complex functionality, let's see how you can implement a hierarchical component.

7.3 *Implementing a tree menu*

Implementing a hierarchical component is slightly more complex than the list example you created. When finished, your tree menu will have the following functionality:

- The ability to expand and collapse nodes that have children so you can navigate in the hierarchical structure
- Indentation at each level to visually indicate the hierarchical structure
- A disclosure triangle at each node to visually indicate whether the node is expanded or collapsed
- The ability to support a single selection or multiple selections from the menu
- The ability to add an icon to the leaf nodes

Figure 7.8 shows how the tree structure looks.

In this section, you'll look at the data model used for the tree model as well as the components required for the tree model to render and function properly.

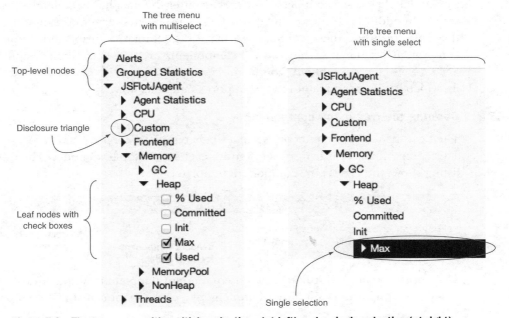

Figure 7.8   The tree menu with multiple selections (at left) and a single selection (at right)

7.3.1   *The tree-menu data model*

Before you get going on the code that makes up the tree menu, let's look at the underlying data model that the component uses, as shown in the next listing.

Listing 7.13   The tree-menu data model

```
Montric.MainMenuModel = DS.Model.extend({
    name: DS.attr('string'),
    nodeType: DS.attr('string'),
    parent: DS.belongsTo('mainMenu'),
    children: DS.hasMany('mainMenu'),
    chart: DS.belongsTo('chart'),

    isSelected: false,
    isExpanded: false,

    hasChildren: function() {
        return this.get('children').get('length') > 0;
    }.property('children'),

    isLeaf: function() {
        return this.get('children').get('length') == 0;
    }.property('children')
});
```

- ◁ Based on Ember Data model object
- Single parent, with one-to-one binding
- ◁ Zero or more children, with one-to-many binding
- Used internally in tree menu
- Helper property for template

You use an Ember Data model object as the data model you send to the `tree-menu` component. A few things are important in the model. First, the server sets up the links between the nodes via the `parent` and `children` properties. Ember Data ensures that the model objects are connected as expected after the data has been loaded from the server. In addition, you've defined two helper properties, `hasChildren` and `isLeaf`, that you use inside the component to make the template shorter and simpler. The component is built up from two subcomponents, a `tree-menu` component and a `tree-menu-item` component. You begin by implementing the multiselect functionality, which you'll extend later to also support single selection.

7.3.2   *Defining the tree-menu component*

The `tree-menu` component consists of a single template, `components/tree-menu.hbs`. This component's only feature is to render each of the top-level nodes. The following listing shows the `tree-menu` component template.

Listing 7.14   The `components/tree-menu.hbs` component template

```
{{#each node in rootNodes}}
    {{tree-menu-node node=node}}
{{/each}}
```

- ◁ Renders component for each node
- ◁ Iterates over each root node

The implementation of the tree-menu component template is simple and should be self-explanatory. You don't have to implement a component class for this component because, for now, no actions are triggered; the default implementation that Ember.js provides is sufficient.

With that out of the way, let's move on to the tree-menu-item component.

7.3.3 Defining the tree-menu-item and tree-menu-node components

The tree-menu-item component is a bit more complex because it needs to support the rendering of the correct disclosure triangle as well as set both the isExpanded and isSelected properties of the node it's representing. The following listing shows the tree-menu-item component template.

Listing 7.15 The components/tree-menu-item.hbs component template

```
{{#if node.hasChildren}}
    {{#if node.isExpanded}}
        <span class="downarrow" {{action "toggleExpanded"}}></span>
    {{else}}
        <span class="rightarrow" {{action "toggleExpanded"}}></span>
    {{/if}}

    <span {{action "toggleExpanded"}}>{{node.name}}</span>
{{else}}
    {{view Ember.Checkbox checkedBinding="node.isSelected"}}

    <span {{action "toggleSelected"}}>{{node.name}}</span>
{{/if}}

{{#if node.isExpanded}}
    {{#each child in node.children}}
        <div style="margin-left: 22px;">
            {{tree-menu-node node=child}}
        </div>
    {{/each}}
{{/if}}
```

Annotations:
- **Renders right-pointing disclosure triangle (collapsed)**
- **Renders down-pointing disclosure triangle (expanded)**
- **Fires toggleExpanded**
- **Renders selectable check box, binds checked property to isSelected property, and fires toggleSelected**
- **Renders each node child as new tree-menu-item component with left-margin space added**

This component template has a lot going on. You fire two actions, toggleExpanded and toggleSelected, and you therefore need to override the default Montric .TreeMenuNodeComponent to catch these actions (see listing 7.16).

Next, you check whether the node has children. If so, you render a disclosure triangle and the name of the node. Both the disclosure triangle and the node name are clickable and fire the toggleExpanded action.

If the node doesn't have children, the node is a leaf node and may be selected by the user. In this case, you render a check box and the name of the node. Both the check box and the name of the node are clickable and fire the toggleSelected action.

A node is expanded if the isExpanded property is true. You need to render the node's children in a similar manner. You iterate over each of the nodes in the children property and render them as new tree-menu-item components. This is what makes the component hierarchical in nature.

Let's take a look at the component's class definition. The following listing shows the `Montric.TreeMenuNodeComponent`.

Listing 7.16   The `Montric.TreeMenuNodeComponent` class

```
Montric.TreeMenuNodeComponent = Ember.Component.extend({          ◁─────────┐
    classNames: ['pointer'],                            Creates SelectableListComponent
                                                         that extends Ember.Component
    actions: {                                 ◁─
        toggleExpanded: function() {                     Implements action's
            this.toggleProperty('node.isExpanded');      hash to catch any actions
        },                                               the component fires

        toggleSelected: function() {           ◁─     Implements
            this.toggleProperty('node.isSelected');    toggleSelected action
        }
    }
});
```

(Implements toggleExpanded action — annotation pointing to the toggleExpanded function)

The implementation of the `TreeMenuNodeComponent` should be familiar to you. As you've seen before, you implement the action's hash, which contains functions for each of the actions that you want to catch. The `toggleExpanded` function does what it advertises and toggles the node's `isExpanded` property between `true` and `false`. Similarly, `toggleSelected` toggles the node's `isSelected` property between `true` and `false`. Now that you have the component working for multiselection, you can build in the single-selection functionality.

7.3.4   *Supporting single selections*

You've now implemented the necessary functionality for a multiselect tree component. Figure 7.9 shows the progress and the component structure so far.

To support single selection, you first need to add a flag that tells the component whether you want to allow multiple selections or only a single selection. You also need to make sure that this property (`allowMultipleSelections`) gets passed down to the `tree-menu-node` component. Although you could rely on simply toggling the underlying model's `isSelected` property when you implemented multiple selections, in the case of single selections, you want the component to assign the selected item to the property that you assign to the `tree-menu` component's `selectedNode` property. As with the `allowMultipleSelection` property, you need to send the `selectedNode` property down to each of the `tree-menu-node` components as well. The following listing shows the updated `tree-menu` component template.

Listing 7.17   The updated `components/tree-menu.hbs` component template

```
{{#each node in rootNodes}}
    {{tree-menu-node node=node
      allowMultipleSelections=allowMultipleSelections action="selectNode"
      selectedNode=selectedNode}}          ◁─     Passes two new properties and an action
{{/each}}                                           to the tree-menu-node component
```

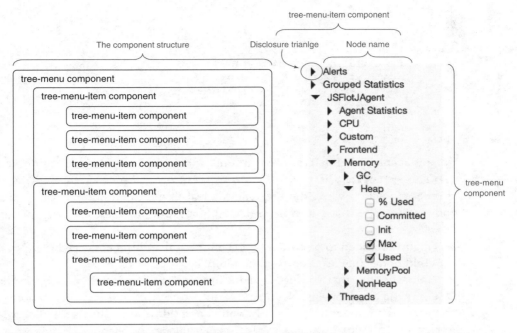

Figure 7.9 The relationships between the `tree-menu` components

You pass the `allowMultipleSelections` and `selectedNode` properties to the tree-menu-item component. In addition, you tell the `tree-menu-item` component that you expect that the `selectNode` action may be fired from the `tree-menu` component.

Next, you need to update the `tree-menu-node` component template to make use of these new properties. The following listing shows the updated component template.

Listing 7.18 The updated `components/tree-menu-node.hbs` component template

```
{{#if node.hasChildren}}
    {{#if node.isExpanded}}
        <span class="downarrow" {{action "toggleExpanded"}}></span>
    {{else}}
        <span class="rightarrow" {{action "toggleExpanded"}}></span>
    {{/if}}

    <span {{action "toggleExpanded"}}>{{node.name}}</span>
{{else}}
    {{#if allowMultipleSelections}}
        {{view Ember.Checkbox checkedBinding="node.isSelected"}}

        <span {{action "toggleSelected"}}>{{node.name}}</span>
    {{else}}
        <span {{action "selectNode" node}}
          {{bind-attr class=isSelected}}>{{node.name}}</span>
```

Annotations:
- If multiple selections allowed, continues as before
- If only single selection allowed, doesn't render check box
- When user clicks leaf node, fires selectNode action

```
        {{/if}}
    {{/if}}

    {{#if node.isExpanded}}                                    Passes selectedNode
        {{#each child in node.children}}                     property and selectNode
            <div style="margin-left: 22px;">                  action to child nodes
                {{tree-menu-node node=child
                  action="selectNode" selectedNode=selectedNode}}    ◁─────┐
            </div>
        {{/each}}
    {{/if}}
```

You add a check that makes sure you render the template as before whenever `allow-MultipleSelections` is true. If `allowMultipleSelections` is false, you fire the `selectNode` action when the user clicks a leaf node. In addition, if the current leaf node is the node that's currently selected, mark that node as blue by appending the CSS class `is-selected`.

Finally, you need to pass the `selectNode` action and the `selectedNode` property to any child nodes that are shown in the template.

Note, though, that you now need a function named `isSelected` in the `Montric.TreeMenuNodeComponent` class, and you catch the `selectNode` action in the `tree-menu` component. To do this, you'll override the default `Montric.TreeMenu-Component` and expand the `Montric.TreeMenuNodeComponent`. The following listing shows the updated `Montric.TreeMenuNodeComponent`.

Listing 7.19 The updated `Montric.TreeMenuNodeComponent`

```
Montric.TreeMenuNodeComponent = Ember.Component.extend({
    classNames: ['pointer'],

    actions: {
        toggleExpanded: function() {
            this.toggleProperty('node.isExpanded');
        },

        toggleSelected: function() {
            this.toggleProperty('node.isSelected');
        },
                                                    Fires action out
        selectNode: function(node) {          ◁───  of component
            this.sendAction('action', node);
        }
    },
                                                    Returns boolean indicating
    isSelected: function() {                  ◁───  if node is selected node
        return this.get('selectedNode') === this.get('node.id');
    }.property('selectedNode', 'node.id')
});
```

So far, so good. You haven't added any code you haven't seen before, so let's move on to the new `Montric.TreeMenuComponent` definition, shown in the following listing.

Listing 7.20 The new `Montric.TreeMenuComponent`

Implements
hash to catch
any actions the
component fires

Takes node
selected by
user as input

```
Montric.TreeMenuComponent = Ember.Component.extend({
    classNames: ['selectableList'],

    actions: {
        selectNode: function(node) {
            this.set('selectedNode', node.get('id'));
        }
    }
});
```

Creates TreeMenuComponent
that extends Ember.Component

Updates selectedNode
property with id of
node selected by user

Here, you catch the `selectNode` action, which receives as input the node that the user clicked. You then assign that node's id to the `selectedNode` property. This property is bound to the value that you gave the `tree-menu` component when you created it, so you can update the user interface directly to tell the user which node is selected.

The only thing left is to add the updated `tree-menu` component to the `alert.hbs` template. The following code shows how you can update the Handlebars.js expression to specify single-node selection and to map the selected node to the `alertSource` property on the currently selected Alert model:

Listing 7.21 Updating the `tree-model` Handlebars.js expression

```
{{tree-menu rootNodes=controllers.admin.rootNodes
  allowMultipleSelections=false selectedNode=alertSource}}
```

Specifying single-node selection, while mapping
the selected node to the alertSource property
on the currently selected Alert model

Figure 7.10 shows the `single-selection` tree menu in action.

You've now implemented a single `tree-menu` component that specifies whether the user can select only a single node or multiple nodes. If the user can select multiple items, then when the user selects an item, that item's `isSelected` property is set to `true`. If the user can select only a single item, then the selected item will be assigned to the `selectedNode` property that the user passed in to the `tree-menu` component.

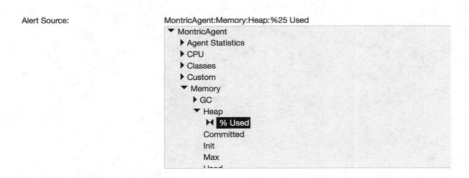

Figure 7.10 The updated `single-selection` tree menu

7.4 *Summary*

The ability to write customized and specialized components that you can easily use in multiple places in your application is an important feature of any front-end framework. The fact that Ember.js makes it easy to include almost any third-party widget library, combined with the ability to use the standard Handlebars.js template functionality, makes Ember.js a suitable framework for writing both simple and complex standalone components that encapsulate the logic and templates that are required.

This chapter has shown how you can create standalone custom components that are built with views and templates, as well as custom components that use the third-party front-end library Twitter Bootstrap. You created both list and tree components and saw how it's trivial to implement simple custom components that use both the Bootstrap CSS class specifications and Bootstrap's jQuery plugins.

In addition, you saw how it's possible, with a few lines of code, to customize a component to transition the user from one route to another in your application. I hope you've seen how powerful and helpful it is to define custom components, not as part of the overall context into which they're placed, but rather as pieces of functionality that can be reused in multiple places both across your application and across multiple applications.

In the next chapter, you'll look at how you can test your application to ensure that you're building the functionality that you intended, while also ensuring that future changes don't break existing functionality.

Testing your Ember.js
application

This chapter covers

- Testing strategies for JavaScript applications
- Using QUnit and PhantomJS for unit and integration testing
- Combining these tools for a complete testing strategy
- Exploring integration testing
- Using Ember Instrumentation for quick performance measurements

Even though JavaScript has matured significantly over the past five years, in a couple of areas you'll notice that you're working with a project that still has some maturing to do. Testing is one of these areas, leaving a lot of the required decisions up to application developers. This chapter outlines how you can successfully test your own Ember.js applications and presents a real-world implementation of one possible test harness.

As with applications written in other languages, you can test your application in multiple ways, including these:

- Unit testing
- Integration testing

161

- Performance testing
- Regression testing
- Black-box testing
- Continuous integration (CI)

You might not need to implement a solution for all of these testing types in your own application. Chances are, though, that you'll need several, even though unit testing and integration testing are the most common types of test harnesses for JavaScript applications.

Depending on what other languages and tools you have previous experience with, you may also find your JavaScript test harnesses to be significantly more involved and specialized for your application and your environment than what you are used to. The tools available to perform JavaScript testing are rather young. In addition, JavaScript has changed so rapidly from a scripting language to a full-featured application framework that building standardized tools to perform testing in this environment is all the more difficult.

That said, there's definitely a light at the end of the tunnel, and we're seeing an increased focus on good testing tools for JavaScript applications.

This chapter presents a complete testing strategy. Throughout the chapter, you'll see examples taken from the Montric project. Specifically, you'll use QUnit and PhantomJS, and you'll see one possible way to integrate these tools to perform both unit testing and integration testing. You'll learn how to use PhantomJS to execute your tests in headless mode, meaning that both the test and the code execute in an environment without requiring a browser. Finally, you'll see how to use Ember Instrumentation to gain quick insight into the performance of your Ember.js application.

Figure 8.1 shows the parts of the Ember.js ecosystem that this chapter examines.

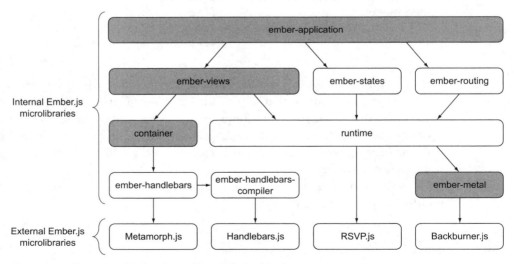

Figure 8.1 The parts of Ember.js you'll work on in this chapter

8.1 *Performing unit testing with QUnit and PhantomJS*

As your application grows and the number of developers working on your project increases, having a logical, sane, and reproducible set of unit tests becomes vital for the continued development of your product. This section shows how QUnit and PhantomJS can be combined to both write and execute your project's unit tests. Before you start writing a real test for the Montric application, you need a clear understanding of these tools and how to use them.

> **NOTE** Download QUnit from http://qunitjs.com, and PhantomJS from http://phantomjs.org. PhantomJS must be installed on your system before you can use it.

The first type of test that you'll likely want to set up is a unit test, so we'll start by looking more closely at QUnit.

8.1.1 *Introduction to QUnit*

QUnit is a framework that lets you write a unit test for your application. QUnit is used by jQuery, jQuery UI, and jQuery Mobile, among others. In fact, the unit tests for the Ember.js framework are mostly written in QUnit.

> **NOTE** Because running tests that require a browser makes testing in a continuous integration (CI) environment particularly difficult, you'll use PhantomJS to execute the tests in headless mode. PhantomJS allows you to run tests without a browser, so structuring your tests to work with PhantomJS makes testing in a CI environment easier to set up.

To verify that QUnit is set up and working properly, you'll create a small unit test. To get started, download the QUnit JavaScript file as well as the QUnit CSS file from the QUnit website, http://qunitjs.com. Create a new HTML file named firstTest.html, which bootstraps QUnit and enables you to execute tests. Place firstTest.html in a new directory on your hard drive. The content of firstTest.html is shown in the following listing.

Listing 8.1   Your first QUnit test

```
<!DOCTYPE html PUBLIC "-//W3C//DTD HTML 4.01//EN"
    "http://www.w3.org/TR/html4/strict.dtd">

<html lang="en">
<head>
    <title>First Test</title>
    <link rel="stylesheet" href="qunit-1.11.0.css" type="text/css"
    charset="utf-8">
    <script src="qunit-1.11.0.js" type="text/javascript" charset="utf-8"></
    script>

</head>
<body bgcolor="#ffffff">
    <div id="qunit" style="z-index: 100;"></div>
```

Includes QUnit CSS file in header of page

Includes QUnit JavaScript file in header of page

Creates div with id qunit in body tag

```
    <script type="text/javascript" charset="utf-8" src="firstTest.js"></
        script>
</body>                                                            ◁
</html>
```
Specifies test to run

As you can see, QUnit uses an HTML page to set up the test. Inside this page, you need to include both the QUnit CSS and JavaScript files along with a `div` element that QUnit uses to display the test results. All the tests that you want to run via the same HTML file need to be specified inside the `body` tag of your HTML page.

> **NOTE**   The HTML page expects to find both the QUnit CSS and JavaScript files in the same directory. If this isn't the case, change this HTML page accordingly.

Next, you need to provide an implementation for the firstTest.js file. You'll create a test that verifies that the integer value of 1 is equal to the string value of `"1"`. The full test script for the firstTest.js file is shown in the following listing.

Listing 8.2   Creating a simple unit test

```
test("Test that QUnit is working as expected", function() {      ◁
    ok( 1 == "1", "QUnit Test Passed!" );   ◁
});
```
Adds assertion as test   **Provides name and callback function**

As you can see, each test is specified in the QUnit `test()` function. The first argument to the `test()` function is the name of your test, and the second argument is a callback function that includes this test's assertions. QUnit uses the name of your test when it reports back the test execution results.

Any assertions that the test requires are created inside the callback function and passed in as parameter 2 to the `test()` function. In this case, you're testing whether the integer value of 1 is the same as the string value of `"1"`, which, in the land of JavaScript, it strangely is.

To execute this test, drag and drop the firstTest.html file into the browser of your choice. This leads to a similar result as shown in figure 8.2.

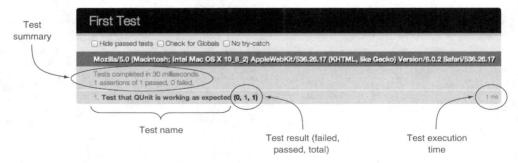

Test summary

First Test

☐ Hide passed tests ☐ Check for Globals ☐ No try-catch

Mozilla/5.0 (Macintosh; Intel Mac OS X 10_8_2) AppleWebKit/536.26.17 (KHTML, like Gecko) Version/6.0.2 Safari/536.26.17

Tests completed in 30 milliseconds.
1 assertions of 1 passed, 0 failed.

1. **Test that QUnit is working as expected** (0, 1, 1)   1 ms

Test name   Test result (failed, passed, total)   Test execution time

Figure 8.2   Executing the firstTest.html file

As you can see, the test results consist of a few elements:

- A header that displays the name of the test. This is the same as the `title` tag of your HTML document.
- Options that let you hide test passes (showing only the failed tests), check for globals, or disable the try-catch feature of QUnit.
- The current browser's user-agent string.
- The time it took to execute all the tests.
- The total, passed, and failed number of assertions.
- The name of each executed test.

QUnit provides a convenient way to get up and running quickly with unit testing, but some key features are missing from this setup:

- Relying on a browser to execute your tests is cumbersome. This is especially true when it comes to setting up and operating a CI environment for your application.
- There's no built-in way to execute this test from the command line.
- Feedback is given via updates to the browser's Document Object Model (DOM), which is hard to extract automatically.

This approach isn't well suited for environments that require CI to work seamlessly whenever a commit occurs to the source code management system. To fix these issues, you'll bring in an additional tool, PhantomJS.

8.1.2 *Executing from the command line with PhantomJS*

PhantomJS is a headless WebKit installation that's highly scriptable via a JavaScript API. PhantomJS works well via the command line, which means that it works equally well when executed through a CI server. The fact that it serves as a headless WebKit installation opens up many interesting approaches when it comes to testing. By using PhantomJS, you can achieve the following:

- Execute your tests from the command line and get feedback on test results.
- Execute your tests against a real WebKit installation.
- Capture screenshots of your web application before, during, or after a test case execution.
- Chain together multiple test scripts and scenarios by using third-party tools.
- Build up a testing pipeline that can be reused for different testing purposes (unit, integration, and performance testing).

PhantomJS is widely deployed in the test strategies of companies around the world. The Ember.js project uses it, as do Bootstrap, Modernizr, and CodeMirror.

To get started, create a test that navigates to http://emberjs.com and verifies that the page's title is as you expect. If so, you'll take a screenshot of the web page and exit the test. Create a file named testEmberHomepage.js, and enter the code as shown in the following listing.

Listing 8.3   Creating a screen capture PhantomJS test

```
var page = require('webpage').create();                          Requires web
var before = Date.now();                                         page module
page.open('http://emberjs.com/', function () {       Opens
    var title = page.evaluate(function () {          http://emberjs.com
        return document.title;
    });
    if (title === "Ember.js - About") {
        console.log('Title as expected. Rendering screenshot!');
        page.render('emberjs.png');                  Renders
    } else {                                         screenshot
        console.log("Title not as expected!")
    }                                                      Logs milliseconds
                                                           of execution
    console.log("Test took: " + (Date.now() - before) + " ms.");
    phantom.exit();                                      Exits PhantomJS
});
```

Fetches page's title → `var title = page.evaluate(function () {`

Verifies title is as expected → `if (title === "Ember.js - About") {`

You should note a couple of important things from this code listing. First, you need to require the modules that you intend to use from PhantomJS before using them. Several modules are available, including the following:

- *webpage*—Makes it possible for your test to interact with a single web page
- *system*—Exposes system-level functionality to your test
- *fs*—Exposes filesystem functionality, as well as access to files and directories to your tests
- *webserver*—An experimental module that uses an embedded web server that your PhantomJS scripts can start

After you've created an instance of the webpage module, load the Ember.js website to execute your test. The test starts by fetching the web page's title via the page.evaluate() function. If the title is what you expect it to be—"Ember.js - About"—the script takes a screenshot of the complete website and stores it in the current directory as emberjs.png.

Before the script finishes, it prints out the number of milliseconds that the test took, making sure to end the script with the phantom.exit() function.

NOTE   To execute the test, you need to install PhantomJS onto your computer. Binaries are available for the most common operating systems, including Windows, Mac OS X, and Linux.

To execute the script, issue the following command:

```
phantomjs testEmberHomepage.js
```

```
Joachims-MacBook-Pro:test jhsmbp$ phantomjs testEmberHomepage.js
Title as expected. Rendering screenshot!
Test took: 16 ms.
Joachims-MacBook-Pro:test jhsmbp$
```

Figure 8.3   Executing the testEmberHomepage.js script

Figure 8.3 shows the result of running the test on my laptop, with Mac OS X installed.

After running this test, you should be able to locate a file named emberjs.png alongside the testEmberHomepage.js file.

Now that you've made sure that you can execute tests via PhantomJS, you can move on and integrate QUnit to run unit tests. Two major issues arise when using QUnit by itself to write unit tests that can be executed by your CI server on each build of your application:

- QUnit requires its own HTML file in which you need to set everything up that the test requires.
- QUnit prints its output straight into the DOM, making it hard for a CI server to figure out whether any tests failed along the way.

By combining QUnit with PhantomJS, you can alleviate both issues. But to do so, you need to build a test harness for executing your test both while writing your application as well as via the CI server build. I'll show you one possible solution for integrating PhantomJS and QUnit before moving on to writing unit tests in QUnit.

8.1.3   Integrating QUnit and PhantomJS

To run QUnit from PhantomJS, you're going to adapt the PhantomJS QUnit integration script from the Ember.js project. Because the run-qunit.js script is rather lengthy, I've broken it into parts. I'm also showing only the most relevant parts. You can view the complete run-qunit.js script in the Montric source code on GitHub.

BOOTSTRAPPING THE INTEGRATION SCRIPT

The bootstrapping of the run-qunit.js script is where you declare what input parameters the script expects and load your test HTML file. This file serves as the integration point between PhantomJS and QUnit and is what allows you to execute the unit tests in a headless manner. The code shown in the following listing can be found at https://github .com/joachimhs/Montric/blob/master/Montric.View/src/test/qunit/run-qunit.js.

Listing 8.4   Bootstrapping the run-qunit.js script

```
var interval = null;                                    Stops PhantomJS
var start = null;                                       when tests pass
var args = phantom.args;                                               Fetches arguments
if (args.length != 1) {                                                to PhantomJS
    console.log("Usage: " + phantom.scriptName + " <URL>");
    phantom.exit(1);                                    Prints correct
}                                                       usage and exits
```

Exits if
tests take
too long

```
                var page = require('webpage').create();
Opens           page.open(args[0], function(status) {
web                 if (status !== 'success') {                      Exits if web page
page                    console.error("Unable to access network");   doesn't open
                        phantom.exit(1);
                    } else {                                     Records current
Calls function if       page.evaluate(logQUnit);                timestamp
web page opens          start = Date.now();
                        interval = setInterval(qunitTimeout, 500);       Sets interval
                    }                                                    for exit
                });
```

You start by defining a variable called `interval`, where you'll store a JavaScript `interval` object. You use this interval to exit PhantomJS after every test has completed successfully or times out. The script then fetches the arguments that are given into the scripts and prints out an error message if the number of arguments isn't equal to one.

In the next section, you open the URL that run-qunit.js is passed in via its first argument. If PhantomJS is unable to load this URL, you print out an error message and exit PhantomJS. Otherwise, you call the function `logQUnit()` via the `page.evaluate()` function.

The last thing this part of the script does is to register an interval to execute the `qunitTimeout()` function every 500 milliseconds. As you'll see next, you use this interval to exit PhantomJS after every test has completed or any test times out.

INSIDE THE TIMEOUT FUNCTION

Before you delve into the execution of QUnit, let's take a closer look at the `qunit-Timeout()` function, shown in the following listing.

Listing 8.5 Exiting PhantomJS via `qunitTimeout()`

```
                function qunitTimeout() {
Indicates           var timeout = 60000;
60 seconds          if (Date.now() > start + timeout) {          Halts test after
for test                console.error("Tests timed out");        60 seconds
                        phantom.exit(124);
                    } else {
                        var qunitDone = page.evaluate(function() {
                            return window.qunitDone;             Checks if QUnit
                        });                                      is done

                        if (qunitDone) {
Clears                      clearInterval(interval);
interval                    if (qunitDone.failed > 0) {
timer                           phantom.exit(1);                Exits with error
                            } else {                            state if test fails
                                phantom.exit();
                            }                        Exits normally if
                        }                            no test failures
                    }
                }
```

The `qunitTimeout()` function is executed every 500 ms via the JavaScript `set-Interval()` function declared in listing 8.4. The script starts by defining the maximum combined number of milliseconds that all unit tests are allowed to take (60,000 ms). It then periodically checks whether this threshold has been breached and exits PhantomJS immediately if it has. This mechanism is added to ensure that test execution doesn't hang or otherwise bring down a CI system.

Within the allowed execution time, the script checks to see whether QUnit is done via `window.qunitDone`. If QUnit has finished, the script clears out the interval that executes the timeout checking. If QUnit reports that any tests have failed, the script exits PhantomJS with an error state. Otherwise, it exits PhantomJS normally.

So far, so good. Next let's look at the `logQUnit()` function.

INSIDE THE LOG FUNCTION

This function registers a number of callbacks into the QUnit runtime to gather the data it needs to print out the results of executing the tests. The most important metric for any test harness is the number of tests that is left in the passed, failed, or not-executed state.

In the following listing, you'll look at only a skeleton of the `logQUnit()` function. Please look at the run-qunit.js script from Montric for the full content.

Listing 8.6 Printing test results with `logQUnit()`

```
function logQUnit() {
    var moduleErrors = [];
    var testErrors = [];                         Holds error messages from
    var assertionErrors = [];                    modules, tests, and assertions

    QUnit.moduleDone(function(context) {              Executes when
        //Log any failures to the moduleErrors Array   module finishes
        //Print Module status to the console
        ...
    });

    QUnit.testDone(function(context) {           Executes when
        //Log any failures to the testError and  test finishes
        //asertionErrors Arrays
        ...
    });

    QUnit.log(function(context) {                     Executes when QUnit
        //Print Assertion error messages to the console   wants to log output
        ...
    });

    QUnit.done(function(context) {
        //Print out any moduleErrors and testErrors
        //Print Stats that show the total, successful and failed
        //tests
        ...
        window.qunitDone = context;
    });
}
```

Executes
when
tests finish

The `logQUnit()` function registers four callbacks into QUnit in order to be notified when QUnit executes the tests. The script keeps track of the results for tests contained in a module, for assertions in a single test, and for single assertions. The script reports back these results after each module along with a summary after all tests have executed.

8.2 Writing a simple Ember.js unit test with QUnit

Writing unit tests for JavaScript applications is different from what you might be used to with other, statically typed languages. Because no standard way exists to set up a JavaScript application runtime, you need to provide a complete application in your QUnit setup. QUnit is set up via an HTML file, as you saw previously in this chapter. Inside this HTML file, you need to bootstrap your entire application, remembering to include any third-party JavaScript libraries that your application is using. After that's set up, you can start writing unit tests for your application.

THE FUNCTION-UNDER-TEST

`Montric.ApplicationController` is used, among other things, to generate readable strings from JavaScript `date` objects that are displayed on a live-updating chart in the application. To format these strings, you can provide a `dateFormat` that tells `Montric.ApplicationController` how to correctly format the date string.

When a user of the Montric application requests a chart, the client side issues an XHR request to the server to fetch the chart data. Montric draws the chart with the values along the y-axis and the time along the x-axis. The dates along the x-axis are formatted according to the user's preferences. Figure 8.4 shows one possible way to format the chart.

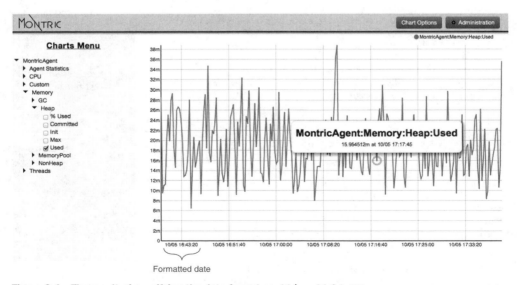

Figure 8.4   The result of specifying the date format as `dd/mm hh24:MM.ss`

The code that converts the JavaScript date into this human-readable date is shown in the following listing.

Listing 8.7 Montric.ApplicationController generateChartString() function

```
Montric.ApplicationController = Ember.Controller.extend({
    dateFormat: 'dd mmmm yyyy HH:MM',

    generateChartString: function (date) {
        var fmt = this.get('dateFormat') || 'dd.mm.yy';

        var dateString = date ? dateFormat(date, fmt) : "";
        return dateString;
    }
});
```

- Specifies default date format string
- The function you are going to write a unit test for
- Gets date format or uses default
- Generates date string or empty string

The `ApplicationController` specifies a default `dateFormat` that it uses to format dates into human-readable form for displaying on a chart. To provide consistency of the dates displayed on each chart throughout the application, the `dateFormat` controls the dates that are presented to the user throughout the application.

Your unit test will test the functionality of the `generateChartString()` function. This function takes a single `date` argument, which it uses to return a valid string representation. If `dateFormat` isn't defined or is `null` at this point, the default `dd.mm.yyyy` date format is used. If the `date` variable is `null` or undefined, you return an empty string. Otherwise, you return the result of the `dateFormat()` function.

Now that you know what the function you're testing does, you can start using QUnit to write a unit test.

BOOTSTRAPPING THE UNIT TEST

The following listing shows the test setup.

Listing 8.8 Testing the generateChartString() function

```
var appController;
var inputDate = new Date(2013,2,27,11,15,00);

module("Montric.AppController", {
    setup: function() {
        Ember.run(function() {
            appController =
    Montric.__container__.lookup("controller:application");

        });
    },

    teardown: function() {

    }
});
```

- Holds date for unit tests
- Holds Ember.js-instantiated ApplicationController
- Houses similar unit tests
- Creates module setup() function
- Fetches and stores Ember.js-instantiated ApplicationController
- Includes teardown() function

Start by defining two variables: one to hold the Ember.js-instantiated `Montric.ApplicationContoller`, and one to hold a `date` object that you'll use throughout your unit tests. The `module()` function allows you to perform some common setup that all tests will require, as well as any teardown functionality that your tests need. As you'll see later, Ember.js provides a simple way to reset your application between each test, meaning that you most likely won't have any special teardown functionality for your Ember.js-based unit tests.

Inside the `module()` function, include both a `setup()` and a `teardown()` function. Inside the `setup()` function, fetch the `Montric.ApplicationController` and assign it to the `appController` variable. It's OK to use the `Montric.__container__.lookup()` function for your unit tests, but you should never, and I mean *never*, use this private function in your production code! Ember.js does a lot of work, trying its best to enforce a clear MVC structure for your application. If you find yourself wanting to use `__container__` in your own application, you should go back and find out where your application logic is combining concerns that ought to be separated.

CREATING THE UNIT TESTS

You're going to create five unit tests for the `generateChartString()` function to verify the following:

1 You were able to get hold of the `Montric.ApplicationController` instance.
2 The default date format formats the date according to the default specification given in the class initialization.
3 Providing a custom date format formats the date according to the date format pattern given.
4 A `null` date format formats the date according to `dd.mm.yyyy`.
5 A `null` date returns an empty string.

The code for all five tests is shown in the next listing.

Listing 8.9   Creating five unit tests for `generateChartString()` function

```
test("Verify appController", function() {                            Verifies appController
    Montric.reset();                                                 isn't null or undefined
    ok(appController, "Expecting non-null appController");
});                                                                  Asserts
                                                                     appController is OK

test("Testing the default dateFormat", function() {                 Verifies
    Montric.reset();                                                 default
    strictEqual("27 March 2013 11:15",                               date
     appController.generateChartString(inputDate), "Default Chart String   format
     Generation OK");
});

test("Testing custom dateFormat", function() {
    Montric.reset();                                                 Verifies custom date
    appController.set('dateFormat', 'dd.mm.yyyy');                   format works
    strictEqual("27.03.2013", appController.generateChartString(inputDate),
     "Custom Chart String Generation OK");
});
```

Resets Montric app before test

```
test("Testing null dateFormat", function() {
    Montric.reset();
    appController.set('dateFormat', null);
    strictEqual("27.03.13",
    ➥ appController.generateChartString(inputDate),
    ➥ "Null Chart String Generation OK");
});

test("Testing null date", function() {
    Montric.reset();
    strictEqual("", appController.generateChartString(null),
        "Null Date OK");
});
```

Verifies null date format generates expected date string

Resets Montric app before test

Verifies null date generates empty string

As you can see, each test starts by calling `Montric.reset()`. This ensures that Ember.js resets the application to a freshly loaded copy. This makes unit testing easier because you don't have to keep track of what each test may have changed in order to successfully write the code for the module's `teardown()` function (see listing 8.8).

Nothing special is going on in any of the five tests, and the code should be readable and easy to understand. In the first test, you use the `ok` assert, which passes if the first argument is *truthy*, meaning that it's not `null`, undefined, or false. Here you're testing whether you were able to retrieve a valid non-null instance of `Montric.ApplicationController`. This test is an important addition to your test module; debugging the cause of failing tests will be easier if you first rule out any problems with retrieving the controller upon which the rest of the tests are built.

For the other tests, the goal is to assert that the `generateChartStrings()` function returns a correct string representation given four different circumstances. For instance, in the second test you verify that the controller's default date format works as intended. In this case, you use the `strictEquals` assert to check whether the formatted date equals `"27 March 2013 11:15"`.

---

strictEquals() vs. equals()

The `strictEquals()` function verifies that the first two arguments are equal by using the strict equality operator (`===`). You could use the `equals` assert to check for non-strict equality, which would use the equality operator (`==`) instead.

The last argument that you pass in to each assert is a string that displays if the unit test fails. Figure 8.5 shows the result of running the unit tests.

```
Joachims-MacBook-Pro:qunit jhsmbp$ phantomjs run-qunit.js http://localhost:8081/index-test.html
calling set on destroyed object
calling set on destroyed object
Module Montric.AppController Finished. Failed: 0, Passed: 5, Total: 5


Time: 390ms, Total: 5, Passed: 5, Failed: 0
Joachims-MacBook-Pro:qunit jhsmbp$
```

Figure 8.5   Executing the unit tests from PhantomJS

As you can see, to execute the unit tests, run the following command:

```
phantomjs run-qunit.js http://localhost:8081/index-test.html
```

> **NOTE** You can find the index-test.html file in the GitHub Repo: https://github.com/joachimhs/Montric/blob/Ember.js-in-Action-Branch/Montric.View/src/main/webapp/index-test.html

The first argument to PhantomJS is the script to execute. The other arguments given are used as input arguments to this test script. In this case, you give the run-qunit.js script the URL that you want to use for executing the QUnit scripts. The run-qunit.js script loads the specified URL and sets up the listeners and hooks that it needs in QUnit to report back the progress of the unit tests as well as any test failures that occur while executing the tests.

Now that you've seen how to use QUnit to test single functions and single classes, the next section explains how to use the same technologies to implement integration testing.

8.3 Performing integration testing

Whereas unit testing is concerned with testing single units of work—broken down to single functions and single classes—integration testing is concerned with integrating different layers of your application and performing wider tests on your application. Depending on your requirements and test setup, you can isolate particular parts of your application to test their isolated requirements, or you can test certain features all the way through the application.

Many tools are available that let you do integration testing at different layers in your JavaScript application. Some of the more popular choices include Mocha, Capybara, Selenium WebDriver, and Casper.js. Because you're already using QUnit for your unit tests, you'll stay with QUnit and PhantomJS and bring in a third library, Sinon.js, which can be downloaded from http://sinonjs.org. I'll refer to Sinon.js as Sinon throughout the rest of this chapter.

The Sinon library helps you fake the parts of the application that you don't want to test for your particular test. You can achieve this in various ways depending on the intended result. Sinon provides the following features:

- *Stubs*—Objects that provide a valid but static result. Regardless of what you pass into the stubs, you'll always get the same response. Stubs also provide input on which methods were executed and their invocation count.
- *Mocks*—Objects that work like Stubs, but which also contain assertions that allow you to test both input and output.
- *Spies*—Objects that allow reporting back the same information as mocks. Whereas mocks provide preprogrammed functionality, spies don't implement fake methods, allowing you to spy only on your methods without changing the functionality.

- *Fake objects*—Objects that act like the real object, but in a simpler way. A common example is a data access object that stores its data in memory instead of in a real database. Note that Sinon doesn't provide this functionality on its own.

You need all these features to implement a maintainable integration testing strategy.

8.3.1 Introducing Sinon

This chapter focuses your integration testing on the client-side application. Because you're not interested in communication with the server side while performing these types of integration tests, this section introduces a mocking framework, Sinon, which enables you to mock out the server-side communications, letting each test specify a fake server-side response. First download sinon.js, sinon-server.js, and sinon-qunit.js, and include them in an index-integration-test.html file.

The Sinon library provides testing spies, stubs, and mocks for any of the JavaScript test frameworks available. For this example, you'll write an integration test that tests the Alert Administration feature of Montric. In short, Montric lets users set up custom alert thresholds for the gathered metrics. The GUI provides the user with the ability to add, modify, and delete alerts from the system. Figure 8.6 shows the point in the application that you'll test.

As you can see in figure 8.6, the user can enter a name for the new alert before clicking the Add button to create the alert. After alerts are registered in the system, the user can then select an alert by clicking it. The selected alert is editable via the form at the right of the list of alerts and can be deleted by clicking the Delete button.

You'll create an integration test to test the capability to add new alerts to the system.

Figure 8.6   The Alerts tab of the Administration view

8.3.2   *Integration test for adding a new alert*

You'll start by writing a test that verifies the capability to add a new alert to the system by entering a name for a new alert and clicking the Add button. You'll verify that this alert is added to the content array of the Montric.AdministrationAlertsController.

The first thing you need to do, however, is to enable the Sinon fake server to stub out any of the Ajax calls. To ensure that the fake server is set up before the Montric application is set up, include the script shown in the following listing inside the index-integration-test.html file just before you load the Montric application.

Listing 8.10   Initializing Sinon `fakeServer`

```
<script type="text/javascript">
    Montric.server = sinon.fakeServer.create();          ◁─┐ Initializes fake server
</script>
```

This code creates a new instance of `sinon.fakeServer`, which you store in the `Montric.server` property so your tests can retrieve the `fakeServer` instance.

After you've ensured that the application won't issue any XHR request to the server, you can start implementing the integration test. The following listing shows the module definition of the test.

Listing 8.11   The alertAdminIntegrationTest.js module setup

```
var alertAdminController;

module("Montric.AdministrationAlertsController", {
    setup: function() {
        console.log('Admin Alerts Controller Module setup');
        Montric.server.autoRespond = true;                          ◁── Tells fakeServer
        Montric.server.respondWith("GET", "/alert_models",              to autorespond
                [200, { "Content-Type": "text/json" },
                    '{"alert_models":[]}'
                ]);


        Montric.server.respondWith("POST", "/alert_models",
                [200, { "Content-Type": "text/json" },
                '{"alert_model":{"alert_source":"null",
                "id":"New Alert","alert_delay":0,
                "alert_plugin_ids":[],"alert_notifications":"",
                "alert_activated":false,
                "alert_type":"greater_than"}}'
                ]);

        Ember.run(function() {
            alertAdminController =
        Montric.__container__.lookup("controller:administrationAlerts");

        });
    },
```

Provides intended response to first request

Provides intended response to second request

Gets instantiated
Montric.AdministrationAlertsController

```
            teardown: function() {
        }
});
```

You start by configuring the fake server to automatically respond to Ajax requests before you create the two Ajax requests that Montric will issue. The first response will be issued when the application is loaded and Montric attempts to load any alerts that might already be stored for that user account. In this case, you're returning an empty array, because this test doesn't require the system to have any predefined alerts. The second response is a fake that simulates the server's reply when a new alert with the name "new alert" is created and sent to the server.

In the final part of the module setup, you're fetching the application-instantiated `Montric.AdministrationAlertsController`, which you'll store in the `alertAdmin-Controller` variable, so it can be used from within your tests.

Next, you'll add a test to verify that you can create a new alert and add it to the controller's `content` array. The code for this test is shown in the following listing.

Listing 8.12 Testing adding new alerts

```
var testCallbacks = {                                    ◁──  Creates container
    verifyContentLength: function() {                         for test callbacks
        Montric.reset();
        if (alertAdminController.get('content.length') > 0 ) {
            strictEqual(1, alertAdminController.get('content.length'),
                "Expecting one alert. Got: " +
                alertAdminController.get('content.length'));
            QUnit.start();                               ◁──  Restarts test after
        }                                                      asynchronous call
    }
};

asyncTest("Create a new Alert and verify that it is shown", 2,
        function() {
    ok(alertAdminController, "Exepcting a non-null
    AdministrationAlertsController");                   ◁──  Asserts we have
                                                              valid instance

    alertAdminController.get('content').addObserver('length', testCallbacks,
        'verifyContentLength');                         ◁──  Adds observer
                                                              to see test result
    alertAdminController.set('newAlertName', 'New Alert');
    alertAdminController.createNewAlert();              ◁──  Simulates clicking
});                                                           Add button
```

- **Verifies alerts increased, ends test**
- **Asserts alert was added**
- **Uses Qunit's asyncTest**
- **Specifies name of new alert**

Because you're testing asynchronous code here, you need to use QUnit's `asyncTest` function. This function executes everything inside the test function, but it won't exit the test until the `start()` function is called. This is handy for testing Ember.js applications, which are, by nature, asynchronous.

The test starts, as always, by resetting the application before it verifies that it was able to retrieve a valid controller from the Ember.js container. Next, update the alert name input box with the text New Alert, before triggering the controller's createNewAlert() function. This is a simple way of simulating a user clicking the Add button, which will call the same createNewAlert() function. This function creates a new Montric.AlertModel object with the ID given in the New Alert input box.

The next part is a bit tricky to test. You want to assert that the alert you created does indeed exist in the list of alerts after the server side has responded. To do so, you must add an observer on the alertAdminController's content.length property. When this property changes, the test invokes the verifyContentLength callback.

After the verifyContentLength callback is invoked, you can assert that exactly one item is in the content array, and that its ID is the one you provided it with, "New Alert". After you've asserted that everything is as you expect, you can safely call the QUnit start() function to progress to the next test.

This test demonstrates one way you can integrate QUnit, PhantomJS, and Sinon to create an integration test harness for your Ember.js-based applications. Most of your integration tests will have a similar setup, depending on the amount of traffic between the client and the server.

Before concluding this chapter, you'll take a quick look at how to performance test Ember.js applications via the built-in Ember Instrumentation implementation.

8.4 Using Ember.Instrumentation for performance testing

You can performance test your Ember.js applications in multiple ways. One way is to use Ember.js's built-in instrumentation API. To use this API, you register which event you would like to get measurements for, and implement a before and after function. In this case, you want to retrieve measurements of the time it takes to render the views for the Montric application.

The following listing shows how to retrieve these performance metrics by subscribing to the render.view event.

Listing 8.13 Measuring `render.view`

```
Ember.subscribe('render.view', {                                    Subscribes to
    ts: null,                                                       render.view event
    before: function(name, timestamp, payload) {
        ts = timestamp;
    },
    after: function(name, timestamp, payload, beforeRet) {          Generates
        console.log('instrument: ' + name +                        message showing
                " " + JSON.stringify(payload) +                    render time
                " took:" + (timestamp - ts));
    }
});
```

Records timestamp before views render →

As you can see, the code is rather simple, starting out by subscribing to the render .view event. An event is triggered just before the view render, as well as just after the view has finished rendering. In this example, you're keeping track of the timestamp in the before() function and using this to print out a log message that shows how long the view took to render in the after() function. An example of the result is shown in the next listing.

Listing 8.14   The instrumentation result

```
instrument: render.view {"template":null,
"object":"<LinkView:ember427>"}
took:6.5119999926537275

instrument: render.view {"template":null,
"object":"<Montric.BootstrapButton:ember434>"}
took:6.587000010767952

instrument: render.view {"template":null,
"object":"<Montric.HeaderView:ember424>"}
took:9.111000021221116

instrument: render.view {"template":"adminAlertLeftMenu"
,"object":"<Ember.View:ember471>"}
took:6.40800001565367
```

As you can see, the output is fairly simple. In this example, you're logging the results to the console, but because you do have this information available inside your application, you can implement interesting strategies to detect possible errors and bottlenecks on the client side. Although this book doesn't cover this, it should be fairly easy to write code that aggregates the information you need from your users, and that periodically sends this metric back to you, server side, for analysis.

You can subscribe to several events, including the following:

- render.view
- render.render.boundHandlebars
- render.render.metamorph
- render.render.container
- * - (all)

Even though the functionality offered by Ember.Instrumentation is limited at this point, it still provides a useful and quick way to gather statistics on the rendering process of your applications. Other, more involved tools are available to perform performance testing, but depending on your needs and requirements, Ember.Instrumentation might be just what you need.

8.5   *Summary*

You can test your JavaScript application by using various approaches. Because the underlying ideas and goals of many of these tools are the same, I've tried to keep the number of introduced libraries and frameworks to a minimum. Although most of the examples in this chapter are based on QUnit, multiple testing libraries are available that cater to differing requirements and test styles.

Because JavaScript as a platform has grown so rapidly over the past few years, the available tools often feel lacking, incomplete, or poorly integrated. This makes implementing strategies for testing your applications at different layers more difficult than it should be, and more difficult than the testing that programmers have become used to from other, more mature languages. That said, the JavaScript tooling business is blossoming, with new and powerful tools emerging at an increasing pace.

This chapter gave you a few ideas about how you can use some of the more popular testing libraries and tools to implement testing strategies for your Ember.js applications. In particular, PhantomJS is quickly becoming the de facto standard for performing headless testing; most of the other libraries and tools have implemented support for it. Over time, it will become clearer which of the available tools gains popularity, enabling easier integration moving forward.

This chapter concludes part 2 of this book. At this point, you should be able to design, write, and test your Ember.js-based applications. You should also have a thorough understanding of the Ember.js core concepts and features. The next part of the book covers advanced topics, including packaging, deployment, and interacting with the cloud.

Part 3

Advanced Ember.js topics

The final part of *Ember.js in Action* presents some of Ember.js's advanced features. You start by learning how Montric is integrated with Mozilla Persona for user authentication. Persona is a complete, open source, and independent user authentication and authorization platform. Even if you won't be using Persona, chapter 9 shows how to integrate Ember.js with your third-party authentication service of choice.

Beneath the surface, Ember.js hides an incredibly powerful engine that ensures that your application's views and templates are always updated whenever the data in the application changes. This engine, often referred to as the Ember run loop, is called Backburner.js and is the subject of chapter 10. Although you can develop Ember.js applications without understanding Backburner.js, knowing what features it provides and how to use its functionality enables you to build an application with better performance and more maintainable code.

The final chapter, chapter 11, takes you through a complete assembly process for your Ember.js application. This is the final step to transition your application from development to production. Implementing a sane directory structure and a proper build tool chain also helps you immensely throughout the development process.

Authentication through a third-party system— Mozilla Persona

This chapter covers

- Using third-party authentication platforms for single sign-on (SSO) with Ember.js
- Integrating and authenticating with Mozilla Persona
- Reauthenticating via HTTP cookies

You're now familiar with the Ember.js architecture, and you know how to use it to structure and build rich web applications. A concept that might not be as clear to you is how to provide a seamless sign-in experience for your application users.

This chapter presents a single sign-on solution by integrating Mozilla Persona. If you haven't heard about Persona yet, you can think of it as a full-featured authentication system that enables your application to authenticate millions of users via their own personal email accounts.

Even though this chapter uses Persona as an example of a third-party user authentication and authorization platform, the lessons learned throughout this

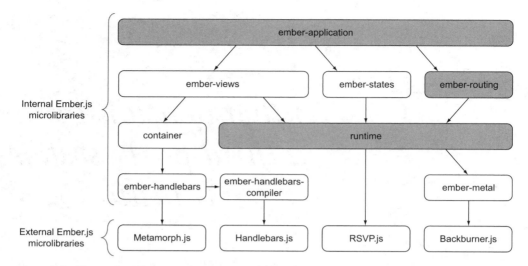

Figure 9.1   The parts of Ember.js you'll work on in this chapter

chapter can be easily adapted to other authentication systems. Because Persona is based on JavaScript, integration with Ember.js applications is easy.

The core idea behind Persona is that your users' online identities should belong solely to them. Persona allows a user to associate one or more email accounts to their identity, which allows them to sign in to a range of websites and applications by using a single username (email) and password. In addition, because Persona is created by a nonprofit organization that thrives on open source, you can gain your users' trust by showing that you're relying on technology from a company that's trusted throughout the open source community.

Using a third-party authentication provider has many advantages. The most significant is that your applications won't have the responsibilities related to keeping usernames and passwords, while supplying secure off-site storage and password hashing, and keeping your users' information safe from hackers.

Figure 9.1 shows the parts of the Ember.js ecosystem that this chapter examines. You'll use the structure of Ember Router to integrate user authentication into your application.

So without further ado, let's dive into what Persona gives you in terms of features and functionality.

9.1   Integrating a third-party authentication system with Ember.js

As previously stated, Mozilla Persona is a full-featured third-party authentication provider that takes care of the following aspects of user authentication and authorization:

- Email registration
- Email validation

- Secure storage of passwords
- Reissuing lost or forgotten passwords
- Any other issues that the user might have in relation to an email address, account, or password

With any third-party web-based authentication mechanism, the user has multiple ways to authenticate toward your system and to log in. For our purposes, we'll look at the three models that need to be implemented in order to provide the user with a smooth login and authentication mechanism:

- First-time login and user registration
- Login via the third-party authentication provider (Mozilla Persona)
- Signing in users via HTTP cookies

9.1.1 *Performing first-time login and user registration*

How you choose to implement the initial login and user registration is largely based on your system's requirements. Montric allows any user authenticated via Persona to register a new account with the system. This account is then marked as new, which means that the user is authenticated with Persona but is still unknown to Montric. At this point, the user is notified that their account is awaiting activation. Because Persona takes care of authenticating that the current user does belong to the given email address, Montric can redirect the user to the user registration page whenever a new user authenticates toward the system. This means that no differences exist between a first login and any subsequent logins to Montric. This is a huge deal for the usability of your application because the application has a single point of entry from the user's point of view.

Montric, however, needs to check the account type of the logged-in user and make sure that any account that has type "new" is redirected to the awaiting activation page. Conceptually, this process is shown in figure 9.2.

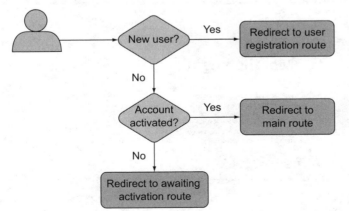

Figure 9.2 Handling new users in Montric

As you can see from this diagram, the application needs to perform two checks. The first checks whether the user is entering the application for the first time. If so, the user is redirected to the user registration route. If the user is already registered, the application moves on to the next check to see whether the user's account is activated. If the user's account is activated, the application redirects the user to the application's main route. If the user's account isn't activated, Montric redirects the user to the awaiting activation route.

Before you move on to see how this can be achieved, let's take a closer look at the Montric router definition, as shown in the following listing.

Listing 9.1   The Montric router definition

```
Montric.Router.map(function() {                                           Directs user
    this.resource("main", {path: "/"}, function() {                       to login page
        this.resource("login", {path: "/login"}, function() {
            this.route("register", {path: "/register"});
            this.route("selectAccount", {path: "/select_account"});
        });
        this.route("activation");
                                                                          Directs user
        //The rest of the Montric router omitted                          to register route
    });
});
```

Indicates main route encompassing all others

Directs user to activation

The Montric application has a top-level route named `main` that encloses all other routes in the application. If Montric is unable to log in the user either via an HTTP cookie or automatically via Persona, the user is redirected to the `login.index` route. This route is responsible for showing the login screen to the user. This login screen is slightly different from the login screens you're accustomed to, because the user will never enter a username or password directly into the Montric user interface. Figure 9.3 shows the Montric login screen.

Figure 9.3   The Montric login screen

After the user is logged in, Montric verifies the credentials received from Persona. These credentials include the user's email address as well as a timestamp, echoed back from the Persona verifier, that shows when the Persona session expires. If the user isn't already registered as a Montric user, they're redirected to the `login.register` route.

Note that a user can take two possible paths to end up on the `login.register` route. The most obvious way is to go through the `login.index` route and click the Sign In with Mozilla Persona button, which redirects them to the `login.register` route if the user isn't already registered as a Montric user. If a user is already logged in to Persona from a previous session and navigates to the Montric application (via any of Montric's valid routes), Montric receives the user credentials from Persona in much the same way as if the user had logged in with Persona via the `login.index` route.

> **NOTE** Mozilla Persona sends the user's credentials only if the user has previously logged in to Montric. This security measure ensures that Persona won't automatically reveal the user's email address to websites that the user hasn't actively logged in to before.

This is an important distinction between traditional authentication solutions and third-party SSO solutions such as Persona.

Figure 9.4 shows the `login.register` screen. The registration form is quite simple. Persona has already authenticated that the user's email address is correct and that the Persona session hasn't expired. Through the `login.register` route, the user is

Figure 9.4   The Montric user registration screen

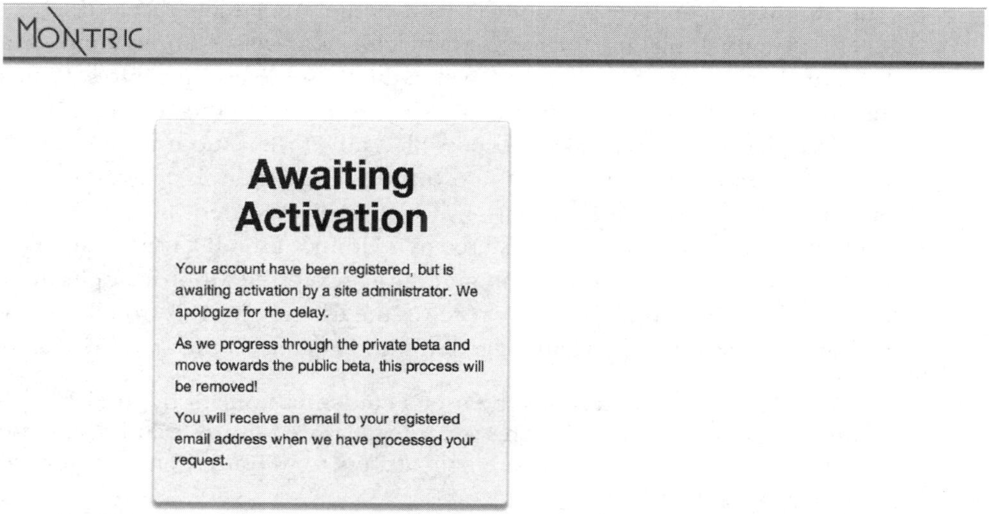

Figure 9.5   **The Awaiting Activation screen**

presented with input fields that let the user set up a name for the new account, as well as fill in their full name, company, and country information. After the Register New Account button is clicked, Montric creates a new account and associates the current user as an administrator of that account.

Because Montric is currently in beta, account creation is limited. The newly created account is locked until a Montric administrator activates the account by changing the account type from `new` to `beta`. The `main.activation` route is shown in figure 9.5.

As you can see, there's little going on in the `main.activation` route. Montric is explaining to the user that their account requires validation and is providing reasons that this is the case. Because the user won't be able to perform any actions inside the Montric application, the application doesn't provide any links or buttons that the user can click to navigate out of the `main.activation` route.

Now that you've seen what the Montric authentication flow looks like, this is a good time to delve into the code and see how authentication and authorization are implemented in the Montric application.

9.1.2   *Logging in to Montric via the third-party authentication provider*

As I've mentioned, users can authenticate themselves against Montric in multiple ways. You'll start by looking at how the user is authenticated via Mozilla Persona, and then look at how the user can be automatically logged in via an HTTP cookie.

Logging in via Persona is a three-step process that involves the user, the Montric Ember.js front-end application, the Montric back-end application, and Persona.

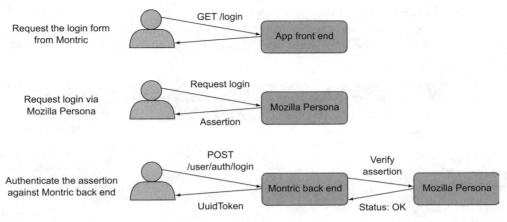

Figure 9.6   Authenticating a user via Mozilla Persona

Figure 9.6 shows the process of authenticating a user via Persona.

Before you can get started, you need to include the Mozilla Persona JavaScript file to your index.html file, as shown in the next listing.

Listing 9.2   Including the include.js Mozilla Persona JavaScript library

```
<script src="https://login.persona.org/include.js"></script>
```
Includes include.js script

This script is most likely the only script (in addition to your analytics script) that you'll include via HTTP/HTTPS. Including this script bootstraps your Persona integration and makes its methods available for use within your own application. The Persona team plans to build Persona functionality right into browsers in the future. The include.js file can therefore be considered a polyfill that ensures that Persona works with browsers that lack built-in Persona functionality.

IMPLEMENTING THE MOZILLA PERSONA LOGIN

The next step involves watching for Persona logins and logouts. This is done by calling `navigator.id.watch()`, in which you provide Persona with three critical pieces of information:

- The email address of the currently logged-in user in your application
- An `onlogin` callback that's invoked when a user is authenticated through Persona
- An `onlogout` callback that's invoked when a user signs out through Persona

Montric has a single controller that takes care of the bookkeeping required to sign in and sign out a single user, called `Montric.UserController`. In order to call Persona early enough in the Montric application startup sequence, you issue a call to `navigator.id.watch()` inside the `UserController`'s init function.

I've split the contents of the `Montric.UserController.init()` function into three listings so you can more easily go through them in detail. The next listing shows the structure of the init function. Listings 9.4 and 9.5 go through the `onlogin` and `onlogout` callbacks.

Listing 9.3   The `Montric.UserController.init()` function

```
Montric.UserController = Ember.ObjectController.extend({        Overrides
    init: function() {                                          Ember.js-specific functions
        this._super();
        this.set('content', Ember.Object.create());            Creates variable for
        var controller = this;                                 UserController instance
        navigator.id.watch({                          Watches for logins
            loggedInUser: null,                       and logouts
            onlogin: function(assertion) {},                    Provides callback
            onlogout: function() { }                            for sign-out
        });
    }
});
```

Initializes content property with new object → `this.set('content', Ember.Object.create());`

Provides callback for successful sign-in → `onlogin: function(assertion) {},`

This listing shows the structure of the init function. It starts by initiating a call to `this._super()` to ensure that Ember.js can set up everything it needs for the controller to operate as intended. Next it initializes the controller's content property to an empty Ember.js `Object`. You'll use this object as a temporary storage object before you're able to fetch a real `Montric.User` object from the Montric back end.

The final piece of code the init function needs to call is `navigator.id.watch()`. Inside this function, you state that the current `loggedInUser` is `null` (no logged-in user). In addition, you provide it with the `onlogin` and `onlogout` callbacks.

The following listing shows the contents of the `onlogin` callback.

Listing 9.4   The `onlogin` callback

```
onlogin: function(assertion) {                                  Provides callback
    Montric.set('isLoggingIn', true);                           with assertion
    $.ajax({
        type: 'POST',                                 Issues POST request
        url: '/user/auth/login',                      with assertion
        data: {assertion: assertion},
        success: function(res, status, xhr) {
            if (res.uuidToken) {
                controller.createCookie("uuidToken", res.uuidToken, 1);
            }

            if (res.registered === true) {                      Fetches user
                //login user                                    of token
                controller.set('content',
                    Montric.User.find(res.uuidToken));
            } else {
                controller.set('newUuidToken', res.uuidToken);
                controller.transitionToRoute('login.register');
            }
        },
```

Sets isLoggingIn to true → `Montric.set('isLoggingIn', true);`

Creates cookie uuidToken → `if (res.uuidToken) {`

Transitions user to login.register route → `} else {`

Provides error handling ⌐→
```
error: function(xhr, status, err) {
    console.log("error: " + status + ": " + err);
    navigator.id.logout();                          ←⌐ Ensures user is
    }                                                    logged out
  });
}
```

Persona passes in an assertion to the `onlogin` callback. You can think of the assertion as an encoded, single-use, single-site password. This assertion contains the information that the Montric back end uses to verify that the response it received from Persona is real. The assertion is also a privacy implementation that Persona uses to keep the user's login credentials out of the browser session. Persona will supply the user's email address only after it receives this assertion in return from the server-side implementation of your web application.

Because you want the Montric UI to tell the user that the application is attempting to log in the user, the first thing you set inside the `onlogin` callback is `isLoggingIn`, which you set to `true`. Next, you need to issue an `HTTP POST` request to the back end with the assertion that you got from Persona.

After the Montric back end responds to the `HTTP POST`, it responds with both a `uuidToken` and a `registered` property.

> ### A look ahead
>
> You'll use the `uuidToken` to set a cookie for cookie-based sign-in in section 9.2. This step is not strictly necessary because Persona keeps the user session active as long as the user is logged in to Persona. But reauthenticating the user via a session-based cookie is faster than going through Persona.

If the back end indicates that the user is already registered with an account, fetch the current logged-in user via a call to `Montric.User.find(uuid)`. If the user isn't associated with an account, redirect the user to the `login.register` route.

VERIFYING THE ASSERTION WITH MOZILLA PERSONA

The back end verifies the contents of the assertion by passing it to https://verifier.login.persona.org/verify, along with the Montric URL. The next listing shows the contents of the message sent to the verify endpoint.

> **Listing 9.5 The message sent to the Mozilla Persona verify endpoint**

```
assertion=<ASSERTION>&audience=https://live.montric.no:443
```

You should note two important points here. First, never authenticate the assertion on the client side of your application because that might expose your user's credentials to malicious third parties. Second, the audience should be defined by the server-side application, not by the client side or by the HTTP header information that you receive from Persona.

If Persona can verify both the assertion and the audience, it responds with a JSON hash containing the user's credentials. The following listing shows the contents of a successful login attempt.

Listing 9.6   The JSON response from Mozilla Persona after a successful login attempt

```
{
    "status": "okay",                                    ⟵┐ Returns status of okay
    "email": "joachim@haagen-software.no",
    "audience": "http://live.montric.no:443",            ⟵─ Returns audience passed in
    "expires": 1369060978610,                            ⟵┐ Indicates when
    "issuer": "login.persona.org"      ⟵┐                    the login expires
}                                       Indicates original
                                        issuer of assertion
```

Supplies user's email address → (points to "email" line)

After you've verified that the user is authenticated by Persona and you have the email address of the logged-in user, the Montric back end associates the user's email address with a unique UUID token, which you'll use to re-log in the user via an HTTP cookie. The response from the Montric back end is shown in the following listing.

Listing 9.7   The JSON response from the Montric back end

```
{
    "uuidToken": "99d21a30-1564-4863-a368-0a890f59532e",  ⟵┐ Token associated
    "registered": false                                       with user
}                                                         ⟵─ Property indicating
                                                            registration status
```

The JSON in this listing is straightforward. The UUID token is generated on the server side after the user is authenticated and authorized as a new user. Montric stores this token as the unique identifier for this user's email address. The `registered` property tells the Montric front-end application whether the user is already registered. Montric uses this information to redirect the user to the `login.register` route if the user needs to register a new account.

Now that you've seen how to authenticate users via Persona, let's see how to use HTTP cookies to provide re-login directly. The advantages of adding this approach are that you reduce the number of HTTP requests between the Ember.js application and your back-end server, and you eliminate unnecessary HTTP requests to Persona if you can already identify the user.

9.2   *Signing in users via HTTP cookies*

As you've seen, you set a cookie named `uuidToken` with a text string that you can use later to authenticate a user without having to call upon Persona. You do this in the `Montric.UserController.init` function by storing the `uuidToken` that you receive in the response from a successful login to the Montric back end.

Logging in via HTTP cookies is not only the fastest option, but is also simpler than logging in via Persona. Therefore, after the user is authenticated via Persona, you want to ensure that as many subsequent logins as possible are made via the HTTP cookie. Figure 9.7 shows the HTTP cookie login process.

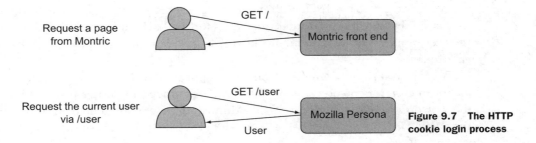

Figure 9.7　**The HTTP cookie login process**

To create both sign-in and sign-out functionality through the use of cookies, you need to provide your Montric front-end application with the ability to do the following:

- Create cookies
- Read cookies
- Delete cookies

In the Montric application, you'll implement these features as three separate functions on `Montric.UserController` because this is the controller that you elected to be responsible for the bookkeeping related to the logged-in user in Montric. This is an appropriate place to put these functions because you want to keep all your user-related functionality inside the single `Montric.UserController` class.

The following listing shows the contents of these three functions.

Listing 9.8　Working with cookies

```
createCookie:function (name, value, days) {          Creates cookie;
    if (days) {                                       expires in x days
        var date = new Date();
        date.setTime(date.getTime()+(days*24*60*60*1000));
        var expires = "; expires="+date.toGMTString();
    }
    else var expires = "";
    document.cookie = name+"="+value+expires+"; path=/";
},

readCookie:function (name) {                          Reads cookie value
    var nameEQ = name + "=";
    var ca = document.cookie.split(';');
    for (var i = 0; i < ca.length; i++) {
        var c = ca[i];
        while (c.charAt(0) == ' ') c = c.substring(1, c.length);
        if (c.indexOf(nameEQ) == 0)
            return c.substring(nameEQ.length, c.length);
    }
    return null;
},

eraseCookie:function (name) {                         Deletes cookie
    this.createCookie(name, "", -1);
}
```

You call `createCookie` from within the `navigator.id.watch()` function when the user is successfully authenticated from the Montric back end (see listing 9.3). When the user signs out of the system, invoke the `eraseCookie` function with the parameter `uuidToken`.

Because you're providing the front-end application with the ability to sign in users based on either a cookie value or via Persona, you need to ensure that you initialize the Persona functionality only if the Montric back end is unable to authenticate the user via the supplied HTTP cookie. The next listing shows the updated `Montric.UserController.init` function.

Listing 9.9   Updating `Montric.UserController.init` with cookie support

```
Montric.UserController = Ember.ObjectController.extend({
    needs: ['application', 'account'],

    init: function() {
        this._super();
        this.set('content', Ember.Object.create());
        var controller = this;
        var cookieUser = Montric.get('cookieUser');
        if (cookieUser == null) {                        ⟵──┐ Initializes Mozilla Persona
            navigator.id.watch({
                loggedInUser: null,
                onlogin: function(assertion) { },
                onlogout: function() { }
            });
        } else {                                         ⟵──┐ Updates the content
            this.set('content', Montric.get('cookieUser'));
        }
    }
});
```

This implementation of the `UserController`'s init function adds a single check to see whether `Montric.get('cookieUser')` has a value. If it does, you update the controller's `content` property with the contents of `Montric.get('cookieUser')`.

You might be wondering where the `cookieUser` comes from. Because cookies are available from the browsers and are part of every HTTP request made from the client application to the server, you can authenticate the user before the Montric application is initialized.

You can perform this authentication early because Ember.js lets you halt application initialization early by calling `App.deferReadiness()`. Inside Montric's app.js file, you've included code that fetches the current user based on the `uuidToken` cookie value. This code is shown in the following listing.

Listing 9.10   Halting and resuming application initialization

```
Montric.deferReadiness();                    ⟵──┐ Halts application initialization

$.getJSON("/user", function(data) {          ⟵──┐ Fetches current user
```

```
    if (data["user"] && data["user"].userRole != null) {          Creates a new
        var cookieUser = Montric.User.create();                    user object
        cookieUser.setProperties(data["user"]);
        Montric.set('cookieUser', cookieUser);
    } else {
        Montric.set('cookieUser', null);            Sets cookieUser to null
    }

    Montric.advanceReadiness();
});
```

You halt the initialization of Montric by calling `Montric.deferReadiness()`. This tells Ember.js to wait to initialize controllers and the router until a call to `Montric.advanceReadiness()` is made. This provides a window inside which you can fetch either data that your application needs (such as the authenticated user), or data that you can use to optimize your application (data that's large or frequently used that you want to prefetch).

In this case, you fetch the current user by issuing an XHR request to the /user URL. If the Montric back end responds with a user object that has an associated `userRole`, assume that the back end has authenticated the `uuidToken` cookie. You can then create a new `Montric.User` object and set the properties that you received from the server. After the new `Montric.User` object is initialized, you can call `Montric.set('cookieUser', cookieUser)`. This tells the `Montric.UserController` that the user was authenticated via HTTP cookies and that you don't need to involve Persona for the current session.

A note about security

Even though Mozilla Persona is a secure authentication provider, all authentication providers are subject to vulnerabilities that you should be aware of. Most vulnerabilities can be avoided by following simple guidelines, but some are harder to avoid.

The Mozilla Identity Team (the people behind Persona) has created a set of guidelines that you should follow when implementing a Persona-based authentication application.

You should at least read through the guidelines given in both the best practices document (https://developer.mozilla.org/en-US/Persona/Security_Considerations) and in the implementor's guide (https://developer.mozilla.org/en-US/Persona/The_implementor_s_guide). Together these outline the vulnerabilities to consider when implementing your authentication solution, while also giving you a walk-through on how to avoid exposing your users.

9.3 Summary

This chapter has presented two possible ways to implement authentication and authorization in your Ember.js application. Through the use of Mozilla Persona, you've seen how a third-party JavaScript-based authentication solution can be integrated into an Ember.js application. User authentication is always a tougher implementation than you might initially expect because you need to consider many edge cases when implementing a proper authentication mechanism in your application.

The advantages of using a third-party authentication provider are many, but the most significant advantage is that your applications won't have the responsibilities that are related to keeping usernames and passwords. In addition to secure storage, password hashing, and keeping your user information safe from hackers, you get all the features related to account creation, editing, and lost and forgotten passwords for free. Persona packs all these features into a single neat package that's fairly easy to integrate into your own applications.

Because Persona isn't based on any social network or other application platform that you might use, Persona users don't have to worry about their personal information leaking outside their authentication mechanism. The only piece of personal information that Persona will ever reveal to your sites is your email addresses.

In the next chapter we'll move on to packaging, deploying, and building cloud-based applications with Ember.js.

The Ember.js run loop— Backburner.js

10

This chapter covers

- Understanding the internal structure of the run loop
- Using the run loop to propagate events
- Using the run loop to improve application performance
- Executing code within a specific run loop
- Executing repeated tasks within the run loop

The Ember.js run loop is a concept unique to Ember.js and is one of the distinguishing features over similar frameworks such as AngularJS or Backbone.js. Even though the name might indicate that the run loop is implemented as a continuous loop, it's not. During the final release candidates of Ember.js, the run loop was extracted into its own microlibrary called Backburner.js. Even though Ember.js now uses Backburner.js internally, the APIs internal to Ember.js, including the run loop API, haven't changed. When I refer to the Ember.js run loop in this chapter, I'm referring to both the Ember.js-specific API and the underlying Backburner.js library. This separation is similar to how Ember.js integrated its other microlibraries, and it ensures that the

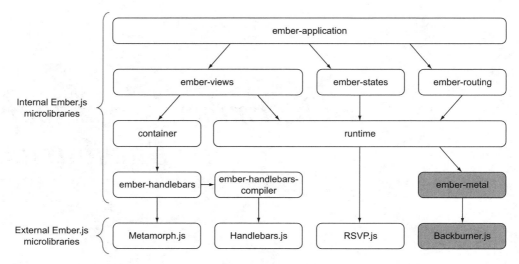

Figure 10.1   How Backburner.js fits in with the rest of the Ember.js framework

APIs that Ember.js offers to your application can remain unchanged, while changes and optimizations to its underlying microlibraries are made.

Figure 10.1 shows how Backburner.js fits in with the rest of the Ember.js application framework.

This chapter explores Backburner.js and how Ember.js uses it to keep your Ember.js-based application responsive and your data bindings up-to-date throughout your application.

You'll start by learning what the run loop is before you look at a sample application enabling you to take a deep dive into the run loop itself. After that's out of the way, you'll take a closer look at how you can interact with the run loop and issue code to execute within the constraints of a run loop.

10.1   *What is the run loop?*

In short, the *run loop* is a mechanism that Ember.js uses to group, coordinate, and execute events, key-value notifications, and timers within your application. The run loop remains dormant until a valid event occurs within your application or until you start one manually via the API.

To further explain the run loop and the role it plays in your application, let's define it in the context of a simple application, the TodoMVC application. Specifically, you'll look at the Ember.js version of the TodoMVC example at http://todomvc.com.

10.1.1   *Introducing the Ember.js TodoMVC application*

TodoMVC is a great project that enables you to explore and compare the various Java-Script MVC libraries and frameworks. Each of the MVC frameworks implements the

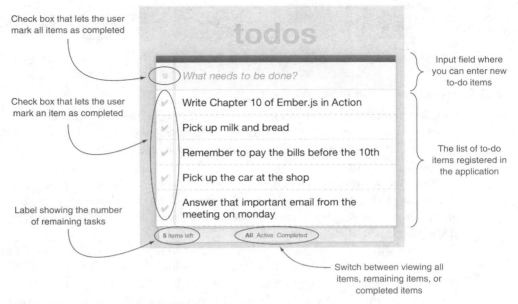

Check box that lets the user mark all items as completed

Check box that lets the user mark an item as completed

Label showing the number of remaining tasks

Input field where you can enter new to-do items

The list of to-do items registered in the application

Switch between viewing all items, remaining items, or completed items

Figure 10.2   The TodoMVC application

same TodoMVC application, and you can go in and look at the source code developed for each of the frameworks. Figure 10.2 shows the TodoMVC application.

The TodoMVC application has several features:

- *Input field*—Using the text field at the top of the application, the user can enter new items into the to-do list.
- *To-do list*—After the user has added at least one item, the items display in a list below the text input field.
- *Mark Task as Done check box*—At the left of each item in the to-do list, a single check box lets the user mark that item as completed.
- *Mark All Tasks as Done check box*—At the left of the text input field, a check box enables the user to mark all remaining tasks as completed.
- *Status label*—At the bottom-left of the screen, a label shows the number of tasks that have yet to be completed.

Let's say a user has added 100 items to their to-do list. Later, the user has finished their chores and wants to mark all the tasks as completed. What happens when the user clicks the Mark All Tasks as Done check box next to the text input field? What you definitely don't want is for the application to update the DOM for each of the 100 tasks, because this is a particularly time-consuming, slow, and expensive task to carry out. This is where Ember.js's run loop kicks in and helps your application structure the events and carry them out in a sane and efficient order.

With this scenario in mind, let's take a closer look at the Ember.js run loop.

Figure 10.3   The Ember.js run loop queues

10.1.2 *The Ember.js run loop explained*

Despite its name, the run loop isn't a loop that executes continuously, but rather it consists of a set of predefined queues, which are placed in an array defining the sequence of execution. Figure 10.3 shows the default queues that are defined in Ember.js's run loop.

By default, Ember.js includes five queues. Unless otherwise specified, any events that are added to the run loop will get scheduled into the Actions queue. You'll learn about these queues, their relationships, and their responsibilities as you progress through the rest of the chapter.

Ember.js does a good job of implementing listeners that fill in these queues whenever appropriate events occur. In rare cases in which Ember.js doesn't add an event to one of the run loop queues, the internal run loop API lets you schedule your own events into one of the queues. If you do something sufficiently unique or complex (for example, implementing your own custom listeners, or working with new technologies such as WebRTC or WebSocket), you're even allowed to create new queues.

In the Ember.js TodoMVC application, when the user clicks the Mark All Tasks as Done check box, that event triggers a new run loop, starting its work on the Sync queue, which contains all your application's actions that involve propagating bound data. At this point, you'll find at least 400 events in the Sync queue:

- A total of 100 events update each of the tasks in the to-do list, marking the to-do item as done by setting the isCompleted property to true.
- The to-do list displays 100 check boxes, one next to each to-do item. These check boxes have their checked property bound to the to-do item's isCompleted property. These binding events account for another 100 entries in the Sync queue.
- At the bottom left of the application is a status label indicating the number of remaining to-do items. This label is bound to the TodosController's remainingFormatted computed property. This property is, in turn, bound to each to-do item's isCompleted property, accounting for another 100 events in the Sync queue.
- Similarly, the Mark All as Done check box at the top-left of the application toggles on or off, depending on whether all items in the to-do list are marked as completed. These events account for another 100 events in the Sync queue.

After the run loop has finished working through this queue, all your bindings will have been propagated out through your application.

Depending on how your application's bindings are set up, the effect of carrying out one binding might lead to new events being added to one of the run loop queues.

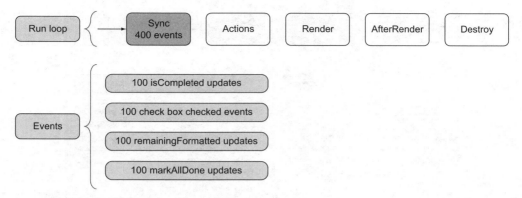

Figure 10.4 The start of the Ember.js run loop

The Ember.js run loop therefore ensures that the current queue, as well as any previous queues, are completely exhausted before moving on to the next queue. Figure 10.4 shows the state of your run loop just after it's been triggered and just before it starts working on exhausting the Sync queue.

Backburner.js starts out by going through all the events added to the Sync queue. When the processing of the events in the Sync queue has completed, Ember.js will have propagated out the bindings and added events to the Render queue, telling Ember.js to redraw all 101 check boxes and to cross out the completed tasks with a strike-through. In addition, the counter at the bottom left of the application has to be updated to show that zero to-do items remain. This accounts for another event in the Render queue.

When the Sync queue is empty, the run loop moves on to the Actions queue. This default queue in Ember.js contains any events that need to be carried out after all the bindings have been propagated, but before the views are rendered into the DOM. The only two events that are specified to go into the Actions queue are the application initialization and RSVP events. (RSVP is the library Ember.js uses internally to interact with promises.)

Figure 10.5 shows the state of the run loop as it starts working on the Actions queue.

Because no items are in the Actions queue and the Sync queue is still empty, the run loop moves along to the next queue.

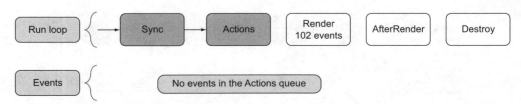

Figure 10.5 After the Sync queue has been exhausted

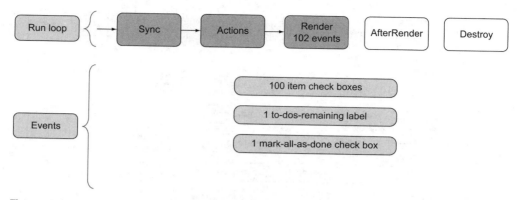

Figure 10.6   After the Sync and Actions queues have been exhausted

The view packages add the two queues Render and AfterRender to the list of queues in the run loop. When the Actions queue is exhausted, it's guaranteed that all your application's bindings have been propagated throughout your application before it reaches the Render queue. This is important, because interacting with and manipulating the browser's DOM tree are among the most time-consuming tasks that Ember.js performs. Having a system implemented that ensures that your application performs a minimum amount of DOM manipulation is critical for your application's performance, especially on mobile devices, which have limited processing capabilities. Figure 10.6 shows the state of the run loop as it starts working on the Render queue.

The Render queue contains events related to view-rendering into the DOM, as its name suggests. It's critical that this queue comes after the Sync and Actions queues, as Ember.js uses its queue sequence to keep the number of DOM manipulations to a minimum during the run loop. After all the bindings have been propagated in the Sync queue and all the pending callbacks and promises have been executed in the Actions queue, everything is ready for Ember.js to start manipulating the user interface.

The Render queue contains DOM-related events, and each item in this queue generally results in one or more DOM manipulations. Most of your views put their render events in this queue. Experience will show you, though, that some views' events need to be scheduled after the Render queue, and this is where—you guessed it—the After-Render queue comes in handy. Figure 10.7 shows the state of the run loop as it starts working on the AfterRender queue.

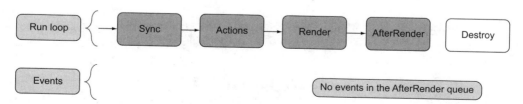

Figure 10.7   After the Render queue has been exhausted

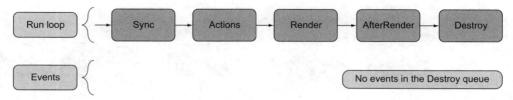

Figure 10.8   After the AfterRender queue has been exhausted

To summarize, the AfterRender queue contains view-related events that need to occur after the standard render events have finished executing. One example of such a view is a view that needs to access the resulting DOM elements, because these elements will be available only after the Render queue is exhausted. Typically, the AfterRender queue is used in views that need to append or alter the contents of an HTML element that's rendered or updated as part of the Render queue. Figure 10.8 shows the state of the run loop as it starts working on the Destroy queue.

After the run loop has finished emptying the AfterRender queue, it moves on to the final Destroy queue. In this queue, events for any objects that need to be destroyed are added. You might be wondering what goes into the Destroy queue. Most often, any views that have been removed from the DOM and aren't needed anymore are added to this queue. This happens when the user navigates from one route to another inside your application or when the state changes so that different parts of a template are rendered into the DOM. Figure 10.9 shows the state of the run loop after the Destroy queue has been exhausted.

The run loop has one more trick up its sleeve, though. Any events in the run queue might cause other events to be scheduled in any of the other queues. Events in the Actions queue might, for instance, schedule new events inside the Sync queue. If an event in the Actions queue manipulates data within your application, that data might have its own observers or computed properties bound to it. If that's the case, new events are added to the Sync queue to ensure that these changes are also taken care of before the run loop moves on to the next queue.

This is an important concept that's critical to the run loop's ability to keep the user interface consistent with the changes while also minimizing the number of DOM manipulations that your application needs to perform: the Ember.js run loop ensures that all previous queues are completely exhausted before it moves on to the next queue.

Figure 10.9   After the Destroy queue has been exhausted

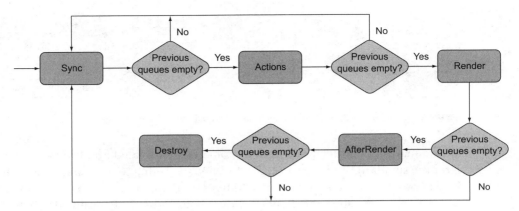

Figure 10.10   The revised Ember.js run loop

Now that you have a clearer understanding, let's revise our conceptual overview of the run loop, as shown in figure 10.10.

Knowing how the run loop is implemented comes in handy after you get past the initial learning curve of Ember.js and your application's complexity grows. By understanding the run loop, you can take advantage of how it works in order to optimize the performance of your application.

I mentioned that the run loop has an API that you can use to interact with the run loop. Through this API, you can execute, schedule, and repeat your application's code within the constraints of the run loop. The next section dives into the run loop API.

10.2   *Executing code within the constraints of the run loop*

You can use various methods to schedule code to execute inside a run loop. Using the run loop API, you can execute code immediately, after a set amount of time, or during the next run loop. You might find this useful when you need to manipulate the DOM elements after the `didInsertElement` function of your views has completed, or when you need to rely on performing actions at a specific interval after your view has rendered. You'll look at examples of each of these scenarios.

If you want to execute code immediately, wrap your code inside `Ember.run (callback)`. Calling this function ensures that your code is executed within a run loop. If no run loop is currently executing, Ember.js automatically starts one. After a run loop starts, the code within the callback executes before the run loop ends. Before the run loop finishes, it ensures that all the queues are flushed properly. As a developer, you can be certain that any events and any bindings that your code affects have been properly executed and that the DOM has been updated after the run loop reaches its end.

10.2.1   *Executing code inside the current run loop*

Executing code in the current run loop is the most common run loop scheduling task you'll write. Using `Ember.run`, Ember.js places the given callback into the default Actions queue.

Listing 10.1 shows an example of attaching a piece of code to the current run loop. In this example, you're implementing part of a view that draws a line chart. Specifically, you're looking at an observer that listens for changes to the view's `chart.series` property. Because the server side doesn't always return a specific color for each series in the line chart, you need to tell the charting library (Rickshaw) to pick a new color from its palette and attach that color to each series without a color already defined. After a new color is added to the series, you need to redraw the view.

Listing 10.1 Executing code in the run loop

```
Montric.ChartView = Ember.View.extend({
    contentObserver: function() {
        var series = this.get('chart.series');
        if (series) {
            var palette = new Rickshaw.Color.Palette({scheme: "munin"});

            series.forEach(function(serie) {            ◁──  Updates color
                if (!serie.color) {                           for each series
                    serie.color = palette.color()
                }
            });

            var view = this;
            Ember.run(function() {                      ◁──  Ensures view
                view.rerender();                              is rerendered
            });
        }
    }.observes('chart.series')
});
```

Observes chart.series property

The preceding view is the main chart view from the Montric application. This view has an observer that listens for changes to the `chart.series` property. If `chart.series` has a value, you ensure that the chart series has a color defined, and if not, you use a new value from the chart library's color palette. After each chart series has been updated, you need to `rerender` the view in order to update the chart present in the DOM. Because you want to ensure that the view is updated properly, you wrap the `rerender` function inside a callback function, passed into `Ember.run`.

But you have other options, which you can use to gain better control of how and when your code is executed by the run loop.

10.2.2 Executing code inside the next run loop

Sometimes you want to make sure that your code executes just after the current run loop has finished. You can do this in two ways. You can either use the special `Ember.run.next()` function call, or you can schedule the code to run in 1 millisecond by using the `Ember.run.later()` function call. In the following listing, you're revisiting the chart series observer from listing 10.1, which has been updated to use `Ember.run.next()`.

Listing 10.2   Executing code inside the next run loop using `Ember.run.next()`

```
Montric.ChartView = Ember.View.extend({
    contentObserver: function() {
        //Code ommited, but same as listing 10.1

        var view = this;
        Ember.run.next(function() {
            view.rerender();
        });
    }.observes('chart.series')
});
```

Executes code inside
next run loop

As you can see, the code in this listing is the same as that shown in listing 10.1, with the exception that you replace the call to `Ember.run()` with `Ember.run.next()`. The signatures for both functions are the same. The effect of this change is that the rerendering of the view waits until all bindings and observers have been properly propagated and until all DOM updates that are scheduled in the current run loop have been properly carried out. This might be useful if you want to apply animations to a DOM element after it renders, and if you need to schedule an event to occur after the events in the Render, AfterRender, and Destroy queues have been carried out.

10.2.3 *Executing code inside a future run loop*

I mentioned that it's possible to use `Ember.run.later()` to schedule code to be executed within the next run loop. In Montric, the application is receiving updated information every 15 seconds. Because you want to keep the user interface updated without the user having to trigger an update action, you need to automatically update visible charts every 15 seconds. Using `Ember.run.later` enables you to implement this type of functionality. The following listing shows an example of how `Ember.run.later()` is used.

Listing 10.3   Executing code inside the next run loop using `Ember.run.later()`

```
Montric.ChartView = Ember.View.extend({
    contentObserver: function() {
        //Code omitted, but same as listing 10.1

        var view = this;
        Ember.run.later(function() {
            view.rerender();
        }, 1);
    }.observes('chart.series')
});
```

Executes code inside
next run loop

Schedules task for 1 ms
after run loop ends

You replace the call to `Ember.run.next()` with a call to `Ember.run.later()` while adding a parameter that specifies the number of milliseconds to wait before scheduling the code to be executed in the next run loop. In this case, you're scheduling the code to execute in the run loop starting 1 millisecond after the current run loop finishes, which is most likely the next run loop.

You might have guessed by now that it's also possible to schedule tasks to be executed at a specific time in the future by using `Ember.run.later()`. By changing the number passed in as the final parameter to 500, the code given executes in the first run loop starting after 500 milliseconds have passed.

In fact, there are many ways in which you can schedule a task at a specified time in the future. So far, you've only been scheduling code into the Actions queue. You might be wondering how to schedule code into one of the other queues or how to schedule a repeated task. This is where `Ember.run.schedule()` and `Ember.run.interval()` come in.

10.2.4 *Executing code inside a specific queue*

Most of the time, you'll want to schedule code into the Actions queue. At that point, all bindings have been propagated and everything should be set up for most of the code that you'd want to schedule to execute inside a run loop.

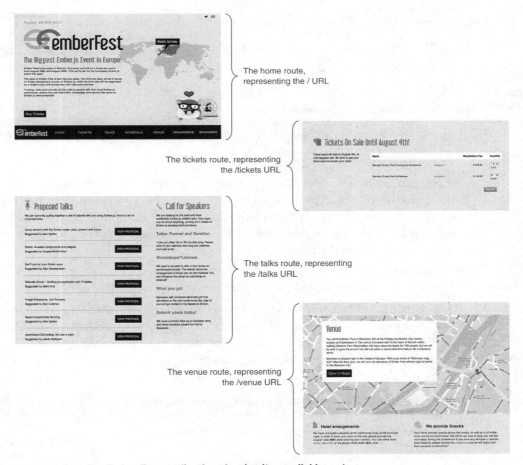

The home route,
representing the / URL

The tickets route, representing
the /tickets URL

The talks route, representing
the /talks URL

The venue route, representing
the /venue URL

Figure 10.11 The Ember Fest application showing its scrollable routes

Once in a while, though, you want to have fine-grained control of which queue you schedule your code in. In the Ember Fest application that you looked at in Chapter 6, you schedule code in the AfterRender queue. The Ember Fest landing page is built from six subroutes that are organized as a single page that the user can scroll down to reveal the contents of the subroutes. As the user scrolls down, the route changes and the URL updates to reflect the user's current location on the page. In addition, if the user enters the application at one of the visible subroutes, the application needs to scroll the page to the correct spot on the page. Figure 10.11 shows a few routes from the Ember Fest application and which routes each part of the website is associated with.

This scrolling functionality is added into each of the subroutes by using `document.getElementById(id).scrollIntoView()`. Consider the code in the following listing.

Listing 10.4   Scrolling to a specific element in the DOM

```
Emberfest.IndexVenueRoute = Ember.Route.extend({                    ◁─┐  Indicates route
    setupController: function(controller, model) {                     │  for /venue URL
        this._super(controller, model);
        _gaq.push(['_trackPageview', "/venue"]);              ◁──┐   Integrates route with
                                                                  │   Google Analytics
        document.title = 'Venue - Ember Fest';
    },
                                                                       Presents
    renderTemplate: function() {                                       nonworking
        this._super();                                                 scrolling example
        document.getElementById('venue').scrollIntoView();    ◁──┘
    }
});
```

Adds scrolling functionality ⟶ (points to `renderTemplate`)

As you can see in the code, you're attempting to scroll the HTML element that corresponds to the ID venue by using the `scrollIntoView()` function. The problem with this code, though, is that the template that the venue element is part of won't be rendered into the DOM when the `renderTemplate` function is executed. The code from listing 10.4 results in the following error message:

```
TypeError: 'null' is not an object
(evaluating 'document.getElementById('venue').scrollIntoView')
```

This obviously isn't what you want. Instead, you want to scroll the venue element into view just after it's been rendered in the DOM. As you may remember, the element is drawn to the DOM inside the Render queue, so try to schedule the code into the After-Render queue by using `Ember.run.schedule()`. The following listing shows the updated code.

Listing 10.5   Scheduling code in the AfterRender queue using `Ember.run.schedule()`

```
Emberfest.IndexVenueRoute = Ember.Route.extend({
    renderTemplate: function() {                                  Schedules code
        this._super();                                            into AfterRender
        Ember.run.schedule('afterRender', this, function(){   ◁── queue
```

```
        document.getElementById('venue').scrollIntoView();
    });
    }
});
```

This example omits the `setupController` code, but it remains the same as before. The only difference is that you now wrap `document.getElementById('venue').scrollIntoView()` inside `Ember.run.schedule()`. The function `Ember.run.schedule()` takes three arguments. The first specifies which queue to schedule the task in, and the second takes the context in which the callback is executed.

Now the preceding code works as expected. When the user enters the `IndexVenueRoute`, the route's `setup()` function is called, which in turn triggers the `renderTemplate()` function. Ember.js internally defers any rendering logic to the Render queue, which includes rendering the template that belongs to the `IndexVenueRoute`. After the run loop enters the AfterRender queue, the venue element that you're looking for is already added to the DOM. At this point, you can scroll the page down to the correct element.

You've looked at how to schedule single tasks into the run loop in different ways, but so far you haven't looked at how to use the run loop to implement repeated tasks.

10.2.5 *Executing repeated tasks with the run loop*

Sadly, Ember.js doesn't implement an `Ember.run.interval()` function. This makes it harder to implement repeated functionality in your Ember.js applications. You can do one of the following:

- Fall back to the standard JavaScript `setInterval()` function, wrapping its contents in `Ember.run()` or `Ember.run.schedule()`.
- Use `Ember.run.later()` and make sure that the callback you pass in recursively adds another call to `Ember.run.later()`.

Listing 10.6 shows how the Montric application implements updating the loaded charts every 15 seconds. `ChartsController` implements both a `startTimer()` and a `stopTimer()` function that create a new interval, store it on the controller, and clear it. In addition to the code shown here, the controller calls the `startTimer()` and `stopTimer()` functions based on the current state of `ChartsController`, as well as the state the application is in.

Listing 10.6   How to execute repeated tasks inside the run loop

```
Montric.ChartsController = Ember.ArrayController.extend({
    startTimer: function() {                                    ◁── Starts interval
        var controller = this;                                         and stores it
        var intervalId = setInterval(function () {
            Ember.run(function() {                              ◁── Executes contents
                if (controller                                         inside loop
.get('controllers.application.showLiveCharts')) {
                    controller.reloadCharts();
                }
```

Starts interval every 15,000 ms

```
        });
    }, 15000);

    this.set('chartTimerId', intervalId);
  },

  stopTimer: function() {
    if (this.get('chartTimerId') != null) {
      clearInterval(this.get('chartTimerId'));
        this.set('chartTimerId', null);
    }
  }
});
```

<---| **Terminates interval**

<---| **Clears and**
    resets interval

You wrap the contents of the interval function inside `Ember.run()` to ensure that that piece of code is executed within the current run loop. This is important because any changes that occur within your interval function trigger a run loop and keep your application's user interface up-to-date.

10.3   Summary

Throughout this chapter, you looked at how the run loop and Backburner.js are used in the Ember.js framework to ensure that your Ember.js-based application is as fast as possible, while staying out of your way as much as it can. In most cases, Ember.js schedules your code into the correct run loop queue without you even knowing that the run loop exists.

That being said, in a few edge cases, knowing how the run loop works and how to use its queues to properly serve your application's needs comes in handy. In these cases, scheduling tasks into the right run loop queue or scheduling code to be run in a future run loop will most likely lead to more-readable code.

You learned that by using the run loop's API, you can schedule tasks into the current run loop or a future run loop. You can also schedule tasks into a specific run loop queue.

Now that you've seen most of what Ember.js has to offer, it's time to take a closer look at how to package and deploy your Ember.js applications.

Packaging and deployment

This chapter covers

- Understanding JavaScript application packaging and assembly
- Creating a project structure
- Minimizing and concatenating files and compiling templates
- Using Grunt.js

JavaScript build tools are, sadly, still at their infancy. A range of products compete to solve the tasks of application assembly: running unit tests, performing linting (ensuring that your JavaScript code is clean), minifying source code, and packaging your application.

The problem with the existing tools is that they tend to be hard to use and give error messages that are hard to understand, even for developers. In addition, the JavaScript community has yet to agree on a standard for managing application dependency and how these dependencies should be bundled with your application. If you're entering the JavaScript world from more-mature server-side programming languages such as Java and C#, the JavaScript build tools and the assembly pipeline leave a lot to desire.

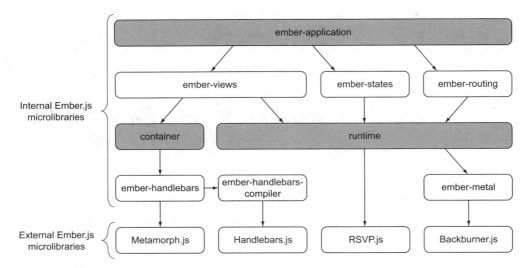

Figure 11.1   The parts of Ember.js you'll work on in this chapter

This chapter is split into two parts. The first part describes the steps that are necessary to assemble and package your Ember.js application into a format that's suitable for deployment and for sending out to your users' browsers. The second part explains how to achieve these tasks by using the tool that's most popular at the time of publication, Grunt.js.

Before you move on, we'll review the parts of Ember.js you'll work on in this chapter, as shown in Figure 11.1.

But first, let's take a closer look at what packaging and assembling modern JavaScript applications entail.

11.1   Understanding JavaScript application packaging and assembly

To use any build tool, you need to properly structure your application's source code files. You can build up this structure in various ways, but most important, you need to keep your source code file types in separate directories. All your JavaScript files need to go either directly into a single directory inside your project or into a subdirectory of that directory. The same is true for CSS files, HTML files, and any other assets that you want to include in your application. Let's look at how to structure an Ember.js application to prepare it for packaging and assembly later.

11.1.1   Choosing a directory structure

As I mentioned, the JavaScript community hasn't agreed on a standard directory structure for JavaScript applications. You're free to name your directories whatever you want. As long as you keep your asset types separate from each other, you'll be able to tell your build tool where to find them later.

On the bright side, the JavaScript community is slowly but surely building up a consensus that eventually will lead to a standard way to define your JavaScript project's directory structure.

Until then, it's wise to follow a few sane guidelines. For my Ember.js applications, I like to separate my assets in the following directories:

- *js/app*—Any self-written JavaScript file that's part of the project.
- *js/lib*—Any third-party JavaScript files. Some of these files might already be minimized.
- *js/test*—Any JavaScript unit tests that are part of the project.
- *css*—All the project's CSS files go directly into this folder.
- *images*—All of your project's images.

NOTE Some build tools require or prefer a specific directory structure. In this case, because you're using Grunt.js, you'll tell Grunt.js where to locate your files. You're completely free to use your own directory-structure style.

Using this directory structure makes it easy for your application, developers, and build tool to find your assets later. Most of these directories are flat, meaning they don't have any subdirectories. This is most likely not the case for the js/app directory, however, as you'll see later in this section.

STRUCTURING YOUR CUSTOM-WRITTEN SOURCE CODE

Having a sane structure for your source code is extremely important. Because I can't stress this fact enough, I'll repeat it: having a sane structure for your source code is extremely important! You've probably seen Ember.js application examples in which all the JavaScript application code resides in a single app.js file. This approach is great and efficient when you're writing small, proof-of-concept or example applications, but if you intend to maintain your application later, and if you're serious about ever deploying your awesome Ember.js application into production, you need to separate your source code into different files.

Other statically typed languages employ a structure that allows you to define only a single entity inside a single file. In my opinion, this is the only sane strategy to use for JavaScript applications, too, but you end up with a lot of files inside your application. To bring a sense of structure to this chaos, you can take one of two approaches: keep objects of the same type together, or keep your features together.

11.1.2 Structuring your custom-written source code

Which of these strategies you choose is up to you, but let's look at how to organize your code both ways and why I recommend keeping your features together.

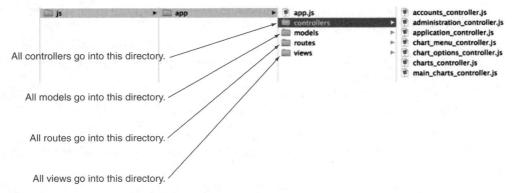

Figure 11.2 Keeping objects of the same type together

KEEPING OBJECTS OF THE SAME TYPE TOGETHER

To keep objects of the same type together, you create directories inside js/app where you collect, for example, all controllers, all views, and so on. This leads to a structure similar to figure 11.2.

You have directories labeled controllers, models, routes, and views. As long as your application is small, this approach is manageable. But even in the example shown in figure 11.2, you can probably see that this approach is hard to maintain in the long run. If you look inside the controllers directory, you'll quickly see that there's no quick and easy way to distinguish between your files and their responsibilities within your application. You can guess that the accounts_controller.js file is responsible for administrating user accounts, but because this directory structure doesn't give you any context for each of your controllers, you won't know for sure until you examine the contents of the file.

KEEPING YOUR FEATURES TOGETHER

The other approach is to define your directory structure bundled into the features that your application provides. For an Ember.js application, any code that's part of a single route within your application lives in the same folder. You then end up with folders named administration/accounts or chart that contain files defining that route's route, controller, and view. Figure 11.3 shows an example of this approach.

The js/app/administration/accounts directory contains all the files that together define the functionality for the administration/accounts route within the Montric application. In addition, you can see directories for administration/alert_recipients, administration/menu, and so on.

This feature-centric directory structure achieves the following:

- Separates your logic into small, maintainable files
- Gives each file a predictable location in your js/app directory
- Reflects your application's main features, making your application easier to maintain in the future while also being easier for new developers on your team to understand

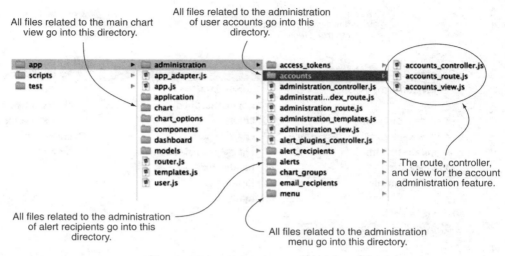

Figure 11.3   Keeping your features together

STRUCTURING THE JS/TEST DIRECTORY

You might wonder what to do with the js/test directory. In my opinion, you should structure this directory in the same way that you structure your js/app directory. You'll end up with directories such as js/test/administration/account and js/test/administration/alerts. As with your js/app directory, structuring your tests in this manner achieves the following:

- Gives you feedback about which feature has failing tests whenever a test fails. If a test is failing inside the js/test/administration/account directory, you can know quickly and without any detective work that you've introduced a bug that affects your account administration.
- Provides predictable locations for your files in your js/test directory.
- Glancing over the directory structure of your tests gives you a sense of which parts of your application are well tested and which parts you should look closer at.

11.1.3   Organizing non-JavaScript assets

Now that you've structured your JavaScript assets, you also need to implement a structure for your non-JavaScript assets such as the contents of the top-level directories and your Handlebars.js templates.

STRUCTURING THE TOP-LEVEL DIRECTORY OF YOUR PROJECT

In my opinion, the top-level directory is reserved for files that define something about your application. This includes—but isn't limited to—the following:

- index.html, which defines the overall structure of your application
- A file describing any third-party dependencies that your application has
- A build file telling a build tool how to assemble and test your application

There's one more directory structure that we haven't talked about: templates.

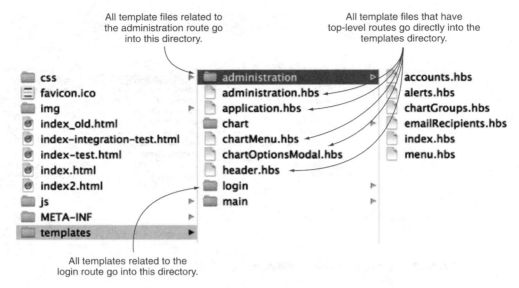

Figure 11.4 **The template directory structure**

STRUCTURING YOUR TEMPLATES

I recommend that you put each of your templates into their own separate files, suffixed with the custom .hbs extension. In fact, you can add any suffix you want for the files, because you'll specify this when you assemble the application. These files should be named after the routes in your application, which achieves the following:

- Separating each template into its own file
- Grouping related templates together into a sensible directory structure that resembles your application's features
- Telling your build tool, via the directory name and filename combination, how to compile your templates into JavaScript code, and, more important, what to call your templates automatically

Figure 11.4 shows the template structure for Montric.

This structure ensures that you end up with a directory named templates, which contains a hierarchical directory structure that exactly maps your application's routes. This is both predictable for the developer and easy for a build tool to use when precompiling your templates into JavaScript code.

Now that you understand how to structure your Ember.js application, let's move on and explore the Ember.js application assembly process.

11.1.4 *Following the Ember.js application assembly process*

After you've structured your application into separate files to make development easier and your application easier to maintain, the assembly process involves combining all your application's assets into single files. All your JavaScript code needs to be combined into one file, and all your CSS code needs to be combined into another file. In addition, each of these files needs to be minimized to cut down on the amount of data that you send across the wire from the server to the client.

To summarize, the JavaScript application assembly process includes the steps listed below. You don't have to know what each step does, or what each means at this point. You'll learn more about each concept in detail as you work your way through the rest of this chapter.

ASSEMBLING SOURCE CODE AND TEMPLATES

Complete the following tasks to combine all your JavaScript files:

1 Find each file inside the js/app directory.
2 Lint each file for common JavaScript errors.
3 Concatenate with previous files.
4 Minify the concatenated file.

Because Ember.js also has templates spread across multiple files, you need to perform the following tasks on your templates:

1 Find each *.hbs file.
2 Assign the contents of each file to Ember.TEMPLATES[dirname/filename] = Ember.Handlebars.compile(fileContents)
3 Concatenate with previous templates.

ASSEMBLING CSS

In addition to the JavaScript and templates, the CSS files also need to be combined and minified. This process involves the following tasks:

1 Find each *.css file.
2 Concatenate with previous CSS.
3 Minify the contents.

Multiple steps are involved in this process, so let's take a closer look at how they're related. The Ember.js application assembly process is shown in figure 11.5.

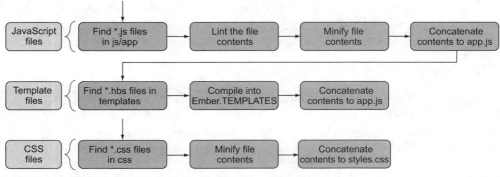

Figure 11.5 The Ember.js JavaScript application assembly process

The preceding figure shows the complete Ember.js application assembly process, which includes assembly of your JavaScript source code, Handlebars.js templates, and CSS files. The goal is to end up with two files: one file (app.js) contains all your application's custom JavaScript, and the other (styles.css) contains all your application's CSS.

Now that you've had a look at how to structure your Ember.js application, let's move on and explore how to use Grunt.js to build and assemble your application.

11.2 Using Grunt.js as your build tool

Grunt.js describes itself as the JavaScript Task Runner. This third-party application, written in JavaScript, runs inside Node.js. Its main task is to automate the process of script minification, linting, running unit tests, and concatenating your application's assets into single files. Grunt.js is built around the notion of a pipeline. This pipeline defines how your application is assembled and tested.

> **Installing NPM**
>
> Because Grunt.js is a Node.js application, you need to have the Node Package Manager (NPM) installed on your system to get started. Head over to http://nodejs.org to install Node.js, and to http://npmjs.org to install NPM.

You'll implement a complete application assembly pipeline with Grunt, which entails the following:

- Bootstrapping the Grunt.js build system
- Concatenating your JavaScript files into a single file
- Applying linting to the concatenated file
- Compiling templates into the concatenated file
- Minifying the concatenated file into a production-ready file for deployment

Grunt.js is plugin-based, and any tasks that you want to perform are executed by a Grunt.js plugin. You'll install the plugin you need for assembling the Montric application as you go through the chapter. You have a ways to go, though, so you'll start by bootstrapping the Grunt.js build system for Montric. After you've learned how to assemble an Ember.js application with Grunt.js, you'll explore the advantages and disadvantages of using Grunt.js.

11.2.1 Bootstrapping Montric's Grunt.js build

Grunt.js expects to find two files inside your application's top-level directory:

- package.json
- Gruntfile.js

The first thing you need to do is add a package.json file, which describes the Montric application, along with any dependencies that either the application or the build pipeline requires. The following listing shows your initial package.json file.

Listing 11.1 The initial package.json file

```
{
  "name": "Montric",
  "version": "0.9.0",
  "devDependencies": {
    "grunt": "~0.4.1"
  }
}
```

Project name → `"name": "Montric",`

Current version of your project ← `"version": "0.9.0",`

Dependencies Grunt needs for assembly ← `"devDependencies": {`

Version of Grunt.js required ← `"grunt": "~0.4.1"`

You need to specify a few details to get started inside the package.json file. This file tells Grunt.js the name of your project, its current version, and any `devDependencies` that Grunt.js requires to assemble your project. You'll add dependencies inside the `devDependencies` section as you build up the Montric assembly pipeline.

Next, you need to add a Gruntfile.js file. This file describes how your application is going to be assembled. The initial Gruntfile.js is shown in the next listing.

Listing 11.2 The initial Gruntfile.js

```
module.exports = function(grunt) {

  // Project configuration.
  grunt.initConfig({
    pkg: grunt.file.readJSON('package.json'),
  });

  // Default task(s).
  grunt.registerTask('default', []);

};
```

Executes any code inside the function ← `module.exports = function(grunt) {`

Reads package.json configuration → `pkg: grunt.file.readJSON('package.json'),`

Places configurations in grunt.initConfig ← `grunt.initConfig({`

Registers default tasks ← `grunt.registerTask('default', []);`

At this stage, your Gruntfile won't be performing any task. But you've added enough information to be able to execute `grunt`. Before you can test your Gruntfile.js and package.json configuration, you need to install the Grunt.js command-line interface (CLI).

Installing the Grunt.js CLI and preparing your application to be built by Grunt

1 Start Terminal (Mac/Linux) or the command prompt (Windows).
2 Enter the following command:

```
npm install -g grunt-cli
```

NPM installs `grunt-cli` into your global environment, allowing the `grunt` command to be executed from any directory in your system. If you are building an application for the first time that already has dependencies specified in package.json, you need to run `npm install` in order to install those dependencies before you move on.

Navigate to your project directory and enter the command `grunt`. When you press Enter, Grunt.js attempts to assemble your application by using the default task that you created previously. The result should be similar to figure 11.6.

```
Joachims-MacBook-Pro:webapp jhsmbp$ grunt

Done, without errors.
Joachims-MacBook-Pro:webapp jhsmbp$
```

Figure 11.6   Executing `grunt`

Now that you have a working Grunt.js setup, you'll add a task to concatenate all your JavaScript code into a single file.

> **NOTE** All the screenshots in this chapter were taken after running the command on my Mac with Mac OS X 10.8, and Grunt.js version 0.4.1. Your output might vary slightly depending on your operating system and version of Grunt.js and Grunt.js plugins.

11.2.2 Concatenating the JavaScript code

Now that you've set up a working application build pipeline, let's review where you are in the assembly process, as shown in figure 11.7.

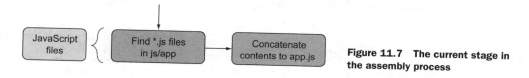

Figure 11.7   The current stage in the assembly process

First, install Grunt.js's `concat` plugin. You can do this via the command line by executing the following command:

```
npm install grunt-contrib-concat --save-dev
```

This downloads and installs the most recent version of the `grunt-contrib-concat` plugin into your project directory. The `--save-dev` parameter tells NPM to also include this version in your package.json file. Figure 11.8 shows the result of executing the preceding command.

After the package.json file has been identified, NPM downloads the `grunt-contrib-concat` plugin. In addition, NPM extends your package.json configuration by

```
Joachims-MacBook-Pro:webapp jhsmbp$ npm install grunt-contrib-concat --save-dev
npm WARN package.json Montric@0.9.0 No README.md file found!
npm http GET https://registry.npmjs.org/grunt-contrib-concat
npm http 200 https://registry.npmjs.org/grunt-contrib-concat
npm http GET https://registry.npmjs.org/grunt-contrib-concat/-/grunt-contrib-concat-0.3.0.tgz
npm http 200 https://registry.npmjs.org/grunt-contrib-concat/-/grunt-contrib-concat-0.3.0.tgz
grunt-contrib-concat@0.3.0 node_modules/grunt-contrib-concat
```

Figure 11.8   Executing `npm install grunt-contrib-concat --save-dev`

including a reference to the plugin you just installed. If you open your package.json file, it should look like the following listing.

```
{
    "name": "Montric",
    "version": "0.9.0",
    "devDependencies": {
        "grunt": "~0.4.1",
        "grunt-contrib-concat": "~0.3.0"              ◁── Adds reference to
    }                                                     version 0.3.0 (or newer)
}
```

To concatenate all your JavaScript code into a single file, extend Gruntfile.js as shown in the following listing.

```
module.exports = function(grunt) {

    grunt.initConfig({
        pkg: grunt.file.readJSON('package.json'),
        concat: {                                  ◁── Indicates configuration
            options: {                                  for plugin
                separator: '\n'
            },
            dist: {                                ◁── Defines location
                src: ['js/app/**/*.js'],                of source files
                dest: 'dist/<%= pkg.name %>.js'
            }
        }
    });
    grunt.loadNpmTasks('grunt-contrib-concat');    ◁── Loads grunt-contrib-
    grunt.registerTask('default', ['concat']);         concat plugin
};                                                 ◁── Registers plugin to
                                                       run in default task
```

Defines string injected between files → (points to `separator: '\n'`)

You added quite a bit of information to your Gruntfile.js file. The most notable addition is the `concat` object, into which you added the configuration required for the grunt-contrib-concat plugin to work. First, define an `options` object, where you can put the options that the plugin will use. In this case, tell the grunt-contrib-concat plugin to append a new line between each of the JavaScript files when it concatenates the files into a single file.

Next, the `dist` object is used to define where the plugin will find the JavaScript files to concatenate, as well as which file to output the results to when it finishes. The `src` property tells the plugin to locate any `.js` file inside any subdirectory of js/app, and the `dest` property tells the plugin to write the concatenated output to a file inside the dist directory. The name of this file is specified in your package.json file as the `name` property. In this case, the final build file is named Montric.js.

Finally, load the task into NPM and add the `concat` plugin to the default task. To assemble your application's JavaScript code into a single file, execute `grunt` at the command line. Figure 11.9 shows the results.

Before moving on, you'll clean up the code inside the Gruntfile.js file. As you can probably imagine, if you

Figure 11.9   Executing `grunt` to concatenate the JavaScript files

add all your plugins directly into the `grunt.initConfig` function, this file soon becomes large and hard to navigate. Let's look at how to extract the configuration of each plugin to a separate file.

11.2.3 *Extracting plugin configurations to separate files*

To keep your main Gruntfile.js file as small and readable as possible, let's see how to extract your plugin configurations into separate files.

Create a new directory called tasks into which you'll place your plugin configuration files. Inside this directory, create a file named concat.js. The content of this file is shown in the next listing.

Listing 11.5   Extracting the concat plug-in configurations into tasks/concat.js

```
module.exports = {                        ◁── Wraps contents inside
    options: {                                module.exports
        separator: '\n'
    },
    dist: {                               ◁── Includes dist object
        src: ['js/app/**/*.js'],              from Gruntfile.js
        dest: 'dist/<%= pkg.name %>.js'
    }
};
```

Includes options object from Gruntfile.js (annotation for `options` block)

You extracted the content of the old `concat` object from the Gruntfile.js file and added it into a `module.exports` object in the new concat.js file. Other than that, the content of the `grunt-contrib-concat` plugin configuration remains the same as before.

Next, you need to tell Grunt.js to use this file instead of the `concat` object. The following listing shows the updated Gruntfile.js.

Listing 11.6   The updated Gruntfile.js file

```
function config(name) {
    return require('./tasks/' + name);     ◁── Brings in file from      Brings in new
}                                              tasks directory          concat.js file

module.exports = function(grunt) {
    grunt.initConfig({
        pkg: grunt.file.readJSON('package.json'),
        concat: config('concat')           ◁── Calls new config
    });                                         function
```

```
  grunt.loadNpmTasks('grunt-contrib-concat');
  grunt.registerTask('default', ['concat']);
};
```

In this step, you greatly reduce the footprint while at the same time increase the readability of the Gruntfile.js file. In addition, you create a mechanism that makes it simple to load new plugins into the Grunt.js configuration.

Now that you've created a simple way of adding new plugins to your Grunt.js assembly process, let's look at how to perform linting to reduce the likelihood of your source code including obvious bugs or bad API calls.

11.2.4 Linting out common bugs

Linting is a process that analyzes your code for common bugs and potential errors. Because JavaScript is an interpreted language, linting also involves syntax verification in the world of JavaScript applications. Figure 11.10 shows where you are in the assembly process.

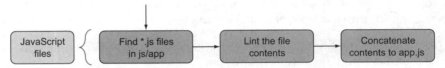

Figure 11.10   Adding linting to the assembly process

To get started, install and add the `grunt-contrib-jshint` plugin. As shown in figure 11.11, you can do this via the command line by executing the following command:

```
npm install grunt-contrib-jshint --save-dev
```

```
Joachims-MacBook-Pro:webapp jhsmbp$ npm install grunt-contrib-jshint --save-dev
npm WARN package.json Montric@0.9.0 No README.md file found!
npm http GET https://registry.npmjs.org/grunt-contrib-jshint
npm http 304 https://registry.npmjs.org/grunt-contrib-jshint
npm http GET https://registry.npmjs.org/jshint
npm http 304 https://registry.npmjs.org/jshint
npm http GET https://registry.npmjs.org/minimatch
npm http GET https://registry.npmjs.org/console-browserify
npm http GET https://registry.npmjs.org/underscore
npm http GET https://registry.npmjs.org/shelljs
npm http GET https://registry.npmjs.org/cli
npm http 304 https://registry.npmjs.org/underscore
npm http 304 https://registry.npmjs.org/shelljs
npm http 304 https://registry.npmjs.org/cli
npm http 304 https://registry.npmjs.org/console-browserify
npm http 200 https://registry.npmjs.org/minimatch
npm http GET https://registry.npmjs.org/lru-cache
npm http GET https://registry.npmjs.org/sigmund
npm http GET https://registry.npmjs.org/glob
npm http 304 https://registry.npmjs.org/glob
npm http 304 https://registry.npmjs.org/lru-cache
npm http 304 https://registry.npmjs.org/sigmund
npm http GET https://registry.npmjs.org/graceful-fs
npm http GET https://registry.npmjs.org/inherits
npm http 304 https://registry.npmjs.org/inherits
npm http 304 https://registry.npmjs.org/graceful-fs
grunt-contrib-jshint@0.6.0 node_modules/grunt-contrib-jshint
└── jshint@2.1.4 (console-browserify@0.1.6, underscore@1.4.4, shelljs@0.1.4, minimatch@0.2.12, cli@0.4.4-2)
```

Figure 11.11   Installing the `grunt-contrib-jshint` plugin

Now that you've installed the `grunt-contrib-jshint` plugin, you're ready to start adding linting functionality to your build process. Create a new file inside the tasks directory named jshint.js, with the contents shown in the following listing.

Listing 11.7 Creating the jshint.js file

```
module.exports = {
    files: ['Gruntfile.js', 'js/app/**/*.js', 'js/test/**/*.js'],
    options: {
        globals: {
            jQuery: true,
            console: true,
            module: true
        }
    }
};
```

Indicates files for linting →

Defines options to jshint ←

The preceding code tells JSHint to perform linting on any .js files inside both the js/app and js/test directories, as well as on the main Gruntfile.js file. Additionally, you provide JSHint with a couple of global parameters.

TIP Multiple options are available for the JSHint project. A complete list can be found at http://www.jshint.com/docs/.

The final step is to include your new jshint.js file in your Gruntfile.js file and add it to Grunt.js's default task. The updated Gruntfile.js is shown in the following listing.

Listing 11.8 Updated Gruntfile.js

```
function config(name) {
    return require('./tasks/' + name);
}

module.exports = function(grunt) {
    grunt.initConfig({
        pkg: grunt.file.readJSON('package.json'),
        concat: config('concat'),
        jshint: config('jshint')
    });

    grunt.loadNpmTasks('grunt-contrib-concat');
    grunt.loadNpmTasks('grunt-contrib-jshint');
    grunt.registerTask('default', ['jshint', 'concat']);
};
```

Adds jshint to Grunt.js configuration ←

Loads grunt-contrib-jshint plugin ←

Adds jshint to default task →

If you run the `grunt` command from the command line, linting will be performed for all your JavaScript source files. Hopefully you won't receive any errors, but most likely JSHint will report a couple of areas where your code could be improved. The result of running the `grunt` command is shown in figure 11.12.

JSHint found a few errors in your source code. JSHint starts by listing the file that it performed the linting on, as well as a status code for the linting process. Next it tells you

```
Joachims-MacBook-Pro:webapp jhsmbp$ grunt
Running "jshint:files" (jshint) task
Linting js/app/app.js...ERROR
[L19:C38] W069: ['user'] is better written in dot notation.
        cookieUser.setProperties(data["user"]);
Linting js/app/application/application_controller.js...ERROR
[L35:C110] W033: Missing semicolon.
        this.get('timezones').pushObject(Ember.Object.create({timezoneValue: '-12', timezoneName: 'UTC-12'}))
Linting js/app/chart/charts_controller.js...ERROR
[L17:C27] W041: Use '===' to compare with '0'.
        } else if (length = 0 || !showLiveCharts){
Warning: Task "jshint:files" failed. Use --force to continue.

Aborted due to warnings.
Joachims-MacBook-Pro:webapp jhsmbp$
```

Figure 11.12   The result of running JSHint

the issue with the code, and then it prints out the code line it has an issue with. This makes it easy for you to go back into your source code and fix the issues JSHint reports.

After you've successfully implemented linting into your build pipeline, you should ensure that your application source code passes the linting process before moving on.

Next, we'll look at how to compile the application's Handlebars templates into a single JavaScript file.

11.2.5   Precompiling Handlebars templates

The templates for the Montric application are located inside the templates directory in separate .hbs files and follow the general structure outlined previously in this chapter. Separating your templates in this manner is great for the maintainability of your application, but in order for Ember.js to understand your templates, you need to precompile them into your application. Figure 11.13 shows the current stage in the assembly process.

Dan Gebhart has created an Ember.js template plugin for Grunt that allows you to do just that. As with any other Grunt.js plugin, you need to install it via the Node Package Manager, which can be done by executing the following command:

```
npm install grunt-ember-templates --save-dev
```

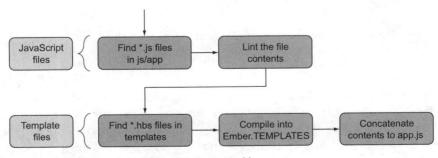

Figure 11.13   Adding file minifying to the assembly process

Figure 11.14   Installing the `grunt-ember-templates` plugin

Figure 11.14 shows the result of installing the `grunt-ember-templates` plugin.

Now that you've installed the `grunt-ember-templates` plugin, you're ready to start precompiling your Handlebars templates. Create a new file inside the tasks directory named emberTemplates.js. The following listing shows the resulting package.json file.

Listing 11.9   The package.json file after installing the `grunt-ember-templates` plugin

```
{
    "name": "Montric",
    "version": "0.9.0",
    "devDependencies": {
        "grunt": "~0.4.1",
        "grunt-contrib-concat": "~0.3.0",
        "grunt-contrib-jshint": "~0.6.0",
        "grunt-ember-templates": "~0.4.10"          ◁──┐  Adds version of plugin
    }
}
```

NPM adds the `grunt-ember-templates` plugin to the package.json file for you, as expected. Next you'll create a file inside the tasks directory, named emberTemplates.js, with the contents of the following listing.

Listing 11.10   The emberTemplates.js file

```
module.exports = {
    compile: {
        options: {                                    ◁──┐  Configures grunt-ember-
            templateName: function(sourceFile) {           templates plugin
                return sourceFile.replace(/templates\//, '');
            }
        },
        files: {
            "dist/templates.js": "templates/**/*.hbs"    ◁──┐  Indicates templates'
        }                                                      location
    }
};
```

Returns name for each template ┄┄►

The emberTemplates.js file looks for any .hbs files inside any of the subdirectories of the templates directory. In addition to the contents of the .hbs files, you also need to tell Ember.js the name of the template you're compiling. You can deduce the template name from the path and filename of the .hbs file, but you need to strip off the `"templates/"` string from the path. You use the `templateName` function for this, replacing any occurrence of `"templates/"` with an empty string.

The final step in precompiling the application's template is to add the `grunt-ember-templates` plugin to Gruntfile.js. The following listing shows the updated file.

Listing 11.11 The updated Gruntfile.js

```
function config(name) {
    return require('./tasks/' + name);
}

module.exports = function(grunt) {
    grunt.initConfig({
            pkg: grunt.file.readJSON('package.json'),
            concat: config('concat'),
            jshint: config('jshint'),
            emberTemplates: config('emberTemplates')
});

    grunt.loadNpmTasks('grunt-contrib-concat');
    grunt.loadNpmTasks('grunt-contrib-jshint');
    grunt.loadNpmTasks('grunt-ember-templates');
    grunt.registerTask('default',
        ['jshint', 'emberTemplates', 'concat']);

};
```

> **Adds emberTemplates.js to our build**

> **Loads grunt-ember-templates plugin via NPM**

> **Adds emberTemplates step to default task**

You've added the emberTemplates.js file to the Grunt.js configuration, told Grunt.js to load the `grunt-ember-templates` plugin, and registered `emberTemplates` as a step for the default build task.

Figure 11.15 shows the result of running grunt.

When grunt finishes, all your templates are compiled into a single file named templates.js, located within the dist directory. But you don't want to have

```
Joachims-MacBook-Pro:webapp jhsmbp$ grunt
Running "emberTemplates:compile" (emberTemplates) task
File "dist/templates.js" created.

Running "concat:dist" (concat) task
File "dist/Montric.js" created.
```

Figure 11.15 Running grunt to compile your templates

to minify and assemble two files for your final deployable application. You can solve this easily by extending your configuration of the concat plugin. The following listing shows the updated concat.js file.

Listing 11.12 Concatenating the precompiled templates into Montric.js

```
module.exports = {
    options: {
        separator: '\n'
    },
    dist: {
        src: ['js/app/**/*.js', 'dist/templates.js'],
        dest: 'dist/<%= pkg.name %>.js'
    }
};
```

> **Adds dist/templates.js for concatenation**

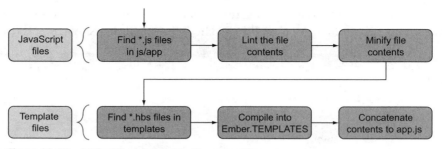

Figure 11.16   Adding file minifying to the assembly process

This concatenates your templates with the rest of the JavaScript application, and your Montric.js file is almost ready for final deployment. Next, we'll look at how to minify the concatenated source code to create a single file that's ready for final deployment to production.

11.2.6 Minifying your source code

Even though the file in listing 11.12 could have been included in a production application, sending JavaScript files like this between the server and the user's browser would be fairly verbose. This is an artifact; you've written the JavaScript code in a way that makes it easy to develop and easy to maintain. The code itself is sprinkled with whitespace, inline comments, and other artifacts that make the code more readable to humans. For a computer, though, this information is useless and redundant. *Minifying* is a procedure that removes as much of this redundancy as possible without breaking any functionality of the application. Figure 11.16 shows the current state of the assembly process.

Grunt uses an application called `uglify` to minify JavaScript code. As with the other Grunt.js plugins, start by installing the `grunt-contrib-uglify` plugin with the following command:

```
npm install grunt-contrib-uglify --save-dev
```

The results are shown in figure 11.17.

As you might expect, this adds a dependency to the plugin inside the package.json file, shown in the next listing.

Listing 11.13   The updated package.json file with `grunt-contrib-uglify` added

```
{
  "name": "Montric",
  "version": "0.9.0",
  "devDependencies": {
    "grunt": "~0.4.1",
    "grunt-contrib-concat": "~0.3.0",
    "grunt-contrib-jshint": "~0.6.0",
    "grunt-ember-templates": "~0.4.10",
    "grunt-contrib-uglify": "~0.2.2"        ◁─┐ Adds grunt-contrib-uglify 0.2.2
  }                                             or newer
}
```

```
Joachims-MacBook-Pro:webapp jhsmbp$ npm install grunt-contrib-uglify --save-dev
npm WARN package.json Montric@0.9.0 No README.md file found!
npm http GET https://registry.npmjs.org/grunt-contrib-uglify
npm http 304 https://registry.npmjs.org/grunt-contrib-uglify
npm http GET https://registry.npmjs.org/grunt-lib-contrib
npm http GET https://registry.npmjs.org/uglify-js
npm http 304 https://registry.npmjs.org/uglify-js
npm http 304 https://registry.npmjs.org/grunt-lib-contrib
npm http GET https://registry.npmjs.org/zlib-browserify/0.0.1
npm http GET https://registry.npmjs.org/source-map
npm http GET https://registry.npmjs.org/async
npm http GET https://registry.npmjs.org/optimist
npm http 304 https://registry.npmjs.org/zlib-browserify/0.0.1
npm http 304 https://registry.npmjs.org/source-map
npm http 304 https://registry.npmjs.org/optimist
npm http 200 https://registry.npmjs.org/async
npm http GET https://registry.npmjs.org/wordwrap
npm http GET https://registry.npmjs.org/amdefine
npm http 304 https://registry.npmjs.org/amdefine
npm http 304 https://registry.npmjs.org/wordwrap
grunt-contrib-uglify@0.2.2 node_modules/grunt-contrib-uglify
├── grunt-lib-contrib@0.6.1 (zlib-browserify@0.0.1)
└── uglify-js@2.3.6 (async@0.2.9, source-map@0.1.25, optimist@0.3.7)
Joachims-MacBook-Pro:webapp jhsmbp$
```

Figure 11.17   Installing the `grunt-contrib-uglify` plugin

Next, you need to configure the `uglify` plugin. Create a file named uglify.js inside your tasks directory with the contents from the following listing.

Listing 11.14   Configuring the `grunt-contrib-uglify` plugin inside tasks/uglify.js

```
module.exports = {
    options: {
        banner: '/*! <%= pkg.name %> <%= grunt.template.today("dd-mm-yyyy")
        ➥ %> */\n'                                          ◁── Defines banner
    },                                                            for top of output
    dist: {
        files: {
            'dist/<%= pkg.name %>.min.js': ['<%= concat.dist.dest %>']   ◁──┐
        }
    }                                                       Configures input │
};                                                          and output file  │
```

In this code, you define two important pieces of information for the `uglify` plugin. The `banner` property specifies the text to display at the top of the final output file. The `files` property defines the output file as well as the input file that the plugin is working on. In this case, you want to work on the destination file that the `concat` plugin created, and you want to create a new file inside the dist directory named Montric.min.js.

This is the entire configuration you need in order to minify your concatenated source file. But before you can build the minified file, you need to update the Gruntfile.js file with the contents of the following listing.

Listing 11.15 The updated Gruntfile.js

```
function config(name) {
    return require('./tasks/' + name);
}

module.exports = function(grunt) {
    grunt.initConfig({
        pkg: grunt.file.readJSON('package.json'),
        concat: config('concat'),
        jshint: config('jshint'),
        emberTemplates: config('emberTemplates'),
        uglify: config('uglify')          ◁── Adds uglify.js file to build
    });

    grunt.loadNpmTasks('grunt-contrib-concat');
    grunt.loadNpmTasks('grunt-contrib-jshint');
    grunt.loadNpmTasks('grunt-ember-templates');
    grunt.loadNpmTasks('grunt-contrib-uglify');      ◁── Loads grunt-contrib-uglify plugin
    grunt.registerTask('default',
        emberTemplates', 'concat', 'uglify']);        ◁── Adds uglify step to default task
};
```

You added the uglify.js file to the Grunt.js configuration, told Grunt.js to load the `grunt-contrib-uglify` plugin, and registered `uglify` as a step for the default build task.

Figure 11.18 shows the result of running `grunt`.

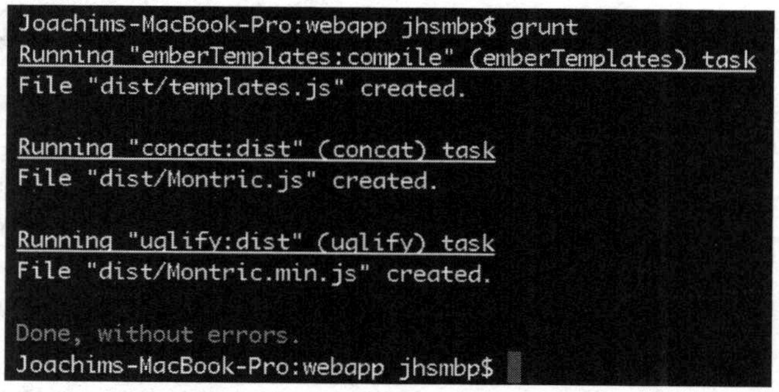

```
Joachims-MacBook-Pro:webapp jhsmbp$ grunt
Running "emberTemplates:compile" (emberTemplates) task
File "dist/templates.js" created.

Running "concat:dist" (concat) task
File "dist/Montric.js" created.

Running "uglify:dist" (uglify) task
File "dist/Montric.min.js" created.

Done, without errors.
Joachims-MacBook-Pro:webapp jhsmbp$
```

Figure 11.18 Running `grunt` to build the final deployable application

At this point, if you look inside the dist directory, you'll find three files, shown in figure 11.19.

Name	Date Modified	Size
Montric.js	Today 6:25 PM	115 KB
Montric.min.js	Today 6:25 PM	76 KB
templates.js	Today 6:25 PM	4 KB

Figure 11.19 The final contents of the dist directory

You could use Grunt.js for other tasks that you'll probably want to investigate further. The task of adding new steps to your build process follows the same outline as described here, and it should be straightforward for you to add new steps to your build process. Steps that you'll want to investigate further are as follows:

- Running your QUnit tests before the concat plugin
- Concatenating and minifying your CSS

The Grunt.js community is large and active, so you should be able to find a plugin that fits your requirements. The Grunt.js project maintains a list of plugins, published at http://gruntjs.com/plugins/.

You've seen what Grunt.js has to offer, but let's run through some of its advantages and drawbacks.

11.2.7 *Considering advantages and drawbacks of Grunt.js*

Grunt.js is a new tool, which is both an advantage and a disadvantage. The advantage is that the tool is tailored to building modern JavaScript applications and has a modern plugin-centric structure. Because Grunt.js is built on Node.js, it's a native JavaScript build tool, and has direct access to a powerful JavaScript interpreter. Integrating Grunt.js with JavaScript-specific tools is easy. You can take advantage of this fact when using the grunt-ember-template function, which uses the Node.js JavaScript interpreter to compile out .hbs templates into JavaScript functions.

But Grunt.js has a few disadvantages as well. Most notably, because of its lenient approach to how plugins can be configured, no standard method exists to configure the operation of the myriad of plugins. If you browse back over the scripts you created inside the tasks directory, you'll see that the scripts have taken a different approach toward how they're configured. You have to peruse the documentation for each plugin whenever you want to change or add configuration properties.

Another drawback, which is the main drawback for me, is that Grunt.js pollutes your project's directory with the file that the build system requires to operate. If you look at your project's directory, you'll find that NPM has created a new directory called node_modules. The contents of this folder are shown in Figure 11.20.

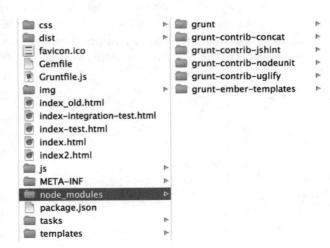

Figure 11.20   The contents of the node_modules directory

The node_modules directory contains any dependencies that you've added to your Grunt.js build, including `grunt`. In fact, this directory takes up 33 MB and consists of more than 2500 files. Although I understand that NPM needs to keep track of which projects depend on which dependency, and which version of that dependency NPM requires, I don't see why NPM needs to store this information inside my project directory. I believe that NPM and Grunt.js could've implemented a structure similar to Maven for dependency resolution. Maven keeps a copy of any dependency that's ever been requested, along with every version of every dependency in a separate directory. But by default, Maven places these dependencies into a ~/.m2/repository directory, which it refers to when building your application.

11.3 *Summary*

Throughout this chapter, we looked at the JavaScript assembly and packaging pipeline. Even though JavaScript is an interpreted language, the fact that you need to deliver your application to your users via a browser over HTTP makes these builds tools necessary. You use the build tools to help develop and maintain your source code. During the assembly and packaging stages, these tools minimize the number of files and the number of bits that you send across the wire between your servers and the users' browsers.

You walked through the steps involved in packaging your application for production deployment. You also saw an example of using Grunt.js build tools. Grunt.js is a Node.js-based build tool, written in the same language as your Ember.js application, and has direct access to a JavaScript interpreter. You use this interpreter when compiling your template files into JavaScript functions.

Now that you've come to the end of the book, I'd like to congratulate you on reaching the end of your journey into learning the basics, the pros and cons, and some of the more advanced features of Ember.js. I'd also like to wish you the best of luck with your continued exploration of Ember.js and your venture into writing truly ambitious web-based applications that push the envelope of what's possible to achieve on the web. Looking back at how Ember.js has evolved since it started out as Sprout-Core 2.0, I'm optimistic that this will be one of the most important frameworks for the web of the future!

index

Secrets of the JavaScript Ninja
by John Resig
   Bear Bibeault

   ISBN: 9781933988696
   392 pages, $39.99
   December 2012

CoffeeScript in Action
by Patrick Lee

   ISBN: 9781617290626
   532 pages, $44.99
   May 2014

HTML5 in Action
by Rob Crowther, Joe Lennon,
   Ash Blue, Greg Wanish

   ISBN: 9781617290497
   466 pages, $39.99
   February 2014

Sass and Compass in Action
by Wynn Netherland, Nathan Weizenbaum,
   Chris Eppstein, Brandon Mathis

   ISBN: 9781617290145
   240 pages, $44.99
   July 2013

For ordering information go to www.manning.com

YOU MAY ALSO BE INTERESTED IN